"Trauma is an emerging field where we seemingly learn more with each passing month. Theology is a timeless field where we want to remain faithful to our faith's foundations. In *Trauma Aware*, Eliza takes us by the hand to orient us to the experience of trauma in light of Christian theology; she helps us explore the timely in light of the timeless. As you process your own profoundly painful experiences or come alongside others doing so, this book will help you find God's comfort for life's most intense sufferings."

—**Brad Hambrick**, pastor of counseling at The Summit Church; author of *Navigating Destructive Relationships*

"Eliza Huie has written the book on trauma that our generation of Christian counselors has desperately needed. She deftly manages a Herculean task in taking a complex topic like trauma—who it impacts, what it is, how to care for those affected—all while remaining imminently accessible to the lay caregiver and the professional counselor. Readers will come away sobered, educated, and encouraged to walk the hard path with those whose lives have experienced trauma, but they will also come equipped with a hope that restores beauty for ashes."

—**Jonathan D. Holmes**, executive director, Fieldstone Counseling

"If you've ever wanted to help someone who is hurting, this book is for you. In these pages penned by an author who lives out what she writes, you will find biblical truth, clinical precision, and practical counsel that will enable you to wisely and compassionately help (and not further hurt) people who are hurting. And in the process, you may (like me) find yourself deeply helped amidst your own hurts."

—**David Platt**, lead pastor at McLean Bible Church, Washington, DC; author of *Radical* and *Something Needs to Change*

T0267744

"We can all greatly benefit from Eliza's well-rounded and God-glorifying approach to trauma. Through these pages, she explores, very practically, the good gifts given us in science, medicine, and psychology so that God may be more glorified in us, body and soul, and that we receive the best in him. She artfully turns an investigation into the dark place of trauma into hope in our loving Savior, Jesus. Patients and providers at my practice benefit from resources like this to learn how best to steward their minds and bodies as they work through traumatic experiences."

—**Dr. Adam O'Neill**, PA-C, DMSc, psychiatric physician assistant and owner of Adam O'Neill & Associates LLC, Washington, DC.

"In a fallen world filled with brokenness, understanding trauma is crucial. In this accessible and engaging resource, seasoned counselor Eliza Huie defines trauma and its impact on the body, mind, and soul. With compassionate skill and researched wisdom, Huie offers practical ways to love our neighbors with informed grace and gospel truth. I will return to *Trauma Aware* again and again—highly recommended."

—**Eric Schumacher**, podcaster; songwriter; author of *The Good Gift of Weakness* and *Ours: Biblical Comfort for Men Grieving Miscarriage*

"*Trauma Aware* provides a wealth of information for Christian helpers who want to learn about trauma and its effects on the body, emotions, mind, and soul. Eliza Huie shares biblical wisdom and practical expertise to spur churches toward becoming safe spaces where trauma survivors can experience healing. This book is a must-read for pastors, ministry leaders, counselors, and people-helpers of all kinds."

—**Beth M. Broom**, LPC-S, executive director of Christian Trauma Healing Network; contributing author to *Caring for Families Caught in Domestic Abuse: A Guide Toward Protection, Refuge, and Hope*

"Eliza Huie draws from her extensive clinical and theological experience to provide the reader with a clear and balanced understanding of the subject of trauma. She uses easy-to-understand terms to show how trauma impacts the brain and the body. Her book does an excellent job of defining what trauma actually is and distinguishes it from events in life that are discouraging, hurtful, even terrible, but don't qualify to be labeled as trauma. Additionally, *Trauma Aware* provides great practical tools that the reader can use immediately when assisting a friend, family member, or church member."

—**Tim Sanford**, MA, LPC, clinical director, Focus on the
Family Counseling Services Department

"The church has needed this book for a long time. In a practical and accessible style, Eliza Huie offers expert advice on how to care for people who have experienced trauma. *Trauma Aware* engages scientific research, draws on current trauma literature, and grounds itself in God's Word to offer an expanded framework for joining people in their trauma recovery. I already know I will be recommending this book over and over again."

—**Esther Smith**, LCPC, director of Christian Trauma Counseling;
author of *A Still and Quiet Mind*

"In *Trauma Aware*, Eliza helps to foster a heart of compassion and comfort for those of us seeking to be 'conduits of care' for individuals who have experienced life-changing and traumatic circumstances. She equips us with biblical truth and with a posture of humility to listen, to respond graciously, and to care deeply. Every Christian should read this book—either as one wanting to help others or one seeking to better understand their own hurt. This book provides a salve of hope and healing through Christ for a broken world. Lord, come quickly!"

—**Jeff Dalrymple**, executive director,
Evangelical Council for Abuse Prevention

"Eliza Huie's *Trauma Aware* offers a profound exploration of the complexities of trauma through a biblical lens. With compassionate wisdom, she guides readers to understand how trauma can impact our lives and how God's grace can heal. Filled with practical tools and biblical insights, Huie equips individuals and churches to address the reality of trauma and seek wholeness. This is the book the church has needed for a long time on this issue."

—**Jason Kovacs**, executive director, Gospel Care Collective

"Trauma studies—and traumatized people—deserve the church's best efforts. In *Trauma Aware*, Eliza helps us minister to the whole person, body and soul. The book evidences her strong case knowledge, maintains a connection to biblical and theological reflection, and engages the broader field with readable surveys and constructive Christian wisdom. We all need to hear this healing calling: moving toward sufferers, bearing burdens, and so fulfilling the law of Christ."

—**Rev. Michael Gembola**, LPC, executive director,
Blue Ridge Christian Counseling

Trauma
AWARE

ELIZA HUIE

HARVEST HOUSE PUBLISHERS
EUGENE, OREGON

Cover design by Faceout Studio, Amanda Hudson

Cover images © Clive Watts / Stocksy; Amanda Hudson / Faceout Studio

Interior design by KUHN Design Group

All names and identifying details in this book have been changed to protect the privacy of individuals. Any resemblance to real persons or situations is purely coincidental, as the stories presented are compilations drawn from various experiences.

Brain illustrations in this book were created using Open AI's DALL·E via ChatGPT, https://openai.com/dall-e-3. All texts and titles added by Eliza Huie.

Box-breathing and breath-prayer images were designed by Eliza Huie using Canva 2024.

For bulk, special sales, or ministry purchases, please call 1-800-547-8979.
Email: CustomerService@hhpbooks.com

This logo is a federally registered trademark of the Hawkins Children's LLC. Harvest House Publishers, Inc., is the exclusive licensee of this trademark.

Trauma Aware
Copyright © 2025 by Eliza Huie
Published by Harvest House Publishers
Eugene, Oregon 97408
www.harvesthousepublishers.com

ISBN 978-0-7369-8892-6 (pbk)
ISBN 978-0-7369-8893-3 (eBook)

Library of Congress Control Number: 2024935694

Printed in the United States of America

24 25 26 27 28 29 30 31 32 33 / KP / 10 9 8 7 6 5 4 3 2 1

To my mother—I love you.

Through you, I've witnessed the power
of God's redemption and grace.

ACKNOWLEDGMENTS

I would be remiss not to take this brief space to express my heartfelt gratitude to my family and friends—your continued encouragements and prayers along the way have been a true gift. I was able to finish this book due to your many prayers. A special thanks goes to my fellow counselors who have provided invaluable feedback on my writing, often at a moment's notice. Your thoughtful insights have been instrumental to this work. And to my husband, who endured many delays so I could write or edit "just one more paragraph." Your patience is a gift that made writing this a reality.

I want to give a special thank-you to Harvest House Publishers and their incredible team for their vision in recognizing the importance of this book. I have no doubt that your conviction that a book on this topic was long needed will be a blessing both to those seeking to help and those seeking to heal.

Last, to the brave hearts who welcomed me into their journeys and courageously shared their stories with me over the years, thank you. You have shown me what it means to enter into the fellowship of Christ's sufferings, and in you I have witnessed the beauty of his redemption. You are the bravest people I have ever met.

CONTENTS

APPENDICES
TRAUMA TOOLS AND RESOURCES

FOREWORD

Elyse Fitzpatrick

I recently sent off a text to my kids. It was entitled, "Trauma I've suffered in the last four years." That text was largely due to my reading of this wonderful book and *finally* deciding to face facts. More about that in a moment.

Who is Eliza Huie, the author of this book? Well, first, Eliza is my friend. Of course, that does not necessarily qualify her to help you learn about becoming trauma aware and informed. But it should tell you that she is a sister in Christ whom I respect and am thankful for. She has dedicated her life to helping those who need a wise, professional, careful, kind, and most of all, Jesus-loving counselor. And, while doing so has been the motivating joy of her life, it has not come cheaply. Aside from the cost of her extensive training, she has chosen to follow sufferers into the fire as they face and wrestle through the trauma they have endured. Why should she expose herself to the horrors faced by others? Because she loves.

In Eliza's ministry to the hurting, she believes it is right to approach each individual as an *embodied soul.* That means that any form of counseling that looks solely to address the soul (though important) while ignoring the body is often both futile and uncharitable. It is futile because it ignores the ways in which the soul and the body unconsciously and unceasingly interact and influence each other. Yes, I am a soul. But I am also embodied, or as Paul put it, I am "clothed" with an earthly "tent" (2 Corinthians 5:1-4).

I do not simply *have* a body. I *am* a body. And the circumstances that I experience I experience as both an immaterial soul (mind, will, emotions) and as a physical body with a brain that processes, encodes, and remembers events. Those who ignore the interplay between the whole self (soul and body), while trying to be helpful, will ultimately struggle to bring wholeness to the very people they seek to serve. We are reactive bodies.

In addition, I do not simply *have* a soul. I *am* a soul. Any method of help that fails to see that there is an immaterial, spiritual dimension to who I am will also fail to bring the wholeness I need. As an embodied soul, I need the living water that comes only from Jesus Christ as he pours out his Holy Spirit upon me (see John 7:37). I need to hear his Word that brings life, and I need to know what it means to be both forgiven and counted righteous by faith. Every day, those who have suffered trauma and, indeed, all of us, are thirsty and need a deep drink of that life-giving water. We are thirsty souls.

We are embodied souls. Not only is it futile to try to help sufferers while ignoring either aspect of this reality, to do this is also uncharitable. It is uncharitable to speak only to the immaterial soul about matters of faith if we ignore the truth that souls are also clothed with a physical body that acts and reacts, often in ways outside of our immediate awareness or control. And it is uncharitable to treat suffering people as though there is nothing more to them than what can be seen and touched.

We are more. We are more than what can be seen. We are more than what cannot be seen. We are embodied souls. Visible and invisible. Quantifiable and ethereal. Both parts acting and interacting in symbiotic union. Even when those aspects seem to conflict with each other, it is clear that God has made us an exquisite creation!

Eliza has thought deeply about that intricate interplay. And that's what makes me so glad she has authored this book for you (and me). Throughout the carefully researched chapters, you will see how wholeness can be found and bestowed through wise and informed counseling. What a gift!

Now, back to that text about my trauma.

In 2020, my 97-year-old mother died. Although she did not live with us, I was responsible for her care and was with her often, increasingly more so as the end drew nearer. Although Richard, my older brother, had lived with her for decades, he was mentally unfit to be her caregiver. And so, much of 2020 was lived trying to answer the questions, "How's Mom today? Does she need anything?" Then, finally, as the end of the year approached, her health began to fail in more obvious ways, and I was with her daily. One day a hospice nurse noted that her blood oxygen level had dropped to 66 percent. We were advised to prepare for her imminent death. One of my sons, Joel, came over and, together with the family, we shared communion with her and sang "Amazing Grace" around her bed. She soon fell into a sleep from which she would never awaken here. Because we were amid the pandemic, our only funeral for her was a gathering with the family at her home. She was gone, but that was just the beginning of my difficulties.

In the months that followed her death, we had to clean out her home and sell it. From the proceeds of that sale, we bought a trailer for my brother to live in on our property. Then, eight months after her death, my brother suffered the first of two debilitating strokes, and once he was released from convalescent care, we had to find and move him into an assisted living space where he would be safe and properly cared for. My husband, Phil, and I would go pick him up frequently to take him to walk at a local park. During this time, I had to arrange for his Social Security retirement benefits, Medicare and Medi-Cal, disability insurance payments, become his representative payee, and make sure that any unusual physical problems were cared for. Then, in September of 2023, less than three years after my mother's death, he died suddenly. I went over to his facility and sat on the floor by his body until the mortuary workers picked him up. That was one year ago this weekend.

Honestly, until I read Eliza's book, I never stopped to put that timeline together or to think about how I had been affected by the deaths of my mother and brother. I never stopped to think about how I had been deeply impacted by these losses, nor about how they had taken a toll on both my body and my soul.

What have I learned about how this trauma impacted my body and soul? What has this book helped me see? I am frequently on edge. I have discovered myself being physically guarding. I am fearful and hypervigilant. I startle often. While this might be the norm for some, it certainly is not the norm for me. I have also always been a person who enjoyed action movies, and onscreen violence never affected me. I cannot watch them now. I find myself feeling afraid and cowering in my seat when I watch the tamest of shows. Even though my mind and heart have been busy with other things, my body has not forgotten. My body remembers what my soul endured: Death is near and can appear at any time.

I am learning to breathe again. And yes, of course, I am going to pursue this further.

So, to Eliza's readers, I say, "I am so glad you are here. I am glad for the people you will help, and I am glad for the way you will be helped." And to Eliza, my friend, I say, "Thank you. Your labor of love is not in vain."

Elyse Fitzpatrick
Author and speaker

EMBARKING TOWARD HOPE

Our perceptions, emotions, and relationships are deeply—and sometimes mysteriously—shaped by the vast intricacies of our experiences, which are woven into the fabric of our life and imprinted in our mind, body, and soul. Life leaves an indelible mark on us and begs us to explore the interplay of our past, present, and future. When trauma becomes a part of our story, the impact can be so confusing and dismantling that it calls into question everything that was once held true. Even someone who loves and follows God can be deeply affected by traumatic events. Rather than permanently shaping our life in a negative way, this disruption can prompt the courageous confrontation of uncertainty, which can aid in discovering hope and resilience in the face of a shattered life.

For Christians desiring to help those who have experienced trauma, the impact of distressing events or circumstances needs to be understood with wisdom, compassion, and unwavering support. At times we struggle to care for people because we aren't sure how to recognize trauma. Other times we might see that trauma is the root of a person's suffering, but we don't know where to go from there. What should care look like? What role does God's Word play? How can we be more aware of what is needed and helpful as believers when supporting others? If you have asked any of these questions, you are not alone, and you are holding the right book.

In navigating the important intersection of faith and trauma care, my purpose is to foster an understanding of trauma, provide practical insights anchored in God's Word, and guide you toward becoming trauma-aware helpers, pastors, counselors, mentors, and friends. This book will equip you with the tools to extend compassionate help, recognize the nuances of trauma, and ultimately walk alongside others with empathy, grace, and the transformative hope found in Jesus.

When Trauma Comes Close

Consider the experience of Tianna, a single woman in her mid-forties. Her story could easily be the story of anyone in your church or circle of friends. Tianna had always been a faithful member of her local church. She attended services regularly, volunteered at church events, and was actively engaged in her small group. She seemed to always have a smile for everyone, and her kind heart was felt by many. But after a series of distressing and traumatic events in her life—including being unexpectantly let go from a job she loved in a downsizing reorganization, and a terrifying house fire a few weeks later—her friends noticed her disposition was changing. Thankfully she was physically unharmed by the fire, but she now feels fearful and hypervigilant much of the time. She is especially fearful at night and has nightmares about the fire often. In addition, the job loss was abrupt and humiliating in how it came about, and left her feeling insecure, rejected, and deeply hurt. Almost eight months later, she still struggled to cope with overwhelming emotions of grief, anxiety, fear, and even depression.

Tianna's friends and fellow church members saw her slowly withdraw from social activities and struggle to function in her daily life, but they felt powerless to help. Beyond praying for her, bringing her meals, and sending her notes of encouragement, they didn't know how to respond to her pain or how to provide the support and care she seemed to need. Some even wondered if she was discontent. Tianna had shared that God had provided a fully furnished apartment for her to live in while her house was being renovated and insurance was covering the costs. However, she couldn't shake the feeling that something bad was about to happen. This led to her feeling distracted and anxious. She found part-time work, and despite taking a cut in salary, was able to make ends meet on the smaller wage. An elder in the church asked Tianna whether she had considered that she might be ungrateful for God's provision. Her friends sought to remind her of God's sovereign plan and questioned why she was pulling away. They didn't understand why she was struggling so much, and neither did Tianna.

Sadly, Tianna's story is all too common. Many Christians, although well-meaning, are ill-equipped to provide effective care and counsel for those who have experienced emotional and psychological trauma. When trauma comes close to people they care about, some may feel uncertain about how to approach the subject, while others worry about saying or doing the wrong thing. They may not even know what to look for or how to determine whether trauma is impacting someone they care about.

What to Expect

This book is written for Christians who want to become trauma aware and learn to provide compassionate care for those who have experienced trauma. It offers practical guidance and biblical wisdom for how to recognize the signs of trauma and how to provide support and care as you walk alongside someone on their journey to healing and restoration.

In these pages, you will hear stories of individuals who have experienced trauma and the ways in which they were helped by those who cared for them. Many of the stories, which are composites, are based on my years of experience as a counselor and a supervisor of counselors. My approach to care has been formed by the deep convictions I hold in the Christian faith, my expertise as a licensed clinical mental health provider, and my nuanced approach to biblically faithful counseling. Shaped by my study of Scripture, my clinical experience, and my heart to see the church equipped, *Trauma Aware* is meant to provide you with a practical approach to understanding trauma, which I trust aligns with the heart of God. Through exploring the complex nature of trauma, its effects on the mind and body, and how it can impact a person's faith and relationship with God, you will become more compassionate and understanding to those suffering from traumatization.

If you are a Christian who wants to make a difference in the lives of those who have experienced trauma, then this book is for you. What you will learn will transform the way you care for others. By becoming trauma aware, you will be able to better support people who have suffered traumatic circumstances, offer hope amidst their pain, and be a light in their darkness. Developing trauma awareness will prepare you to provide compassionate care and support to those who have endured life's most challenging circumstances, and to empower them on their journey toward healing and resilience. As you dig deeper into the pages of this book, you will discover valuable insights and practical strategies that will not only transform your understanding of trauma, but also ignite a profound sense of compassion and purpose as you encounter stories like Tianna's.

One final note as you start this book: I stumbled into the world of writing—I am an accidental author of sorts. While I hadn't anticipated I would write a book on this topic, my hope is that I'll adequately share with you the wealth of experience I have acquired from years as a licensed counselor, particularly within ministry contexts. This has not only given me a distinct perspective but has also allowed me to hone my expertise on this topic, providing me the opportunity to share insight not often found among Christian resources. With that said, I approach the pages ahead with a blend of humility and confidence born from a genuine passion for and practical involvement in the subject matter. I pray that God would use the skills and experience he has given to me to help others. This book is an invitation into a conversation that I trust will be insightful as well as accessible.

I make no claim that this book is exhaustive. My goal was not to create an all-encompassing work, but rather, for this to be an accessible, informative, and useful resource for those who want to learn more about how to identify trauma and care for those affected by it. Every chapter and section could have easily been expanded into its own book. More can and should be said on the topics covered here. But I hope and pray this book will make a great starting point for those who desire to learn how we can care for those touched by trauma.

This work stands as my heartfelt contribution, not boasting in its sufficiency but aspiring to extend compassionate wisdom and practical help. I hope it plays a role in raising interest in this topic, which is often overlooked in the church. May it be a catalyst for deeper understanding, empathy, and most importantly, action in our collective journey of supporting those affected by trauma. If you make it all the way to the final page, let me thank you in advance for hanging in there with me—I hope you come away feeling that you are more attuned to the profound impact of trauma and better recognize the pressing need to address it within the context of the church so that we become and stay trauma aware.

PART 1

BECOMING AWARE

The scope of trauma care is vast and varied, encompassing a spectrum of approaches that address the individual's physical, emotional, and spiritual suffering. While it's common for Christians to prioritize spiritual care, an exclusive emphasis on this aspect may limit the effectiveness of overall care. A more well-rounded approach acknowledges the impact of trauma on the body and other areas that make up the whole person. Awareness of how trauma manifests in various facets of an individual's life equips friends and caregivers to provide more holistic and effective support.

Even so, crucial assistance for trauma survivors lies within the realm of God's compassionate care. In the forthcoming pages, you will discover insights to enhance your awareness of the impact of trauma. This awareness will equip you to extend support to those in need of care, which, anchored in the truths of the Bible, expresses God's love.

Care of this kind necessitates a humble reliance on the Lord as you seek his wisdom in areas that may elude your full understanding.

Becoming more aware of trauma and its impact is a vital pursuit for Christians. A good starting point involves exploring the complexities of the body and brain. Drawing from the wisdom of our Creator, the guidance of his Word, and insights from science and medicine, you will be amazed at the remarkable resilience of human beings. But more than that, as you engage with this exploration in the upcoming pages, I trust it will cause you to marvel at God's intricate design of the human body. I am confident that this journey will strengthen your conviction that trauma awareness is essential for the church, equipping us to provide thoughtful and effective care.

CHAPTER 1

WHAT IS TRAUMA?

When I was five years old, my brother ran me over with his bicycle in an intentional act of sibling rivalry. What started as a standoff on one of the trails of our forested property ended with my injury. The single-track path was big enough for only one of us, and we were both unwilling to move off the clear-cut trail onto the uncleared shrubbery and weeds to allow the other to pass.

My brother came down the trail on his bike as I went up it on foot. I squared my stance and jammed my hands on my hips for extra emphasis, even though we were about to meet. He continued to approach with increasing speed and force, daring me to challenge him. It was a challenge I readily accepted! I asserted my dominance in a clear, single-word command, which I shouted with defiant authority: "Mooove!"

My demand fueled his determination to win this dual and his seven-year-old legs pumped the pedals of his bike even faster—his little sister would not have the last word. I didn't think he would actually run me over. But he did. Well, mostly. I abandoned my position and dove off the path just as his front tire grazed my knee. I was not seriously hurt, but the unfortunate encounter threw me off the trail as he whizzed by. It wasn't the scrapes I received on my skin that hurt most, but rather, the blow to my pride.

My only consolation for the humiliating defeat was that our mother took my side. I was, after all, the only one bleeding, and he was supposed to have watched out for his younger sister (even if she did instigate the crime by being annoyingly bossy). This moment in my childhood might have been completely forgotten by the passing of time except for a small scar that remains on my knee to this day. I recovered from the wounding—my knee probably healed faster than my pride—but the scar on my body is the link to the memory of what happened that day on the trail.

The Wounds of Trauma

In many ways, our bodies tell the story of what happened to us. The wounds of life can leave visible scars, like the one on my knee from my unsuccessful dual with my brother, while emotional wounds leave their mark in other ways. Distressing and difficult circumstances can mark us with internal pain or emotional damage. Although visible scars may fade, when the hurts of past situations don't diminish with time, we may find ourselves experiencing the effects of trauma.

Trauma is a term that comes from a Greek word (τραῦμα) that literally means "wound." This is a good description of what trauma is: a wound. A deep wound. A wound sometimes invisible to others. Trauma is an injury that can be misunderstood and requires specific care to heal. One's healing from the wounds of trauma is best aided by the wise and humble attentiveness of another, someone who is willing to create a safe place for the traumatized. Like the scar on my knee, wounds do heal when given the appropriate care. The scar may remain, but the pain no longer stings. Similarly, even when it comes to emotional wounds, the healing process has much to do with the type of care one receives.

Psychological Trauma

There are various types of traumas, and this book will concentrate on what is known as psychological, or emotional, trauma (terms that can be used interchangeably). Psychological trauma is not isolated to one specific type of event. The many categories into which trauma is divided certainly demonstrate this. For example, sexual trauma, medical trauma, complex trauma, attachment trauma, religious trauma, and betrayal trauma are just a sampling of the most common types of psychological traumas. These can also overlap and intersect, and the effects can vary from person to person.

In the pages ahead, you will be given a clear definition of psychological trauma as well as hear stories that will bring to light the true nature of its impact. These accounts, which I mentioned are composites, are based on years of personal experiences in helping others. The stories will help to provide a clear understanding of the extensive impact of trauma. It is my utmost priority to approach this topic with compassion, to illuminate the far-reaching effects of trauma, and to offer biblical hope to those who may have experienced trauma.

While this book mainly focuses on psychological trauma in general, it is important to acknowledge various subtypes of this trauma that also deserve attention. Though these subcategories of emotional trauma are not exhaustive and are explored only in brief below, this information serves as valuable insight for supporting individuals who have experienced these forms of psychological or emotional wounding. This foundational awareness will equip you to approach the broader landscape of trauma with a more informed perspective that provides you with an awareness of the various categories of trauma.

Generational Trauma

Generational trauma or intergenerational trauma refers to the lasting impact of difficulties faced within families over multiple generations. The theory is that the traumatic magnitude of the situation can be transmitted to the younger generations. This can be manifested in many ways. For example, a great-grandfather who was beaten or regularly humiliated in his younger years because of the color of his skin could develop a deep sense of hopelessness that his condition might never change. He cannot change the color of his skin, after all. To cope with this hopelessness, he would simply accept whatever came to him. This hopeless acceptance might be seen in future generations as passivity or apathy as it relates to improving their circumstances, or it could also be seen in a lack of ambition about the future.

Other examples of generational trauma have been investigated in the children of Holocaust survivors. For example, a young woman who was placed in a concentration camp in Germany may have learned to cope by "cutting off" her emotions. Because of this, she may interact with others in an emotionally distant fashion even after the traumatic situation ended. As she builds a family of her own, the coping that kept her alive during the war may show up in emotional detachment when things get hard at home. When her children experience painful emotions, she may tell them not to cry or avoid talking about what is upsetting, and instead, she may focus on changing the situation that caused the distress. This approach teaches her children to avoid or suppress the emotional pain that may make relationships tumultuous to navigate, to say the least.[1] This model continues for future generations, inferring that feelings should be suppressed.

Not only does the trauma that a person experienced have the potential to impact generations to come, but the ideology of the victimizers can also be passed on to future generations.

Consider what researcher J.P. Gump shares regarding slavery in

America: "There is little in slavery that was not traumatic: the loss of culture, home, kin…sense of self, the destruction of families, through the sales of fathers, mothers, offspring, physical abuse, or even witnessing the castration of a fellow slave."[2] Traumatization did not end with slavery for Black Americans. What is now known as racial trauma continued to be propagated through prejudice after freedom was granted. This prejudice was equally dehumanizing through the enacting of Jim Crow laws. While the civil rights movement paved the way to expose continued racism in America, Black people still faced traumatic realities in day-to-day life. Racial prejudice remains in some of the people and the systems of a country largely shaped by enslavement and discrimination. We are learning that these traumatic experiences were perpetuated from one generation to the next and the ongoing impact can extend to communities as well.

Race-based and generational trauma is not isolated to African Americans. Racial oppression began early in America with the mistreatment of Native Americans. After the Spanish brought the first slaves to the Carolinas in 1526, the brutal treatment of people based on race became prevalent with dreadful acts of genocide and displacement against many Native American tribes. Racial trauma continued with the discrimination of ethnic Jews, Muslims, Asians, and others and it lingers to this day in hate crimes and prejudice against immigrants and refugees. The effects of racial trauma are palpable, lingering in the lives of those who have experienced it, and passed down through generations despite the passage of time.

Complex Trauma

Complex trauma has to do with the amount of time a person was exposed to a stressful or adverse situation. The trauma-inducing situation often begins in early childhood and involves interpersonal relationships, specifically relationships where there should be a trusting and nurturing connection. Unlike typical emotional trauma, complex trauma is characterized by repeated and chronic incidents such as abuse or neglect. Taking an Adverse Childhood Experiences (ACE) assessment can help determine whether complex trauma may be a factor in an individual's life. This assessment quantifies exposure to various adverse experiences during childhood and provides insight into the potential long-term impact on a person's emotional well-being. However, it is important to note that while the ACE assessment provides valuable insight, it should not be used as a diagnostic tool, and an evaluation by a qualified professional is essential for accurate diagnosis and appropriate care. For more information on the ACE assessment, see Appendix B at the back of this book.

Complex trauma can lead to difficulty in forming secure relational attachments and can also have a negative impact on a person's ability to regulate their emotions. Complex trauma often has a more profound and enduring impact compared to trauma caused by a single isolated event. It brings its own unique challenges. Effective care for individuals with complex trauma will often require a counselor who can recognize the unique challenges posed by prolonged exposure to adversity and is trained in trauma-informed approaches.

Supporting someone with complex trauma requires patience, empathy, and understanding. Friends, family members, or helpers can be supportive by being a reliable presence who listens and supports the person while being willing to work at a pace most tolerable for the one who has suffered the trauma. If you are walking with someone for whom complex trauma is a reality, you also want to be seeking out consultation for yourself so you know how to care for them well. Pray for wisdom and pray for them regularly. If they are open to it, pray with them and welcome them into a community where they can find acceptance and grace.

Religious Trauma

Religious trauma refers to the psychological or emotional distress stemming from harm done either in religious communities or through religious teachings. Unlike general emotional trauma, religious trauma involves harm caused by religious beliefs, practices, or communities in which rigid doctrines, spiritual abuse, or judgment were expressed.

Distinctively, religious trauma has a negative impact on a person's view of self and of God. This kind of trauma deeply impacts their worldview and their trust of those in positions of spiritual leadership as well as religious institutions and systems. People who have experienced religious trauma often have deep questions related to faith and spirituality that may lead them to turn from beliefs they once firmly held.

Christians whose intentions may be to offer comfort can sometimes add to the distress of one who has experienced religious trauma by offering pat answers to the person's struggle. Hastily saying things like, "You need to forgive and forget," or "This is all in God's plan," or "You just need to find the right church" can prove unhelpful or even detrimental. That's because these types of responses oversimplify the impact of religious trauma and imply that a simple faith is all that is needed to resolve deep wounds. Forgiveness, trusting God, and connecting to a community of believers are important and yet these topics must be approached with wisdom. It's essential for believers to care for those impacted by religious trauma with sensitivity, acknowledging the complexity of their experiences and avoiding simplistic answers that may inadvertently cause further harm.

Vicarious Trauma

Another type of psychological trauma worth mentioning is vicarious or secondary trauma, which can happen when someone is exposed to another person's trauma. This is common among first responders, medical doctors, therapists, and caring friends or family members of a trauma survivor. Vicarious trauma refers to the emotional impact experienced by people who are indirectly exposed to the trauma of others. This trauma often occurs in those whose role is that of caregiver, mentor, counselor, pastor, or friend to a person who has endured trauma. These helpers absorb the pain and suffering of others.

The pain of people's stories has an impact on helpers. Regardless of your role, if you sit with someone and hear the atrocity of their story, you are permeable and you will be affected. This absorption of a person's story can cause you to have your own doubts. It can also cause you to experience emotional distress and impact your own sense of well-being. Hearing someone process their experience of being in an automobile accident might cause vicarious trauma that may result in increased anxiety while driving or pervasive thoughts about potential accidents. Similarly, learning about someone who has survived a violent assault may lead to heightened fear in seemingly safe situations, nightmares related to the details of that assault, or an increased overall sense of vulnerability.

Because empathetically engaging with others' traumatic experiences has the potential to traumatize those in caregiving or supportive roles, it is essential to be mindful and proactive in self-care. Vicarious trauma can lead to compassion fatigue or burnout, and helpers must be proactive in caring for themselves as they care for others. Enter conversations prayerfully. Spend time in the Word meditating on who God is and his faithfulness to take care of his own. Prioritize spiritual disciplines and rhythms that emphasize truth and hope to counterbalance the discouraging and dreadful stories you might hear when walking with those who have endured trauma. In the resource section of this book, you will find the Compassion Fatigue and Burnout Assessment that I created to assist helpers to gauge how well they are doing as they care for others (see Appendix C). Take the assessment whether you are feeling symptoms of vicarious trauma or not. Retake it regularly if you are in the role of helper or caregiver for those who may have experienced trauma.

As you can see, trauma is a complex and multifaced topic. As we delve more deeply into an understanding of what trauma is and how it can manifest in people's lives, we will focus specifically on psychological trauma, regardless of its origin. Let's begin by briefly surveying the history of trauma in the field of psychology.

Trauma's History

Before the year 1980, there was no official diagnosis of post-traumatic stress disorder (PTSD). The most common diagnosis of its kind was nicknamed *shell shock* and was given mainly to men suffering from the long-term effects of war. In her book *Trauma and Recovery*, Judith Herman explains, "The soldier who developed a traumatic neurosis was at best a constitutionally inferior human being, at worst a malingerer and a coward." She goes on to state, "Some military authorities maintained that these men did not deserve to be patients at all, that they should be court-martialed or dishonorably discharged rather than given medical treatment."[3]

Women were also treated poorly and often exploited as "objects of study,"[4] leading to compounding traumatic experiences. In fact, the earliest psychological term used to describe what we now recognize as trauma was *hysteria* and, sadly, the treatment lacked understanding and compassion.[5] It is believed that *hysteria*, a word derived from the Greek word *hystera*, which means "uterus" or "womb,"[6] is the first mental health disorder attributed to women and characterized by extreme excitability and emotional overflow.[7] The connection between hysteria and hysterectomy is likely not missed here, and sadly, one prescribed cure for hysteria in women was removal of the womb, which was thought to be the source of the problems experienced. Women who experienced trauma exhibited disturbing symptoms ranging from extreme emotions to catatonia often occurring after the woman experienced sexual exploitation or rape. The attention given to them by experts was often rooted in curiosity or psychological exploration rather than compassion.

Hysteria was also recognized in men and significant shame was attached to both women and men given this diagnosis. Galen of Pergamon, an ancient Greek physician, noted that "hysterical passion is just a name but varied and innumerable are the forms which it encompasses."[8] The diagnosis of hysteria meant "that the individual is suffering from some persistent form of wickedness, perversity, or weakness of the will."[9] Considering the context of a cultural era where the equality of women was drastically incongruent and the promotion of a machismo characterization of what it means to be a man was propagated, social pressure often caused sufferers to retreat into silence and stigmatization. This left them feeling unheard, disbelieved, and shamed. Sadly, the earliest forms of treatment were not only exploitive but also reckless. Patients were given shaming threats and punishments in efforts to provoke change. Herman shares the reports of a soldier who, unable to speak due to traumatization, was treated with electric shocks to his throat and told to "remember you must act as the hero I expect you to be."

Herman describes how societal pressure influenced the psychiatric field to change the focus away from understanding the traumatized. As "medical interest in the subject of psychological trauma faded," the presences of long-lasting psychiatric patients "became an embarrassment to civilian societies eager to forget."[10] But trauma does not dissipate with silence; instead, it grows. People continued to suffer alone with the memories of the horror they experienced.

It was not until the end of the Vietnam War in 1975 that significant changes began to occur. The distressing symptoms experienced by combat veterans served as a catalyst for trauma research as the post-traumatic effects of soldiers became the focus for understanding trauma. But traumatization existed long before this and psychology now affirms that reality. Marc-Antoine Crocq, a French psychiatrist and leading expert in generalized anxiety disorder, wrote a scholarly article on the history of psychotraumatology and cited many early historical and literary sources that give depictions of trauma. He started the article recognizing that civilization's earliest literature acknowledged the psychological impact that witnessing atrocities such as war and death can have on people. In proving his point, he quoted the Bible, stating, "We are reminded in Deuteronomy 20:1-9, military leaders have long been aware that many soldiers must be removed from the front line because of a nervous breakdown which is contagious." He then cites this:

> When you go out to war against your enemies, and see horses and Chariots and an army larger than your own... the officers shall speak further to the people and say, "Is there any man who is fearful and fainthearted? Let him go back to his house, lest he make the heart of his fellows melt like his own."[11]

The purpose of this biblical instruction was not to affirm what is now known as psychological traumatization; however, it does demonstrate that God understands our frame and he recognizes that when we see and encounter terrifying situations—for instance, horses and chariots and armies larger than our own—it has an impact on our experience. It has the possibility to not only make our own heart faint, but the hearts of those around us as well. A better understanding of trauma can help us know how to respond to people wisely and compassionately. We do not need to repeat the history of the past when it comes to our approach to trauma. We can learn from it and take a humble approach of embracing that sometimes there is much more going on than we know or understand.

We tend to judge what we don't understand. This was the case for early trauma sufferers. Doctors judged that trauma victims were fragile people who had a frenzied temperament, or they viewed them as a diagnostic curiosity that challenged their clinical skills. Society judged them as an embarrassment to be kept out of sight and out of conversations. Even the church has judged trauma victims as being unfaithful Christians or unbelievers, often causing ostracism. In the thirteenth century, the church embraced the "theory of demonical possession leading to treatment by exorcism and finally torture."[12] Remnants of this approach remain in religious thought today and lead to painful stereotyping and marginalization of those who experience traumatization. Certainly spiritual warfare exists, but there is great error in casting judgment upon someone without a careful consideration of all possible factors.

The stigmatization is not only external. Trauma survivors judged themselves as weak and unable to explain or control their distress. This often led to them feeling "hopeless" and being "dead inside." What was needed was for them to be seen as people whose suffering was worthy of compassionate attention.

With the early years of psychological care marked by practices and methods that were often unhelpful and reckless, and with the field of psychiatric research and care casting sufferers in a negative light, the treatment of psychological trauma lacked empathy or overall respect and honor for the patients. At the same time, the church was also uncertain of what to make of trauma survivors, treating them as people who lacked self-control, were uncooperative, or even demon possessed. To top it all off, at that time, the care and research of trauma focused mainly on how to stop the symptoms that manifested physically. The treatments then were often counterproductive, making matters worse for the patient and sometimes even retraumatizing survivors. Nothing addressed the inner dimensions of injury. There was little concern for what might have happened to them to cause the distressing symptoms.

Much has changed in the clinical world today. Psychiatrists, psychologists, and counselors have grown significantly in their understanding of trauma. There have been remarkable changes and advancements in psychological care based on clinical research, which has led to more sensitive therapeutic approaches.

Will the church follow a similar path? For more than half a century, the church has been essentially uninformed and ill-equipped to offer care to trauma survivors. Despite advancement in biblical and Christian-based counseling models, trauma has remained a subject of mystery—and sometimes suspicion—and faith-based resources have been few. Often the priority of personal holiness can cause pastors, lay counselors, and helpers to be hesitant to label something as trauma when it looks similar to sinful behavior. A female church member who chooses to watch the Sunday gathering online might be viewed as forsaking the assembly for not being physically present when it appears she has no justifiable reason to watch from home. The teen who will not look the pastor or youth leader in the eye when they talk could be seen as disrespectful to spiritual leadership. The man who gets distressed when someone is sitting in his regular seat is seen as angry when he moves around the sanctuary rapidly looking for a new seat. The student who struggles to stay in his class or connect socially may be seen as noncompliant or socially awkward.

While each of these could look like a willful or stubborn response, a greater understanding is gained by learning more of the story. The woman is triggered because church is where she was repeatedly sexually molested as a child. She longs to be in church with others, but when she has attended, fear has gripped her through the entire sermon—to the point she's struggled to recall what she heard.

The teen who avoids eye contact lived with a highly abusive and ranting father until his mother fled with the teen to keep him safe. He remembers receiving a severe beating for looking his father in the eye, a gesture his father told him was not only disrespectful but also a challenge to his authority.

The man who appears angry is no longer comfortable sitting anywhere he cannot see the exit after surviving an active shooter incident in his office building.

The student was adopted at four years old. The country he came from was known for cold and distant caregivers and his orphanage was no exception. He was given only minimal attention beyond feeding and bathing when needed. Social and relational connection do not come easily for him. Though he is now in high school, he struggles with distressing social anxiety and can only tolerate limited amounts of social interaction.

We must always take sin seriously, but if we are going to change how the church cares for the traumatized, we must expand our understanding of what besides sin might be driving people's actions. We must become compassionately curious people who avoid assumptions and seek to learn more. Christians must become invested in people's stories, and we must become more aware of other potential factors at play. Helpers must become students of trauma to usher in needed change. Reading this book is one step in that direction. I believe more than ever that the church desires to grow in trauma awareness. The need for resources on the topic of trauma will continue to be in demand, and I hope this book is just one of many that you, as a helper or friend, might read.

Thankfully, improved methods of care and research continue to change in the psychiatric world as well. Positive traction for trauma survivors started to be seen after 1980 when the American Psychiatric Association added PTSD to the third edition of *Diagnostic and Statistical Manual of Mental Disorders* (DSM-III).[13] Since that addition, there has been an increasing emphasis on comprehending the effects of trauma, as well as a growing effort to provide compassionate care and assistance to those who have experienced it. Much of the research is focused on how the brain is impacted by trauma and how symptoms are experienced physically, emotionally, and relationally. But the brain is complex and memory networks are just shy of mysterious. To say we are still learning about trauma will likely be a statement that will ring true for decades to come.

With improvement in psychiatric care and advancement of a more compassionate approach to trauma care developing, Christians now have more opportunity than ever before to improve their understanding of trauma and trauma care. Every encounter with trauma is an opportunity to show the love of Jesus to those who are suffering. It is an opportunity to affirm that the God who created them does not condemn them for having physical and emotional responses to terrible situations, but rather, he understands.

> **Every encounter with trauma is an opportunity to show the love of Jesus to those who are suffering.**

Becoming trauma aware will require a compassionate and holistic approach to people. We may not fully comprehend the experience of a trauma survivor—in fact, they may not fully comprehend it either—but we can seek to learn. In gaining more knowledge about trauma and learning a person's specific story, we can prevent further emotional harm and exemplify a kindhearted response, much like the way Jesus loved and cared for those who were in deep need of help. This is an approach that will require us to embrace a Christlike demeanor toward sufferers, while at the same time acknowledge that we are all learners in the process. Let's begin with a deeper dive into what trauma truly is and expand our understanding of how it manifests in our lives.

The Impact of Trauma

The word *trauma* and various forms of the word (*traumatic* or *traumatized*) are, at times, tossed out flippantly in conversation to overstate the impact of certain relatively minor events. People will say they were traumatized when they receive a bad haircut, were asked to introduce themselves in front of a large group, or when they lost or misplaced a sentimental object. While everyone's experiences are unique, and what may seem insignificant to one person may be more significant to another, these circumstances, though upsetting, embarrassing, or frustrating, are likely not going to cause lasting emotional distress.

The American Psychological Association describes trauma as "an emotional response to a terrible event like an accident, rape, or natural disaster."[14] This definition, however, is often expanded to include the more comprehensive experience that trauma sufferers face. Professor Preston Hill, influenced by psychiatrist Bessel van der Kolk, describes trauma in a concise yet accurate way when he says trauma is an "inescapable stressful event that overwhelms someone's coping mechanisms."[15] The simplicity of the definition captures it well. Trauma overwhelms us and leaves us unable to cope.

The Substance Abuse and Mental Health Services Administration (SAMHSA), however, offers a more robust definition, which can also be very helpful in understanding trauma. While I appreciate simple definitions, such as those offered by Hill and van der Kolk, this one will better serve you in understanding what is meant when the word *trauma* is used in this book. They define trauma as resulting "from an event, series of events, or set of circumstances that is experienced by an individual as *physically* or *emotionally* harmful or threatening and that has lasting adverse effects on the individual's *functioning* and *mental, physical, emotional, mental,* and *spiritual* well-being"[16] (emphasis added).

From this definition and the emphasized text, you can see that traumatic events impact the whole person. Trauma can wound both physically and emotionally, and the signs of traumatization can manifest in many areas of a person's life. This definition also emphasizes that the impact is lasting and distressful.

Judith Herman, again in her book *Trauma and Recovery*, goes further in explaining the impact of trauma on a person. She states,

> Traumatic events called into question basic human relationships. They breach the attachments of family, friendship, love, and community. They shatter the construction of the self that is formed and sustained in relation to others. They undermine the belief systems that give meaning to human experience. They violate the victim's faith in a natural or divine order and cast the victim into a state of existential crisis.[17]

As you read that description, can you see how what she is describing could mean that even a steady Christian might question things they firmly believe when trauma hits? Trauma can cast deeply held beliefs into the shadows of doubt.

Another word that will be helpful for us to understand is *traumatization*. Traumatization is a term used to describe the negative impact a traumatic event or series of events has on a person's life. Traumatization captures the state in which a person is now living, taking into consideration their exposure to trauma and the various ways trauma impedes their capacity to function optimally in their daily life. Experiencing a traumatic event does not necessarily mean that a person will become traumatized. We will discuss why that is in future sections of this book. The experience of trauma and its impact on an individual's well-being can vary significantly. It is essential to recognize that there is no one-size-fits-all approach to addressing the effects of traumatization.

Trauma can cast deeply held beliefs
into the shadows of doubt.

One last explanation is that of the phrase *trauma response*. When you think of a trauma response, you may have in mind certain behaviors or thought processes that are mainly negative. Maybe you think of someone hyperventilating or becoming physically agitated. Or maybe you think of someone becoming paranoid or hypervigilant. You might think of reactions or thoughts that need changing and are unhealthy. Allow me to redefine your understanding of a trauma response.

When someone goes through a traumatic experience, in order to survive, they must do something. Maybe it is resisting an attacker (fight), running from a burning building (flight), or pretending to be asleep when a drunk parent comes home (freeze). Any of these choices could be different based on the circumstances faced, but whatever is done is done for survival. That is resiliency at work— adapting in whatever way is needed to endure. Their response to the trauma keeps them alive. So now when a current situation triggers a memory or emotion experienced in the traumatic past, the body goes back into survival mode. Committed to keeping the person alive, the body seeks to provide whatever was needed previously when the trauma first happened.

When seen in this context, we realize a person's trauma response is a way of adapting for survival. It is the body's way of choosing to survive once again. To put this as a colleague of mine once did, sometimes our body doesn't get the message the war is over. This is in part because the body doesn't always distinguish between the distress caused by the memory or the distress triggered by the actual event and will activate this survival response either way, even when there is nothing presently threatening the individual. In essence, an actual threat, a perceived threat, and a remembered threat can get the same reaction from the body. That is a trauma response.

From these definitions and descriptions, we can see the impact trauma can have on a person's life. What you've read up to this point may have resonated with you in connection with your own life or the life of someone you care about, and you may be wondering what can be done. This book will guide you into a better understanding of what it means for Christians to understand trauma and what help looks like for the sufferer. As you read, be prayerfully open to what the Lord might teach you about your own story or the story of someone who has gone through trauma.

Looking again at the definition of trauma from SAMHSA, and recalling that traumatic events "violate the victim's faith in a natural or divine order and cast the victim into a state of existential crisis," then the church ought to set out to learn all it can about trauma and how to help survivors. The church ought to be the place where people turn when their faith is given a painful blow. Traumatized people are helped when the church learns what trauma is and how it affects the lives of those who have experienced it. But definitions are not enough. There are unique reasons why believers need to understand trauma, and we will look at those reasons in the coming pages. In doing so, we will continue to expand our understanding of trauma. But let me first clarify who this book is for.

A Note to My Readers

While this book will benefit both the helper and the sufferer, it is written primarily for those who are walking with others and who desire to be more informed and educated about trauma. You will find both biblically and scientifically based direction to help you better prepare to care for the traumatized, and if you are someone who has been through trauma, I believe you will find help and hope here as well. This resource is an attempt to help the church, the body of believing brothers and sisters, better understand trauma. But I am certain that some will be reading this to better understand their own story of trauma. With that said, before we go any further, allow me to briefly address both of these readers.

To the fellow helper:

This book aims to equip you to become a helpful part of the healing process for those who have experienced a traumatizing event or situation. Whether you are a friend, family member, mentor, pastor, counselor, or whatever your relationship to the trauma sufferer, you have the potential to offer comfort and support. You don't need a formal degree or a certification to make a difference in the life of a person with a trauma story. However, it is essential to be well informed regarding the impact of trauma, well informed about how trauma might manifest in someone's life, and well informed about how to respond with empathy and compassion. *Trauma Aware* will provide you with just that. I have prayed for you, trusting you will become a better helper through what you read here.

To the sufferer:

If you have picked up this book as one who has experienced trauma, I am so glad. I hope and believe you will find the content of these pages of great benefit. But let me make one significant suggestion: Let me encourage you to seek the support of a trusted friend or mentor by asking them to read this book together with you so that you have a companion to walk with you as you process what you are learning. Go slowly and allow yourself time to do this processing. If you are a follower of Jesus, you are never alone and you can trust God to help you and care for you. May the words of Isaiah 42:3-4 encourage you:

> He will not break the bruised reed, nor quench the dimly burning flame. He will encourage the fainthearted, those tempted to despair. He will see full justice given to all who have been wronged. He won't be satisfied until truth and righteousness prevail throughout the earth, nor until even distant lands beyond the seas have put their trust in him (TLB).

Welcome to this journey. I have prayed for you.

CHAPTER 2

WHY WE MUST UNDERSTAND TRAUMA

Life can bring various unexpected challenges and difficulties. The human experience is not promised to be carefree and easy, and so it becomes imperative to explore the profound realm of our deepest sufferings. Trauma is often a misunderstood and underestimated force that shapes lives in myriads of ways. Within this chapter, we will explore three compelling reasons we need to understand trauma. They are as follows: First, we will confront trauma as a universal human struggle, calling upon the command to love those who bear its weight. Second, we will grapple with the perilous consequences of ignorance, acknowledging that a lack of understanding can inadvertently be hurtful. Finally, we will consider trauma not merely as an experiential challenge but as a poignant opportunity for the gospel, illuminating the path toward healing and redemption.

Reason #1 We Must Understand Trauma:
To share a common human struggle in love.

The caller ID came up as Mercy General Hospital. Alan had never received a call from them before. No one in his family was sick. His heart seemed to pause as he touched the "accept" button on his phone.

"Mr. Jones, are you the father of Christopher Jones?"

The caller's words hung in the air as Alan's thoughts started to race.

He last saw his son at the breakfast table that morning. They had exchanged a few words about what Chris would do that day. Chris had described a typical summer day for a teenager—a quick drive to pick up a friend, skateboarding in the park, maybe some video games, and then back home to mow the lawn once the sun was not so hot.

Holding his breath, Alan affirmed Christopher was his son.

"Your son has been in a serious accident."

As Alan listened to the caller, he felt as if time was moving in slow motion. The questions flooded his mind faster than he could process them. He had to go to the hospital! He began to hunt for his keys as he tried to listen to what was being said about his son, but he was having a hard time keeping up. His mind was racing and paralyzed at the same time. He could feel his heart pounding. He interrupted the voice on the other end in a desperate cry: "Is Chris okay? Will he be okay?" Any further delay in learning the answer to that question was unbearable for Alan.

My guess is you read the paragraphs above with rapt attention. You may have found yourself more riveted to this account than to anything else you've read so far in this book. You likely felt yourself pulled into the story as it unfolded. Why? Because as humans, we all have our share of struggles and difficulties that we encounter in life, and we can readily identify with the panic felt in a crisis situation. Even if our stories are not exactly the same, we can all relate to moments like Alan's. Part of being human is being subjected to challenging and painful circumstances and the impact they have on us. Our common experience of suffering has a way of drawing our hearts toward others even when we have no direct connection with them. We care and we want to express it. In addition, as Christians, we are commanded to love, and love compels action.

Understanding trauma is important because, despite the various and sometimes unique circumstances that bring about the trauma, the effects that it has on people are shared by many. In some way or another, you relate to life's distressing events even if they are not your own circumstances. Whether it is your neighbor, your co-worker, someone in your family, or someone at your church who has experienced trauma, you have an opportunity to love them amid their struggles and connect with them through care and support.

As Christians, we are called to love people. Paul directs us to "walk in a manner worthy of the calling to which you have been called, with all humility and gentleness, with patience, bearing with one another in love" (Ephesians 4:1-2). One common problem is we think we know how to love people and we assume we know what they need even before we know their full story. The truth is, we won't love people well if we don't understand what they have been through and how their circumstances have affected them. I mentioned earlier that throughout this book, I will share stories from my past counseling sessions in an effort to help us grasp the importance of why we must understand trauma. These stories are real, but they have been adapted to protect the privacy of those who have suffered, in some cases, unimaginable atrocities. Some of the stories exemplify long-term exposure to repeated distress, abuse, or suffering. Others are about people who have endured a single catastrophic event. Each person whose life I explore will share two similar realities: First, their lives are marked by traumatization. And second, they are people we are called to love.

Regardless of how trauma entered a person's world, a compassion-ate approach will require you to learn to understand their experiences so you can love and care for them well. In doing this, you will follow in the path of Jesus, who was moved with compassion when he saw people suffering (Matthew 9:36). Consider the stories in this book and the stories of those you are walking with as invitations. They are invitations to understand. They are invitations to become curious in an effort to learn what life is like for others so you can offer essential care. The stories are also invitations to compassion. Trauma opens a door for Christlike compassion and tenderhearted care to be offered. With a little equipping, you will be able to extend wise care that will demonstrate your awareness of the impact of trauma.

Every trauma story you encounter is an invitation. At bare min-imum, you are being invited to lend your ear and listen empatheti-cally. But the invitation may ask for more from you. It may ask you to open your heart and seek to tenderly offer support and care into circumstances you may not fully understand. This is a necessary invitation, for we are all human and are susceptible to the horrors of this world. We never know when we might find ourselves facing a call from the local hospital or experiencing an event that can bring trauma into our own life.

We need to understand trauma because it is an issue faced by people, and we are called to love people. We are called to bear one another's burdens. As we delve deeper into the world of trauma and explore how we can be of support through difficult times, we will then be able to help lighten the load others are carrying (Galatians 6:2).

Trauma opens a door for Christlike compassion
and tenderhearted care to be offered.

Reason #2 We Must Understand Trauma: To avoid minimizing or worsening someone's suffering.

Last year, I took a pretty bad fall down the stairs in my home. Thankfully I didn't break any bones, but my elbow took the brunt of the impact. Within only a few seconds of the fall, my elbow had swelled up so that it looked like I had a golf ball under my skin. I didn't give much attention to my elbow at first, but attended to other aches and pains in my body caused by the fall. But after a week of significant tenderness in my elbow, I went to the doctor. The visit revealed I had ruptured the bursa sac surrounding my elbow. My doctor informed me that though it would heal, the wound was significant, and I would need to give it appropriate attention and care. I was surprised to learn that rupturing the bursa sac can lead to serious infections, and I was grateful he was more attentive to my elbow than I had been. I had admittedly minimized the injury.

After seeing my doctor, I followed his advice for care, and my elbow eventually started to heal. At the time of this writing just over a year later, my elbow has mostly healed, though it is still tender when bumped too hard.

More recently, however, I took another fall. Not down my stairs but off a hammock I had hung incorrectly. As it turned out, the same injured elbow broke my fall. This time, the fall itself was not bad at all—more of a clumsy tumble. Because the previous wound had made my elbow all the more sensitive, this minor fall caused the pain to resonate again upon impact. I ended up reinjuring or retraumatizing the same spot.

This can happen with emotional trauma. If we don't seek to understand a person's story of trauma, we may unintentionally make less of their pain or retraumatize them as we unknowingly *touch* areas of their life that are tender. We also need to understand trauma because, to put it simply, we don't understand it. We may use the word *trauma* to describe someone's experience, but we may not fully grasp its true meaning or the potential consequences of labeling something as traumatic. In some ways, it makes sense that we do not understand trauma because it is a topic that is only recently receiving significant research. If you recall, I shared earlier that the diagnosis of PTSD was not recognized in mental health care until 1980, exposing our lack of understanding of the disorder in years past. Because the church commonly trails behind the latest developments in science and medicine, it is not surprising that trauma is a newly addressed topic for the church.

The landscape of trauma care continues to change rapidly. With further research, advancing methodologies, and the use of imaging like functional magnetic resonance imaging (fMRI) and two-photon excitation microscopy (TPEF), which allows us to see activity in the brain *in vivo*, we are learning more and more about trauma and its impact on the brain.

Understanding how trauma changes or affects the brain has led those in the psychotherapy world to approach people differently. Instead of asking, "What is wrong?," the question has now become, "What happened?" This needed shift alone is an advancement in our understanding, but we (specifically the church) still have a long way to go. What is most encouraging is that these methods of viewing the brain (fMRI and TPEF) are expanding our comprehension of how trauma's impact on the brain can be repaired through care, treatment, and therapy.

Understanding trauma starts with being able to recognize it. But recognizing trauma is not always easy. The good news is you don't need a high-tech brain scan to see it. By learning the various ways trauma can manifest in someone's life, you can become a better student of what happened to that person and notice how it affected them. I created a resource called the Basic Trauma Questionnaire-15 (BTQ-15).

This brief questionnaire and the instructions for administering it can be found in Appendix A. We will look further at common symptoms in Part 2 of this book. However, knowing symptoms isn't the only way to grow in your understanding and awareness of trauma.

One of the first ways you can become more trauma aware is by learning to ask helpful questions and engage in healing conversations. Some people are naturally more curious than others and when they encounter something they don't understand, they ask questions. The questions are not interrogative or accusatory. They simply have a desire to learn more about people and their stories. This creates a space for people to feel understood.

Too often, when we don't understand things, we impose our own experience, judgment, convictions, or assumptions on the person or their situation. These biases can get in the way of being curious. When we don't understand something, we more easily misjudge it. When this happens, we can end up viewing a traumatized person's story through the lens of our own misunderstanding rather than through the experience of their suffering. This can unintentionally end up causing more pain and deeper traumatization. If there is anything that should put us in the posture of being the learner, it is encountering a suffering person. Resist the temptation to assume you understand. Instead, become compassionately curious. Take time to ask questions. If you are uncertain of what to ask, I will share some possible questions as you continue in this book. One good way to become adept at asking insightful questions is to observe and learn from those who excel in this aspect.

If there is anything that should put us
in the posture of being the learner, it is
encountering a suffering person.

Jesus was masterful at asking questions. With Jesus, questions were invitations to be known. He is God, which means he does not lack information, nor does he need to be taught or enlightened about anything, especially his own creation. We see in Scripture how he knew the thoughts of people (Matthew 9:4-5; 12:25; Mark 2:8; Luke 5:22-23; John 2:24), yet he asked questions. He drew people out by being curious: "Who do people say that I am?" "Do you want to be healed?" "Who touched my clothes?" "Where are your accusers?" As Jesus asked questions, people were given the opportunity to share their stories, better understand themselves, and better understand God. We want to do the same. Let your questions be avenues of better understanding for you and the one you are caring for.

If you struggle to know what questions to ask, here is a short list:

- Are there any emotions or thoughts you have been grappling with that would be helpful to talk about?

- Is there anything or anyone that gives you comfort as you process what happened?

- Is there anything that is triggering for you that I should know about as we talk?

- Are there particular times, people, settings, or memories that make it easier or more challenging for you to open up about your experiences?

- Is there any Scripture passage that is a comfort for you as you consider your experience?

- In what ways do you think your spiritual, emotional, or physical life has been affected by trauma?

- How does your body respond when you think about the trauma?

- Are there parts of your body that you notice hold tension more than others when you talk about what happened?

- In light of the traumatic experience, how have your feelings and thoughts about God evolved over time, if at all?

- How are you feeling about being with me and talking about your story?

As you walk with someone, it is important to understand the *emotional, physical,* and *spiritual* impact their traumatic experience has had on their life. The questions above start to explore this, but it is also important to go slow and take whatever time is needed to discover how these three areas are often affected in diverse ways.

We are embodied souls, which means our bodies are affected by what we deeply believe, and what we deeply believe impacts our bodies. This is what it means to live out embodied faith. Our bodies and our faith are interconnected. Sometimes our feelings and faith match. Other times what we believe doesn't align with what we feel. This doesn't mean we lack faith; rather, it may be we are experiencing what it means to be embodied and living in a world where suffering and struggle are part of life.

John Murray, a great theologian who also served as a professor at Westminster Theological Seminary until 1966, taught that man is a bodily creature, and therefore, it is biblical and right to say that man is a body rather than man has a body.[1] Murray grasped the importance of the body and taught accordingly. We need to bring back this teaching to our churches today. We need to talk openly about the importance of the body in ways that are not only connected to spiritual worship or Christian obedience but also to our experience in a fallen world. We need to have conversations about the body that acknowledge how our bodies communicate our experiences to ourselves and others. Trauma is a matter of emotional, physical, and spiritual importance because these aspects of our lives are divinely interconnected.

The Prevalence of Trauma

Statistics show that more people will be exposed to a traumatic situation in their lifetime than ever before. More than two-thirds of people will experience a traumatic event by the time they are 16 years old.[2] A research study conducted by the Department of Epidemiology and Psychosocial Research found that more than 70 percent of respondents to their survey reported experiencing at least one traumatic event.[3] Trauma has become a reality of life.

The increased exposure may certainly be due, in part, to how accessible traumatic events are to us via our smartphones and computers. A natural disaster happens, and we are shown multiple firsthand videos of the destruction people endured. A shooting takes place, and every news platform broadcasts the devastating scenes as the main headline. A person is victimized, and the raw video footage of the event becomes a viral video for all to see. We not only see traumatic events in the news and on social media, but thanks to our smartphones we can watch and rewatch them, zooming in to the details or pausing to examine the specifics of the horrifying event. In these ways, our world has become more filled with trauma than ever.

We never know when trauma will hit but we do know it is abounding. We must grow in our understanding of it so we can wisely move into a person's experience and not add to the pain people have already endured. Sometimes we add to a person's trauma by missing the weight of what they have endured. Just because something is not traumatizing to one person doesn't mean it won't be traumatizing to another. We may not understand the impact of the trauma even when we know the details of it. This should motivate us to better understand trauma so we can better comprehend the weight of what people have endured.

Let me raise one caution here: In a world that is eager to compare and keep score, we must be careful not to compare people's experiences of suffering. Just because someone's trauma doesn't seem all that serious to you or if you know of worse situations, this does not mean their experience was not deeply painful. When we view trauma as only fitting into catastrophic categories, we not only diminish the suffering people have endured, but we also classify trauma into categories we should not. Remember, something was traumatic to a person because it was experienced as an inescapably stressful event and going through it overwhelmed their ability to cope. I urge you to avoid the pitfall of dismissing something as not traumatic if someone else could have perhaps coped with it better, or if it does not seem as stressful as another situation. Resist the temptation to compare various circumstances because doing so dismisses a person's suffering.

Be Aware of Retraumatization

Even more serious than diminishing a person's pain is doing and saying things that compound the trauma. Retraumatization is the reactivation of emotional distress linked to a previous traumatic experience in a way that has a compounding impact. This happens when an individual is exposed to circumstances (including conversations) that amplify the original traumatic experience and intensify the emotional, physical, or spiritual challenges they face in coping with the effects of the original traumatic event. Retraumatization can cause a resurgence of the pain and stress experienced and provoke setbacks in the healing process.

One well-meaning and common way Christians can unintentionally retraumatize people is by expecting others to be okay with physical touch or close community engagement. A church should be a warm and welcoming place where brothers and sisters are excited to see one another, but we should not assume everyone wants to be touched or treated in the same way. A common situation that happens when we are not trauma aware is that we can do or say things that are intended to be helpful but end up being hurtful.

An empathetic touch might be intended to express care and compassion, but it could be an unwelcome trigger for a trauma survivor. A comment about a person's looks might be meant as a compliment, but it could cause triggering discomfort. Asking detailed questions about a person's life or family, before you have developed a trusting relationship with them can also be distressing to a person who has experienced trauma. Our unintentional interactions could compound the struggle and the pain a person is carrying when we are not more aware of their stories.

For trauma survivors, entering a church where physical forms of contact—such as hugging, shaking hands, or other socially acceptable gestures—are commonplace can be challenging and distressing. Past traumatic experiences can contribute to heightened sensitivity to touch, making such interactions uncomfortable. Churches can create a more inclusive and trauma-informed environment by raising awareness about the potential of diverse needs in their congregation. Encouraging the congregation to offer alternative forms of greetings like verbal acknowledgments or respectful nods can provide trauma survivors with a safer, more supportive space to participate in worship and the church community. Implementing this in your small groups as well can lessen the possibility of church becoming a stressful event for a trauma survivor.

Training for those in leadership can be helpful, including suggestions for alternative ways to greet congregants and useful questions that help the leadership set the example for the church. Simply asking permission is the best way to approach these interactions, such as, "Are you okay with a hug?" Questions with options are also helpful, such as, "Could I shake your hand or is hello sufficient?" "Are you a hugger, or do you prefer a smile when I see you?" "Do you want me to hold your hand as I pray for you, or is standing beside you more helpful?" At first you may feel awkward about asking these kinds of questions, but when you do so, you are fostering an atmosphere of compassion and understanding that will help trauma survivors feel more accepted and respected.

But it isn't only in church that circumstances of retraumatization can happen. I would guess that you, too, have had situations in which you were hurting, and a well-meaning friend sought to cheer you up with a little comic relief. They joked about lighthearted things, hoping to brighten your day. Or maybe someone attempted to care for you by offering words of counsel, suggesting you "stop dwelling on the past," or they lovingly encouraged you to "move on." Your friends might have had good intentions. They wanted to help, but the impact of their words might have caused you to feel invalidated and even unsupported.

On one occasion, I was the giver of such words, and I am grateful the friend I spoke them to was willing to let me know how hurtful they were. She had been through a very painful breakup due to severe abuse happening in the relationship. She had been so controlled in the relationship that, despite clear physical and emotionally abusive actions, she had felt trapped. Thankfully, with the help of supportive friends, she fled the relationship.

Afterward, though she was attending weekly counseling sessions, she began to feel overwhelmed by how much trauma she was coming to realize she had endured. She expressed her weariness to me about how difficult and exhausting the counseling process was. As her friend, I could see that as hard as things were, she was truly making progress. As I listened to her share her feelings with me, I wrongly assumed she was telling me she was going to quit seeking counsel. Wanting to encourage her, I jumped in and said, "You can't quit counseling, though." We continued to talk, yet I sensed her slowly retreating from the conversation. A few days later, she called me to tell me how hurtful my statement had been. In her relationship, her ex-boyfriend had told her what she could and could not do, and in that moment, I had done the same by telling her she could not quit seeking counsel.

I was so grateful my friend had shared that with me. I realized how, to her, my words were similar to the words she had heard in her abusive and controlling relationship, which had brought up familiar feelings of dread. My words had caused a wave of fear to come over her and were retraumatizing.

The more you understand trauma, the less likely you are to retraumatize a person. But as you can see, even with an awareness of the impact of trauma, mistakes can still happen. We must be aware of this possibility and proceed with caution.

Avoiding Common Pitfalls

When we don't understand trauma, our efforts to show care can inadvertently minimize or dismiss a person's struggle and leave them feeling more isolated and alone. Our intent may be to care, but to be trauma aware means exercising caution when we show our care. One way to make sure your words or actions had your intended impact is to do a conversational check-in. When you intend to help or encourage someone, whether you are aware of any trauma in their life or not, a conversational check-in positions you to better care for them and avoid the possibility of retraumatization.

*To be trauma aware means exercising
caution when we show our care.*

You can do this by simply asking how what you just said affected them. Start by letting the person know you want to care well for them, and you want their feedback on how your interactions are going. Choose one of the questions below to ask. This type of interaction requires humility and a willingness to learn. Be prayerful as you enter this interaction. You are there to hear the impact of your words or actions, not to substantiate them. Avoid the temptation to defend yourself. Taking a humble posture will build relational trust and will pave the way for future conversations in which you may be able to offer further clarification or justification if needed. But for now, be genuinely curious and ready to hear and learn. Had I done a conversational check-in with my friend, she probably would have been able to at least clue me in to the fact that my words were hurtful.

When you do a conversational check-in, you want to affirm you are there to help but you need the other person's input regarding whether or not your care is helpful. Let them know you want to get feedback along the way during the conversation. Choose one of the questions below, and use it to check in on how the conversation is going:

1. How are you feeling right now after what I just said?

2. What did you think about what I just said?

3. Were any of my actions toward you helpful? If so, how? Were they hurtful in any way? If so, how?

4. Did I say or do anything that made you feel uncomfortable?

5. Is there anything you would like to share about how what I just said or did affected you?

6. What could I say or do differently next time to make you feel more cared for when we meet?

7. Is there anything we talked about today that has left you feeling unsettled?

Again, this is not the time to defend anything you've said. Your goal is to check in with the other person about how helpful your interaction with them was. You are there as a learner. It does not mean their assessment is correct; they may have missed your intent. But no matter how good your intention was, if the impact is negative or unhelpful to them, it will not matter what you meant, especially if it is left in this state. You must be invested in learning how your care is impacting them. Do a check-in, learn what you can, then take the situation to the Lord and prayerfully ask him to help you know how to better care for your friend.

Reason #3 We Must Understand Trauma: To open opportunities for the gospel.

As a licensed counselor with specific trauma training, I have occasionally been invited to provide care in crisis situations that happen in various communities in the US and around the world. With every major news headline of a catastrophic event, a call often goes out to mental health care workers who are equipped to provide trauma care. Thanks to the ability to hold sessions online, counseling can begin immediately. In some of these situations, people are still enduring the traumatic event while care is being provided. Counselors have reported holding online sessions with people in their disheveled homes after a natural disaster, or with people living in war zones while artillery shells can be heard in the background.

Perhaps you are wondering whether it is helpful to provide care while the trauma is still happening. The answer is yes, it can be very helpful. Specific trauma-care protocols used as closely as possible to the traumatic event have been shown to lower the negative impact of the event and allow processing to begin, even while the trauma continues. These various protocols have been used with great success on combat veterans and others who have experienced trauma. However, as effective as these methodologies and technologies are, they are only a temporary fix. That is not to say the effect of the care will wear off, but rather, that it provides relief only in the immediate circumstance.

While we should do what we can to alleviate a person's pain and suffering, it is Jesus who can bring deeper and more profound healing. He not only provides comfort in this life but also offers eternal liberation from all suffering. It is essential to realize that outside of the compassion of God, the comfort of Jesus, and the help of the Holy Spirit, every approach to healing is temporary. As Christians, we seek to relieve pain. That is what compassion does. When we point the hurting and broken to Jesus, we hold out eternal hope and healing. There is no quick fix in trauma care, but he is the long-term sustainable solution for all our pain.

A compelling rationale for comprehending trauma arises from the fact that the gospel provides the essential hope individuals need in a world full of atrocities. When we begin to grasp the intricate and multifaceted nature of traumatic experiences—how they can affect individuals emotionally, psychologically, and spiritually—we become more cautious with people's stories. This, in turn, provides the opportunity for the church to extend lasting hope to those enduring such sufferings. While this is excellent motivation, we still have a long way to go in becoming trauma aware.

Trauma survivors need to know that their past has not ruined their future. God can heal even the most devastating realities of life. The Hebrew name *Jehovah Rapha* is usually translated "the God who heals." In Jesus, God became a man, bringing healing and restoration to us through his life, death, and resurrection. He is our healer and our sympathetic Savior. The cross is evidence that Jesus can empathize with being threatened, mistreated, abandoned, betrayed, and deeply wounded. He can empathize with the most painful circumstances we face, and he provides healing (Isaiah 53:5; Hebrews 4:15).

Trauma survivors need to know their
past has not ruined their future.

"Effective trauma care always starts with empathy. Although we may never empathize with trauma survivors as fully as Jesus, we must continually express that we have a desire to understand the wounds of trauma such as we are able."[4] It is this Christlike compassion driven by empathy that sets the stage to invite the hurting unbeliever to know this sympathetic Savior. The church has the hope that a traumatized world needs. In the words of Diane Langberg, let us consider that "a look at suffering humanity would lead to the realization that trauma is perhaps the greatest mission field of the twenty-first century."[5]

In Part 3 of this book, you will learn practical ways the church can become a safe place for those whose lives are marked by trauma. It is worth noting that the church has not been completely unwilling to learn how to provide appropriate care. Trauma can be tricky and can manifest in confusing ways. A person who has experienced trauma can exhibit a range of effects. You may be familiar with some of the more common signs of trauma, including flashbacks, bad dreams, or hypervigilant reactions. These are indeed indicators. However, other common effects of traumatization can manifest in ways that are easily mislabeled. Being distracted and disorganized, socially awkward or uncomfortable, or having digestive sensitivity, high blood pressure, medically unexplained chronic pain or illness, a deep guilt or shame, or a change in convictions or beliefs are just a handful of signs often missed by the inexperienced helper.

Caring starts with knowing. And when love for our wounded brothers and sisters in Christ is the catalyst for our interaction, then the church is positioned to be one of the safest places for trauma survivors seeking to hold on to their faith. But that is not the only reason we need to be more trauma aware.

The church has the hope that
a traumatized world needs.

Equally important is the fact that understanding trauma equips the church to be more effective in making disciples. We have the hope a traumatized world needs. Our God stands ready to save, to be a father to those who call out to him in repentance and faith. He leaves the 99 to pursue the one who is in greatest need.

The Bible offers a clear picture of God's tender care for the wounded: "You, God, see the trouble of the afflicted; you consider their grief and take it in hand. The victims commit themselves to you; you are the helper of the fatherless" (Psalm 10:14 NIV). God is a refuge and a source of protection for his children. He knows and keeps every one of their tears. They matter to him—they are never lost. Where they may have contributed sinfully to their situation, there is forgiveness. Where there has been mistreatment, he will deliver justice even when this world does not. Where there is continual pain and regret, he promises to one day make all things new.

In this chapter, we have delved into some key reasons we must seek to better comprehend trauma. Understanding trauma is essential because it allows us to compassionately resonate with the struggles people endure, better positioning us to fulfill the call to love people. By grasping trauma's nuances, we ensure that we don't inadvertently diminish a person's pain or unintentionally retraumatize them. Moreover, growing in our understanding of trauma presents extraordinary opportunities for the gospel to touch lives in profound ways. Through a heightened awareness of trauma, we can become better equipped to provide the care survivors truly need. All of this paves the way for creating contexts in which Christians can be conduits of care, making the church become one of the safest places for trauma survivors.

CHAPTER 3

TRAUMA AND THE BRAIN

The human body is an amazing creation. The intricate systems and processes that ensure our survival occur precisely, and yet they function largely unnoticed by us. Think of it like an amazing symphony. As we go about the ins and outs of our day, each movement is composed in complete harmony with all the others. The conductor of this symphony of creation is the human brain, which directs every detail of our existence and brings everything together in a masterful way.

Biologically speaking, the brain is not only conducting our actions and reactions, but also constructing the framework for how we process life. It is the architect of the pathways of both conscious and unconscious thought and action, and the interpreter that helps us to make sense of everything that enters our world. With billions of neural connections taking place, our brains are the most active part of our body.

Trauma strikes a minor chord in the orchestra creating a dissonance that reverberates through the whole of our person. To better comprehend trauma, we must have a good grasp on the brain's remarkable complexity and how it responds to and is affected by traumatic experiences.

To gain a deeper understanding of how trauma affects the brain, it is crucial to explore the inner workings of our brain and the complex systems designed to ensure our safety and survival. This knowledge will not only help us to grasp the effects of trauma but can also prevent common misconceptions surrounding it. By delving into the functions of the brain, we not only become more attuned to the impact of trauma but also gain insight into our own reactions to life's circumstances. In essence, learning about the brain not only enhances our awareness of trauma but also provides valuable self-awareness regarding our behavioral responses.

There are many ways to explain the brain. To name a few, its complexities can be broken down into regions, lobes, and hemispheres. However, even those general categories merely scratch the surface of its intricacies. In this chapter, you will become more acquainted with the brain to better grasp its remarkable design and function as it relates to trauma, survival, and resiliency. We will also explore some elements of neural function, which will lead us to explore the brain/body connection and enhance our awareness and understanding of trauma's impact.

Any attempt to understand trauma is incomplete without addressing the body, and addressing the body starts by going to the central operating system of it—namely, the brain. This amazing synthesis of the brain and body demonstrates the masterful work of our Creator. These next several pages will not only be an exploration of neurology through a broad-spectrum look at the brain and its systems but will also lead you to affirm that we are indeed fearfully and wonderfully made (Psalm 139:14).

Any attempt to understand trauma is incomplete without addressing the body, and addressing the body starts by going to the central operating system of it—namely, the brain.

To unravel some of the mysteries of how the brain responds to trauma, it's crucial to grasp the functions of the different areas of the brain that contribute to our reactions to situations. Understanding how these areas operate will shed light on which part of the brain takes center stage during traumatic experiences. Knowing this is the key to understanding how to provide appropriate care. In addition to function, a basic understanding of brain development is also needed. While none of this is simplistic, what I present here aims to provide an overview that should offer sufficient clarity for a basic understanding, though it will fall short of being comprehensive.

When discussing our ability to understand the brain, Bill Bryson, author of *The Body: A Guide for Occupants*, concludes that "there is a huge amount we have left to learn and many things we may never learn. But equally some of the things we do know are at least as amazing as the things we don't."[1] With that in mind, let's embark on a brief exploration of the brain and trauma.

A Simple Three-Part Explanation of the Brain

As we explore the brain's role in understanding trauma, we will delve into three crucial components: the brainstem, the limbic system, and the prefrontal cortex. Each of these integral regions will shed light on what happens in our brains when we are exposed to traumatic circumstances and how what happens is meant to keep us alive. This chapter includes images to help illustrate the areas of the brain we will be discussing. The images are for general reference purposes rather than scientific representation. The explanations given will be more of an informal stroll than an exhaustive expedition. I will touch only on the essentials, providing digestible glimpses into how these three components collaborate, and will not go into the vast complexities of brain science. However, I have found a little biopsychological education goes a long way in helping people make connections to their struggle.

The Brainstem

To assist us in comprehending the development and function of our amazing brains, a metaphor may prove helpful. The brainstem is like a reliable engine that powers the most basic operations of our mental machinery. It is the foundation that regulates essential functions and automatically keeps the gears in motion for life and survival.

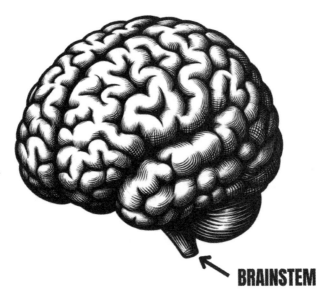

BRAINSTEM

The brainstem is the basis of physical and neurological functioning.

The brainstem is the first part of the brain to mature, and it powers the initial stages of our mental machinery. It is responsible for automatic movements—things like breathing, blinking, swallowing, digestion, heart rate, and blood pressure are regulated and controlled there. The brainstem is fully developed when a person is born and is already regulating the unconscious functions essential for life. When my first child was born, no one told me just how intently invested I would be in watching a little human breathe. As a new mother, every time my baby slept just a bit longer than expected, I repeatedly checked on him to confirm his little chest was rising and falling. This reassuring rhythmic movement continued peacefully without any conscious effort on his part, nor was it dependent on his mother's watchful eye. This automatic life-sustaining activity was regulated by his trusty brainstem. When this part of the brain is most active, a person can be described as being in the *survival state*.[2]

You don't do anything to initiate the activities controlled in the brainstem. They are happening right now, even as you read, without you even noticing. You have been breathing, blinking, digesting, and more. Although you can influence these actions, they will, however, regulate and adjust based on the messages received by other parts of the brain.

The amazing design of the brainstem reveals God's care. If we had to actively engage the functions that our brainstems do automatically, we would be exhausted and would never be able to sustain ourselves because we could never rest. The reality we can go to sleep while our brainstem stays busy working to keep our lungs breathing and our heart pumping is a reminder that our God sustains us through his creative design of our brains. For this reason, we can say with the Scripture, "In peace I lie down and sleep" (Psalm 4:8 NIV)—not only because God watches over us, but also because of how he designed our brains to keep us alive in the most rudimentary and complex ways.

The Limbic System

The machine doesn't stop there. As development progresses, we move on to the limbic system, which gives heart and soul to our functioning. Here emotions ignite, memories form, and our experiences are etched into the very fabric of our being.

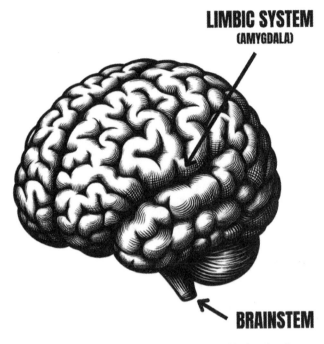

LIMBIC SYSTEM
(AMYGDALA)

BRAINSTEM

The limbic system is fundamental to emotional and behavioral responses.

Imagine the limbic system as a complex network of connections that infuses life with meaning and gives us direction on how to respond both for survival and for deep and expressive engagement. Like an artist adding vibrant hues and defining brushstrokes to a painting, the limbic system injects emotions and fuels our responses, creating a complex masterpiece of experiences that shape our life.

The limbic system, which includes the amygdala, the hippocampus, the thalamus, and more, begins to develop during the first few years of life and is usually fully mature by early childhood. It goes through a time of rapid development during the toddler years, explaining the emotional outbursts as well as the unfiltered expressions you often see in this stage. This part of the brain is responsible for emotion, motivation, aspects of behavior, long-term memory, and the fight, flight, or freeze responses. It is also involved in processing and responding to sensory information. It plays a significant role in regulating basic functions such as sleep and appetite, and is associated with the experience of reward and pleasure. When this part of the brain is most active, a person is described as being in the *emotional state.*[3]

The limbic system helps us in our ability to resolve conflict, maintain friendships, and have the motivation to learn new things. Within this part of the brain is the amygdala. The amygdala gets its name from the Latin word for *almond* because of its almond shape. More accurately, it could be referred to as amygdalae due to their plural nature; we have one in each hemisphere of our brain. These twin clusters of neural cells are located in the center of the limbic system and play a significant role in trauma responses. "On the basis of experiences, your amygdala creates emotional memories—both positive and negative—that you don't necessarily have an awareness of."[4] These memories will determine your responses. "The amygdala weighs in and says something like, 'The last time you met a guy like this, it didn't turn out well,' or 'This seems like one of those nice people.'"[5] This does not mean the messages will always suitably match with the situation at hand, but it is your amygdala that draws on prior experiences to provide you with the possible interpretations and responses.

The amygdala is our God-designed protector. It signals the body on how to react when threatened. It is vigilantly on the lookout for potential harm and signals the body on what to do to be safe. This activity, described as neuroception, refers to the subconscious process of detecting danger. The amygdala comes to your aid throughout your day, anytime you get that uneasy feeling walking to your car late at night, get startled by a sudden loud noise, or have that concerned feeling when you haven't heard from a loved one as they travel. Stemming from the amygdala, all of this happens automatically and influences our emotions and behaviors.

The Prefrontal Cortex

The final part of the brain to understand for our focus here is the cortex (or prefrontal cortex—these terms are often used interchangeably). This part of the brain is the last to develop, and while it undergoes significant maturation starting at around age 12, it is not fully developed until around our mid to late twenties.

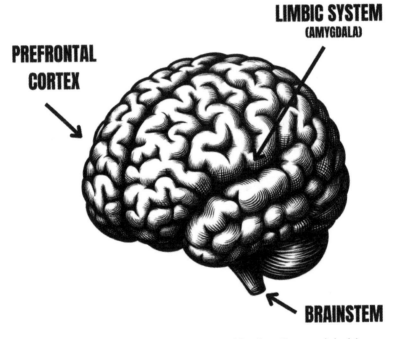

The prefrontal cortex regulates higher cognitive functions and decision-making.

The cortex represents the pinnacle of our cognitive abilities. Connecting the dots in the various messages from the brainstem and limbic system, the cortex provides the intellectual reasoning needed to allow for foresight and reasonable decision-making. This not only fuels our imagination but provides problem-solving prowess unlike any man-made machine or computer.

Whereas the limbic system gives heart and soul to our functioning, the cortex, like a well-oiled machine, executes the operative responses. The cortex engages higher-order functions such as perception and cognition. More specifically, the prefrontal cortex is responsible for intelligently regulating thoughts and emotions and initiating executive functioning. The prefrontal cortex is highly involved in judgment and evaluation and assessing the potential outcomes of actions. It is what helps you make decisions based on your experiences and goals. It analyzes information and facts to assist you in making logical and rational decisions. This part of the brain is highly involved when you learn and process information. When this part of the brain is most active, you can be described as being in the *executive state*.[6]

The prefrontal cortex is what helps us respond logically and adapt to situations with rational and calculated responses. However, these valuable capabilities are not immune to trauma's impact. The frontal lobe, which is part of the cortex, is where we mull around anxious thoughts and explore all the possible outcomes of what is burdening us. This part of the brain has been described as having "the ability to predict future events and imagine their consequences—unlike our pets, who seem to sleep peacefully without anticipating tomorrow's problems. Worry is an outgrowth of anticipation of negative outcomes in a situation. It's a cortex-based process that creates thoughts and images that provoke a great deal of fear and anxiety."[7] Both fear and anxiety can stem from enduring something traumatic as the mind holds past negative experiences and can create an amplified sense of dread about future events. This can lead to dysregulation, characterized by persistent feelings of unease or catastrophizing behaviors. Trauma can cause a person to become hypervigilant and overanalyzing as a means of self-protection. Because trauma calls into question beliefs people hold dear, the promises of God can become muted in the traumatized brain. The good news is that trauma's impact is not fixed, but with well-informed care, those precious promises and essential beliefs can take on deep meaning once again when processed in a regulated brain.

Putting It All Together

Together, the brainstem, limbic system, and cortex are some of the essential components of the extraordinary mental engine we call our brain. It is a state-of-the-art machine that collaborates in unison, shaping who we are and how we interpret and navigate the world. This remarkable creation not only keeps us alive but also helps us to give meaning to the life we live.

All this matters because when you encounter a threat or perceived threat, your brain functions differently than when you are in a place of calm and safety or in the process of learning or critical

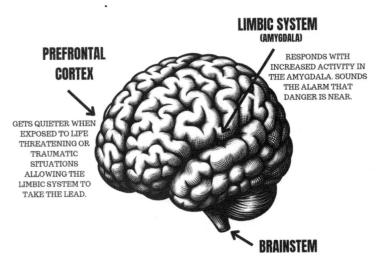

PREFRONTAL CORTEX

GETS QUIETER WHEN EXPOSED TO LIFE THREATENING OR TRAUMATIC SITUATIONS ALLOWING THE LIMBIC SYSTEM TO TAKE THE LEAD.

LIMBIC SYSTEM
(AMYGDALA)

RESPONDS WITH INCREASED ACTIVITY IN THE AMYGDALA. SOUNDS THE ALARM THAT DANGER IS NEAR.

BRAINSTEM

INSTINCTIVELY KICKS IN TO REACT TO THE AMYGDALA'S ALARM.

These three regions interact and influence one another to regulate decisions, emotions, and behaviors.

thinking. God designed our brains with incredible adaptability to keep us alive despite traumatic situations. "Trauma is not a flaw or a weakness. It is a highly effective tool of safety and survival."[8] We've learned how the brainstem keeps us alive by automatically controlling functions like our heartbeat, our breathing, and all the functions of our organs. The limbic system also works automatically to keep us alive. Traumatic events activate the limbic system and send the brain and body into action. In these situations, the functions of the cortex quiet down, allowing more mental space for more necessary life-sustaining actions. With the yielding of the cortex, the limbic system, along with the brainstem, takes the lead. The amygdala comes in full force and pumps hormones through the body, which provide needed energy and strength to allow you to respond with immediate and automatic action.

The Brain's Response to Distressing Events

Learning how parts of the brain work together and react to circumstances can be helpful, but examples of what it looks like can bring it all to life. Here are a couple of amygdala-driven responses from situations that may be familiar to you.

When a car in oncoming traffic starts to veer into your lane, it is your limbic system that activates to help you respond instantly, causing you to turn the steering wheel, hit the horn, or slam the brakes (or maybe all three) to keep you from colliding with the veering car or anything else. It is your amygdala in the limbic system that provides you with the additional energy and strength needed to rush toward the child who is attempting to climb on the table and is about to fall.

Certainly, your cortical brain could assess the make and model of the car and seek to calculate how significant the impact would be based on how heavy the car is and how fast it is headed toward you. It could run through a list of options to instruct the child to climb more effectively to prevent falling, but none of that is helpful in the moment.

God wired our brains so that in threatening situations the functions of the cortex take the back seat and the limbic system takes over to ensure safety and survival become the top priority. All this happens while the brainstem keeps our body's systems going without interruption.

The cortex will eventually play a needed role in the processing that takes place on the other side of the event. How soon or how well that happens after experiencing something distressing or horrific plays a part in whether the experience becomes traumatizing or not. I hope you are seeing just how important the brain is when it comes to understanding trauma and how a person responds to traumatic events.

All this brain activity happens at lightning-flash speeds and is executed in, through, and with your body. For this reason, anyone seeking to become more aware of the impact of trauma must have, at minimum, a general understanding of the brain/body connection. This reciprocal relationship is crucial. In future sections of this book, we will revisit these concepts to explore how these components of the brain are actively engaged in two systems, shedding essential light on how and why individuals respond to trauma and what we can do to help someone who has been traumatized. For now, we will go a little deeper into understanding the brain by looking at the neural systems that are activated in traumatic situations.

Two Essential Systems

Now we are going to turn to two very important systems in the brain that will help you better understand trauma's impact.

The two essential brain systems we will focus on here are the sympathetic and the parasympathetic nervous systems. These systems are both a part of the autonomic nervous system (ANS). Knowing more about these two systems and how they function will be instructive in helping someone work through what might feel like uncontrollable trauma responses. This knowledge will also help the person you are caring for to know that they are not "crazy," "damaged," or "broken." Sadly, these are all terms traumatized people have used to describe themselves to me. Rather, they are experiencing what most often happens when the brain perceives a threat.

The brain's nervous system is made up of billions of nerve cells called *neurons*. Neurons are electrochemical messengers that make connections at lightning speed, causing you to act and react. The various types of neurons all have unique jobs; here is a small sampling of their functions:

- Sensory neurons. As you can probably guess, these nerve cells send information from the eyes, nose, ears, mouth, and skin to the brain so that we can experience life through our senses.

- Autonomic neurons. These regulate involuntary functions like heartbeat, digestion, and respiratory rate, and keep us alive.

- Motor neurons. These carry messages away from the brain to the body to activate both voluntary and involuntary movements.

- Mirror neurons. These nerve cells are essential for experiencing empathy and building connection with others. They help us understand others' actions and emotions by mirroring observed behaviors.

These and other types of neurons in the autonomic nervous system (ANS) are all actively firing and wiring into essential connections that affect the way we think, learn, feel, move, and behave.

The ANS is part of the central nervous system made up of billions of neurons transmitting information throughout your body. This complex system controls many of the processes in your body that happen automatically. Breathing, blinking, heart rate, blood pressure, sweating, digestion, and more are controlled by the ANS, which has three distinct divisions: the sympathetic, the parasympathetic, and the enteric (or gastroenteric) nervous system. As mentioned above, we're going to focus on the first two systems and their relationship to one another as they play a significant role in the impact of trauma and how it is processed.

The sympathetic and parasympathetic nervous systems, which are at the root of how a person responds to trauma, are both tonically active systems. *Tonically active* means "constantly or continuously functioning." This nonstop tonic activity is continually seeking regulation or restoration of health or well-being. This means these two systems of the ANS always provide some degree of input to the body for our good. The rate at which brain cells send signals in both systems can either increase or decrease based on what is needed for homeostasis. *Homeostasis* comes from the Greek word translated "same" or "steady," and it refers to the condition that a system needs to establish and maintain stable conditions for survival.[9]

The result of being tonically active means different regions in the brain may be enhanced or inhibited as needed. This is seen in the activation of the amygdala and the quieting of activity in the prefrontal cortex. This characteristic of the ANS enables the body to more precisely regulate functions and responses as needed. Without this balancing act of tonic activity, the input from our brains would only continue to increase.[10]

While the functions of the ANS happen automatically, this does not mean you cannot influence and adjust the automatic responses in these two systems. You can, and the influence you can have on the ANS will be the focus of some of the practical guidance provided in this book. Scientific research affirms that one of the most significant ways we influence the ANS is through breathing. However, our breathing not only influences the ANS but is also affected by our emotional states.

> Breathing behavior is, for example, highly influenced by emotional states. This behavior is greatly affected by negative (panic, anxiety, and pain) and positive emotions (pleasure, love, and relief)...Breathing disturbances, such as hyperventilation and an increased sigh frequency, are characteristic of panic disorders. And...hyperventilation is possibly causal for the initiation of panic.[11]

To illustrate how breathing can influence the sympathetic nervous system, consider this. Imagine if you were to breathe short, quick breaths as you read the next few paragraphs (don't do it—only image what that might be like).

This change in breathing would influence your sympathetic nervous system, which would cause a chain reaction in your body as your brain sends signals to the rest of the body based on your changed breathing. Your body would respond by elevating your heart rate, sending more of your blood to your core, and you would feel the effects of that. You might get lightheaded, feel out of breath, or begin to experience dizziness. That illustrates how even though this system is automatic, it is not outside of your conscious influence.

In learning about trauma, it is essential to not only understand the sympathetic and the parasympathetic nervous systems but also how one can influence them. Because these systems are directly linked to the symptoms experienced by trauma survivors, a good understanding of both systems increases your ability to help trauma survivors to alleviate trauma symptoms. For this reason, let's take a little more time to get a clearer understanding of both systems and what they do.

The Sympathetic Nervous System

The sympathetic nervous system (SNS) prepares your body for action. It focuses on increasing available energy. The SNS is vigilantly attuned to any signs of sudden stress or any semblance of threat, real or perceived. When these circumstances arise, one of the ways the sympathetic nervous system responds is that it speeds up the heart so your body can quickly send blood to wherever it is most needed. This preparation is necessary for action. It initiates the provision of more blood to the arms or legs for more strength or for protection. Then blood is also sent to the vital organs for survival. This is both an offensive and defensive act of self-preservation. These responses cause hormones to be released because of synaptic firing in the brain, which then cues the adrenal glands to react. Hormones such as adrenaline and cortisol give the body a power boost, which allows your muscles to have needed strength and responsiveness to prepare your body to ready itself for the situation.

Activating the SNS

When your brain perceives a threat, the sympathetic nervous system is activated. This whole process is referred to as the fight, flight, or freeze response and can happen when you are in a situation of distress or threat. The threat can be relational or circumstantial and can include the horrific reality of abuse, rape, robbery, accidents, natural disaster, and the like. It is also what is activated when you are seeking refuge after disturbing a hornet's nest or when you are nervous and about to go on stage to deliver a talk.

During a recent hike, I unexpectedly came upon one of the biggest timber rattlers I have ever seen. The sound of the snake's rattling tail caused me to stop and stay completely still until I could determine the best way to stay out of striking range. Thank you, SNS, for initiating the freeze response, which kept me from a potentially perilous encounter. The sympathetic nervous system not only prepares the body for action with a boost of energy, but it can also keep you from acting too hastily by inhibiting other functions. This inhibition, seen in the freeze response, is your brain preparing your body to survive whatever danger is present. Digestion and salivation are slowed because these are not necessary functions to saving your life or protecting you from harm. Have you ever had a dry mouth when you were asked to give a speech or talk? That is a result of your sympathetic nervous system being activated. If you have ever been unable to eat when you were nervous or anxious, that is a result of your sympathetic nervous system becoming triggered.

Activation of the sympathetic nervous system also turns up the volume in the limbic system, which we learned automatically quiets the cortex at the same time, causing your responses to be more emotional and less rational.

Other physical reactions that take place when the sympathetic nervous system is activated include:

- Dilation of the pupils (maximizing field of vision)

- Inhibition of saliva (slowing digestion)

- Acceleration of the heart rate (giving more blood to the body)

- Dilation of the bronchi (providing faster intake of oxygen)

- Conversion of glycogen into glucose (creating energy)

- Secretion of adrenaline and other neurotransmitters (providing a power boost)

- Inhibition of bladder contraction (eliminating excess weight)

Remember that all of this is the body's response to distress, and its purpose is to aid in keeping you alive. However, the brain's automatic response does not always know the difference between being chased by a bee and being chased by someone in a dark alley. In the same way, the action of talking with your boss about a raise may cause a similar response as when you talk to an emergency dispatcher after calling in to report an accident you encounter on a highway. Just because the sympathetic nervous system's responses are automatic doesn't mean that there isn't anything you can do about them. That is where knowing about the second system in the ANS comes in handy.

The Parasympathetic Nervous System

The parasympathetic nervous system works in opposite ways as the sympathetic nervous system. Rather than giving the body energy, the parasympathetic nervous system conserves it and prepares the body for rest. This system aids in digestion and in the ability to process information. Whereas the sympathetic nervous system is predominant in situations where fight, flight, and freeze responses are needed, the parasympathetic nervous system is predominant in situations where rest, digest, and process responses are needed.

The parasympathetic nervous system is a network of nerves that help to relax your body after periods of stress or danger. It also helps run life-sustaining processes, like digestion, during times when you feel safe and relaxed.[12] Essentially it calms you down, regulates your body, and allows for the absorption of nutrients. It's your parasympathetic nervous system that makes conversation on a first date a little easier after dinner once digestion has begun, versus the often awkward and anxious feelings you have when you are first seated at the table. It is working for you at the end of the day as you sit on your couch and relax or when you feel a comfortable yawn coming on. You can experience the results of your parasympathetic nervous system in the feeling you have after a satisfying meal, a long hot bath or shower, a walk in the park or along a beach, or when you watch a sunset, receive a comforting hug, or have a genuine moment of laughter with a friend. You may even sense hints of parasympathetic activation as you read about the above situations and remember some of the feelings that accompany them. Other physical reactions that the parasympathetic nervous system controls include:

- Constricting of the pupils (allowing for better focus and attention)

- Stimulation of saliva flow (causing digestion to begin)

- Slowing of the heart rate (preparing for rest)

- Constriction of the bronchi (breathing becomes easier and slower)

- Stimulation of the stomach, pancreas, and intestines so that the digestive system stimulates bile release (processing of food)

- Contraction of the bladder (allowing for longer periods of rest)

Activating the PNS

In the same way that you can activate the sympathetic nervous system by taking short, quick breaths, you can also activate the parasympathetic nervous system by taking slow, controlled breaths. Take a deep breath through your nose right now. Fill your lungs as full as you can, and just when they are at their fullest, take one small, quick breath (like a sniff). Now let the breath out through your mouth as if you are sighing. How did that feel? Try it one more time. Breathe in through your nose. When your lungs are full, add one more small, quick breath in, and then without effort, let out the breath through your mouth, allowing your shoulders to relax as your lungs release the breath. Congratulations—you just activated your parasympathetic nervous system! Chances are you feel a bit more at rest or more relaxed than you did before. This is called the *breath sigh*, and you will learn more about it and other calming exercises in the next chapter.

Remembering Activates

It is essential to know that when you ask someone to remember anything that had an emotional impact, you will restart whatever system was most active at the time of that memory. Whether it is a good memory of a favorite holiday location or a distressing time of sorrow or pain, bringing up that memory can bring up the somatic responses associated with that memory as well. What is recalled, however, is not the actual event but a memory of the event. The memory is a link to what happened.

Memories, however, are never exact replicas of what happened. They are shaped and influenced by our experience of the event. "Recalling one's past is not like replaying a videotape of one's life…When we remember an event from our past, we reconstruct it from the encoded elements distributed throughout the brain."[13] This includes the emotions, the sensations, and the reactions. In trauma, the sympathetic nervous system becomes activated and can stay active or be reactivated in triggering situations or with reminders of that trauma. It is important to know that as you talk with someone who has survived trauma and they share their story, their SNS will likely become reactivated. This reactivation of the SNS makes it essential for you to know how to activate the PNS to ensure you don't leave them more upset than when they first started talking with you.

When trauma is unprocessed, a person's body can experience some of the same responses when they talk with you as they did during the traumatic event. Trauma is unprocessed when someone has yet to ascribe accurate and healthy meaning to the event. Trauma is processed when the distressing event is integrated into their lives, resulting in transformed and adaptive responses to the memories, which, in turn, allows for a sense of closure and emotional healing. Scripture—which communicates the truth of God's love and care for his children—is a powerful resource in helping transform responses to memories. I call this redemptive information processing, which we will learn more about in Part 2. For now, we will look at practical exercises that will help with addressing the body's response to trauma.

The Body Tells the Story

The body will tell the story through sensations and reactions. Because of this, when you are caring for people who have gone through traumatic situations, it is helpful to know how to activate the parasympathetic nervous system, as mentioned previously. This is done in the context of a trusting relationship of care, in which the person has agency and is in an environment that is free of threats. Agency simply refers to the individual's ability to have a voice in the relationship and to express their comfort with the process without fear. Activating the parasympathetic nervous system when a person shares about a past traumatic event can take that person from a stress response to a rest response even while sharing the distressing memory.

I noted earlier breathing slowly can activate the PNS. Another simple way to activate it is by paying attention to the story the body is telling and attending to what it needs. If the body is upset, it needs calming. In the counseling world, we say a person is dysregulated or regulated. A regulated person is responsive and in control of their reactions, which allows for your care to be well received. Dysregulation and regulation can be seen in both emotional and physical responses. Often you will see dysregulation happening in the body as a person begins to feel distressed.

Calming Through Grounding

The most direct way to activate the PNS is through the senses. Engaging the senses is a means of grounding a person. Grounding involves helping them reconnect with the present moment and their surroundings. This is done to help someone feel less overwhelmed. Trauma can cause a person to detach from their circumstance as a means of survival. This detachment may be mental, emotional, or physical, or a combination of all three. The detachment may have been needed in the moment of trauma to survive but can inhibit processing afterward. Grounding aims to add a sense of stability and control, counteracting the effects of trauma and allowing a person to better process what happened.

One of the most effective ways to help ground a person is through engaging the senses. Below are some suggestions for engaging the senses in ways that will help to ground and regulate a person when you are helping them process their story of trauma.

1. Sound: Play calm music softly in the background as you talk. Sometimes a quiet room can cause distress—this can happen when there are silent pauses during a conversation in which a person is recalling their story. Check in to see if the music is helpful or distracting. You can also play gentle nature sounds as an alternative. Occasionally draw the person's attention to the music or calm sounds. Ask them to notice how their body feels when they focus on what they hear.

2. Smell: Use aromatherapy. You don't need to have a shelf full of essential oils to utilize the sense of smell to calm the nervous system. Various scents are naturally calming to the body. Air fresheners with natural essences of pine, citrus, mint, or neutral smells can help to lower tension. You can brew tea or coffee to introduce a subtle aroma into the room. Offer a cup of tea or coffee and ask the person to hold it to their nose and notice how they feel as they slowly inhale. As with the music, be sure to check whether the scent is comforting or distracting or elicits any negative feelings.

3. Touch: Have tactile resources in the room. Therapy putty or stress balls are great for this as are fidget toys. I keep a basket full of items like these in my office. I grab one regularly so if the person I am talking with needs one, they are not alone in squeezing a ball, shaping putty, or fidgeting with something while we talk. Having soft pillows or throws on the chairs is another way to utilize the sense of touch to help steady a person. Sometimes people feel better when they can place a pillow on their lap while they talk. It may be that it is settling to hold something, or the pillow creates a natural barrier that helps the person feel safe.

4. Taste: Hard candies, chocolate, or small bottles of water are helpful to have available. Once again, hot tea or coffee are also good options. They are more than just ways to be hospitable—they give a person the opportunity to ground themselves through their senses. Most people do not realize that activating the sense of taste or other senses causes us to be more present with our body.

5. Sight: Draw the person's attention to objects in the room. It helps if the room you meet in is comfortably decorated and includes things that can catch their eye without being distracting. Plants, unique pictures, clocks, or other décor can help someone to pay attention to something visually for grounding.

Calming Through Breathing and Movement

Grounding isn't the only way to help calm the nervous system, though it is effective. Another excellent way to activate the parasympathetic nervous system is through breathing. We discussed this earlier, and you may be wondering why breathing is so helpful. Breathing activates the body's relaxation response. Slow, deep breaths signal the brain that all is well by causing the blood to become more oxygenated and inhibits the production of stress hormones, promoting a sense of calm throughout the body. This happens naturally every time you yawn. The next time you yawn and someone asks you if you are tired, you can tell them, "No, I'm regulating my nervous system."

Deep breathing and grounding exercises can be employed to help bring someone's nervous system back into balance. In addition, movement can be a means to calm a person who is feeling the impact of an activated sympathetic nervous system. Take a short walk outside of the counseling office or the room you are meeting in. Or stand and stretch for a minute, then resume the conversation. At first it may feel unnatural or uncomfortable to do these activities with people you are seeking to help if you haven't been doing them, but they get easier to do when you repeat them often. Soon they can be a regular and natural option to consider when someone you are working with is distressed. These calming practices help the brain to regulate. When people engage in these exercises in counseling settings, they will do them when they find themselves activated outside of counseling settings.

Hope Amid Suffering

Understanding trauma's impact on a person requires a general knowledge of the divine design of our brains. In the same way that it is beneficial to understand the interconnectedness of the gears and circuits in a complex machine, when you know the neural mechanics at play in trauma, you are better positioned to make sense of people's responses and understand trauma's disruptive impact on them. In addition, understanding how one can influence and alter the responses of the sympathetic and parasympathetic nervous systems can augment hope.

Seeing how negative symptoms may be related to the brain reacting to a previous traumatic situation can normalize a person's experience and brings much-needed encouragement. Learning these things also points our hearts to a loving God who knows how to take care of the body he created. Trauma disrupts God's design for healthy functioning; however, God's grace is often found in the amazing way he designed our body, particularly our brains, to help us survive traumatic events. One of the most significant truths a trauma survivor needs to be reminded of is that they did indeed survive. God designed their amazing brain and body to do what was needed to get through the situation. That encouragement can bring a needed lift to the heaviest realities of people's lives.

CHAPTER 4

TRAUMA AND THE BODY

I n 2014, Dr. Bessel van der Kolk, a medical doctor and the founder and medical director of the Trauma Center in Brookline, Massachusetts, published what became seminal work on understanding and treating trauma. One reason his book *The Body Keeps the Score: Brain, Mind, and Body in the Healing of Trauma* became a bestseller is that Dr. Van der Kolk explained what many people were experiencing either in the counseling room or in their own bodies as they lived life in a broken world shattered by sin. Your body tells the story of what you have been through. Your body keeps track of each event and ensures what was experienced is not forgotten. Like the server in a pickleball or volleyball match, your body keeps count and calls out who is in the lead: you or the trauma you've been through.

The Brain/Body Connection

Becoming trauma aware requires an understanding of not only the brain but the whole body. "If you are not aware of what your body needs, you can't take care of it. Simply noticing what you feel fosters emotional regulation, and it helps you to stop trying to ignore what is going on inside you."[1] Knowing what the body needs opens the opportunity for help that is more holistic.

Our minds are created to do more than simply comprehend the world around us; God made us to live out that comprehension in our body. The mind and the body are deeply connected. In the scientific world, this connection is called *neurobiology* and is one of the ways we experience embodiment. If neurobiology seems like a big word, let me put it simply: Neurobiology is how the brain and its systems work together with the body. The reality of trauma demands we grasp just how interconnected our lives are. When something has an impact on us, it affects us emotionally, spiritually, mentally, relationally, and physically.

As we seek to become more aware of trauma's impact on the whole person, we must have an understanding of the brain as well as the body. However, whereas the previous chapter was more informational, this chapter will be more practical. Use this chapter as a toolbox filled with exercises that can help a person whose body is dealing with the negative impact of trauma.

Remember: The fact that we are embodied means whatever we experience, we do so *in* and *with* our bodies. When we care for people, it is essential we do not bypass the body. "Healing must always happen where the wound has occurred,"[2] and while trauma's wounds impact the heart and mind, they are always held in the body.

> *The reality of trauma demands we grasp*
> *just how interconnected our lives are.*

Breathing to Help the Body

In my house hangs a piece of calligraphic art that consists of simple black-and-white script of various handwritten lettering styles with one message. Over and over, in various forms of creative lettering, the entire artwork repeats the sentiment "Don't stress." As your gaze descends on the repeated message, a solitary word in vibrant red interrupts the monochrome cadence—"Breathe." Amid trying to convince yourself not to stress, this artistic reminder is indispensable. This poignant artwork, given to me by the artist, depicts a powerful revelation, a revelation discovered in my counseling room together. As we face the continual challenges of life, we need more than cognitive repetition ("Don't stress"). To counteract the stresses we face, we must attend to what our body needs. The simple yet essential need is this: We need to breathe.

Hopefully you picked up on the importance of breathing when we discussed the activation of the parasympathetic nervous system in chapter 3; now we will expand on that here as we explore the body.

In her practical book *Breath as Prayer: Calm Your Anxiety, Focus Your Mind, and Renew Your Soul,* author Jennifer Tucker shares how she began to understand the value of breathing when faced with distressing situations.

> "Breathing is the bridge between the brain and the body." I first heard these words from psychiatrist Dr. John Bocock, in our first visit with him. Our daughter had been diagnosed about a year earlier with Generalized Anxiety Disorder and suffered from severe and frequent panic attacks, and his first bit of professional advice was centered on breathing and the power of the breath, especially as it relates to managing anxiety.

Tucker captures, in laymen's terms, what medicine and science have confirmed breathing accomplishes: "Breathing gives us a way to hack into our own brain and nervous system!"[3] The way we breathe has a significant impact on how we respond to and engage in life's circumstances, including the circumstance of trauma or post-trauma. I will share a few ways to help you effectively engage breathing to help bring calm to a person who is experiencing distress. These exercises are helpful not only for those living with the impact of trauma in their life, but also for all of us as we go through stressful and upsetting situations.

In chapter 3, we discussed how breathing quickly activates our sympathetic nervous system. This activation, triggered by the change in breathing, causes the release of hormones in the brain. This then causes the body to react in accordance with what it assumes is a threat. In a similar fashion, we explored how we could activate the parasympathetic nervous system by taking slow, controlled breaths. Hopefully you engaged in the slow breathing exercise shared in that chapter.

I now want to share more specific ways you can help a person activate the parasympathetic nervous system through breathing. The purpose of doing this is to help calm the body, something anyone who walks with trauma survivors must know how to do well. You do not need to have a degree or letters before or after your name to utilize these techniques. Breathing is something every living person is qualified to do and teach. I do, however, want to encourage you to try the exercises for yourself first before you use them with those who are experiencing distressing symptoms related to trauma, anxiety, or stress.

Box Breathing

One type of slow, intentional breathing is called *box breathing*. Box breathing can be described as a series of steps you take as you breathe and is a helpful calming exercise. Your goal is to slow your breath and allow the incoming oxygen to reach your furthest extremities (something rapid breathing does not do). Each step lasts four counts. You can use the image below, or any square or rectangular object in your line of vision. Follow each side of the object or the image below with your eyes as you count out each breath:

1. Breathe in as you slowly count to four.

2. Hold your breath to a slow count of four.

3. Breathe out to a slow count of four.

4. Before breathing in again, count slowly to four.

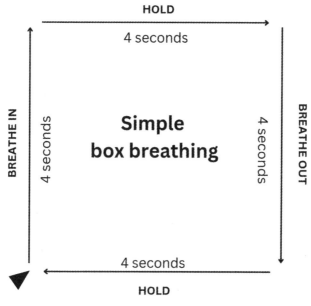

Follow the arrows as you breathe.

Scripture-Based Box Breathing

I have created a variation of box breathing that can be helpful for Christians to practice. Combining Scripture with this exercise rather than counting allows for the mind and heart to engage. It is also a way to help you memorize a favorite passage. I have memorized several verses merely by pairing them with box breathing. Here is an example of how to do that.

1. Breathe in as you slowly recite part of a favorite verse.

2. Hold your breath and recite the next part of the verse.

3. Breathe out slowly as you recite the next part of the verse.

4. Before breathing in again, recite the remainder of the verse.

Here is an example of Scripture-based box breathing with Psalm 23:1:

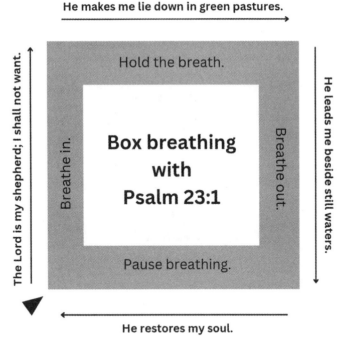

Pair the words of Scripture with your breath.

I have adapted this helpful exercise to better serve Christians seeking to incorporate their faith into this calming practice. Scripture can be a source of peace for believers. Most of us have favorite verses we cling to during difficult seasons. By pairing these verses with breathing, we attend to our spiritual and emotional well-being. For more on box breathing, including additional examples for how it can be done, see Appendix G at the back of this book.

Breath Prayers

There is another similar practice that utilizes deep breathing and Scripture, often called *breath prayers*. In breath prayers, there is no focus on counting or sustaining the breath. Instead, you slow down your breathing as you progress, and make each subsequent breath a bit deeper than your current breath while pairing the breath with Scripture. Inhale while mentally rehearsing part of a Scripture verse, and then when you exhale, mentally rehearse the remaining part of the verse. This practice allows your body to become calmer as you focus your mind on truth. It is important to first affirm that Scripture is indeed a source of calm for a person. Some people may have

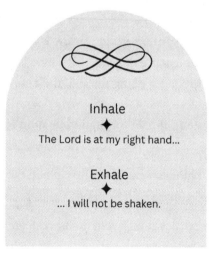

Inhale
✦
The Lord is at my right hand...

Exhale
✦
... I will not be shaken.

This is an example of a breath prayer based on Psalm 16:8.

had Scripture weaponized against them or used in a manipulative way. If Scripture was closely connected to a person's past trauma experience, cautiously explore whether it would be helpful to engage this exercise before proceeding.

For more examples of breath prayers, see Appendix G at the back of this book or consider Jennifer Tucker's book *Breath as Prayer*.

Breath prayers are most effective when practiced on a regular basis. Encourage those you are helping to use them as part of a daily routine—when they first wake up, during a daily devotional time, or at night as they settle into bed.

Breath Sigh

Another exercise to activate the parasympathetic nervous system and calm the body is a breath sigh, more formally called the physiological sigh. Research by Drs. David Spiegel, Andrew Huberman, and Melis Yilmaz Balban highlights a specific breathing pattern that can help regulate your nervous system.[4]

You may have already participated in a breath sigh in the last chapter when you read how to activate your parasympathetic nervous system by changing your breathing. Below is a more detailed, step-by-step guide for engaging this breathing exercise, which includes alternative options for breathing through the nose or mouth.

1. Take in a long inhale through your nose (or mouth, if necessary).

2. Once your lungs are full of the first inhale, take in a second short inhale (like a sniff or gasp).

3. Then fully exhale through your mouth, extending the exhale until your lungs are emptied.

If there is any issue breathing through the nose, the breathing can be done through the mouth. In situations where breathing through the mouth is problematic, the breaths can be done through the nose.

> The second inhale in the double inhale is "really important," Huberman says, allowing for not just the intake of more oxygen, "but also the offload of carbon dioxide." And the exhalation is critical, too, activating the parasympathetic nervous system, according to Spiegel, which then slows down your heart rate and has an overall soothing effect on the body.[5]

You can repeat this exercise as needed. Remember, it is important to not only know the exercises but to have practiced them yourself before you share them with someone you feel could be helped by them.

Breathing, while hugely effective, is only one way we can wisely address the body's response to the trauma and stress we encounter. We must also become more attuned to our bodies to know what they need. There are numerous other ways the body tells the story of trauma, and we must attend to what is needed without reservation. As one writer observed,

> So many of us were taught to fear, abhor, or disconnect from our bodies. As a result, we may mistreat or neglect them. Yet ultimately, we must learn to live in our bodies if we are to pursue wholeness and integrated lives in which we are connected to ourselves, others, and God. We must begin to listen to what our bodies are telling us about what has been done to them and what we are doing to ourselves.[6]

How you respond to what your body is telling you is an essential step to healing from what has traumatized you. One way to become more aware of what the body is experiencing is to do a body scan. This can be a means of relaxing the body, and it can also be a way to become more attuned to where stress is affecting your body.

How you respond to what your body is telling you is an essential step to healing from what has traumatized you.

Body-Scan Awareness Exercise

Trauma counselors often use body-scan exercises to help their clients build awareness of how their body is processing or holding distressing memories. This exercise is also helpful for noticing tension or discomfort in the body that may be connected to trauma or stress. While many find the exercise calming, some individuals who experience chronic pain or have endured body trauma may find it uncomfortable. To alleviate any possible discomfort, you can pair the body scan with rhythmic tapping or sounds. This is referred to as bilateral stimulation (BLS). Studies have revealed that BLS activates a person's parasympathetic nervous system and decreases their fear response.[7]

Here's how the exercise works: Either with or without BLS, take a minute to go through each of the steps below and notice where you had tension that you hadn't been aware of before the exercise. As you do the exercise, give your body what it needs. Do you need to adjust the position your body is in? Do you need to take more time to soften tight muscles? Do you need to stretch or massage any tense muscles? Take the time to respond to what your body is telling you as you scan it.

Once you have become familiar with this exercise yourself, you'll be able to guide another person through it. Always check in and see if the exercise is helpful to them as they do it. Let them know that you can stop at any time, if necessary. The steps below can serve as a helpful guide to doing the body-scan exercise.

> **Step 1:** Settle into a comfortable position. This works best when you can sit in a comfortable chair with your feet on the ground and your back can comfortably rest on the chair. Start by taking in a deep breath. Then breathe normally. Feel the sensation of your breath moving in and out. Gently focus on the rhythm of your normal breathing.

> **Step 2:** Starting at your head, bring your attention to the top of your scalp. Notice any sensations you feel here. Scan your head from the very top and move down, noticing any tension. Consider the area around your temples, or your forehead between your eyebrows, or your jaw. Is there tension in any of those places? If so, take in a slow, deep breath, and as you exhale, imagine the tension releasing.

> **Step 3:** Moving down from the face, see if there is any tightness in the neck or shoulder regions. If you feel any stiffness or stress, take in a deep breath, and as you exhale, allow the muscles to let go.

> **Step 4:** Now pay attention to your arms and hands. How do they feel? Are the muscles in your arms tight? Are your fingers relaxed? Take in a deep breath and imagine sending the breath to that area with your inhale. Then, when you exhale, see if you can release any tension.

Step 5: Shift your attention to your chest and back. Feel the rise and fall of your chest as you continue to breathe. As you scan, take note of whether you come across any stiff muscles. When you do, inhale slowly, then ease the stiffness with the exhale.

Step 6: Turn your attention now to your abdomen and hips. Do you feel any sensations here? Are you holding any tightness in these areas? Breathe in to that space and let go as you exhale.

Step 7: Mentally move down to your legs and feet. Notice how they feel. Are any muscles tense or fatigued? Take in a deep breath and imagine those feelings melting away as you exhale.

Step 8: Now take a moment to tune in to your entire body as a whole. How does it feel after the body-scan exercise? Do you need to make any other adjustments to become more comfortable? One last time, see if you can sense any lingering tension anywhere in your body. If you do, simply take the time to breathe in to those areas and allow them to relax.

For more directions on doing a body-scan exercise, I have included additional scripts in Appendix H at the back of this book.

The body is an essential component when it comes to processing trauma. It can be the entry point to helping someone whose life has been affected by trauma. Often the body will communicate where words are lacking, revealing what the mind has hidden. Because of this, trauma care must address the body.

Often the body will communicate where words are lacking, revealing what the mind has hidden.

More Than *Our* Body

While the exercises in this chapter are helpful for calming the body, there is more that is needed. As believers, addressing trauma should also include the body of another. Jesus became a human. He took on a physical body and subjected himself to traumatic atrocities in his own body for us. His broken body opened the possibility of total healing from the horrors that life in this world holds.

It is important to recognize complete healing does not need to happen for a person to experience fullness in life or relief from trauma's symptoms. There are some memories that will always be terrible, and expecting a traumatic past to be neatly wrapped up and tied with a bow can compound the hurt people have already endured.

There are many wounds that last a lifetime, and there are tears that will remain to the last day (Revelation 21:4). But on that last day, Jesus himself, the one whose body holds the scars of trauma eternally, will wipe away every tear, and death and trauma will be no more. Because of what his scarred body endured for us, our wounds will one day be completely healed. As one writer observes,

> The problems we experience *with* our body were never ultimately going to be solved *in* our body. We may be able to ameliorate some aspects of our bodily brokenness—we can cure some ills and ease some pains. But we cannot fix all that has been broken. The only hope for us is the body of Jesus, broken fully and finally for us. And by looking to his broken body, we find true hope for our own. In Christ, our bodies are no longer identified by what we do *with* them, or by what others have done *to* them, but by what Jesus has done *for* them. And so we await "the redemption of our bodies" (Rom. 8:23) with patience. And in the meantime, we

learn what it means to use our bodies for our new master and savior.[8]

Embracing the Connection

Until that day, when all is redeemed, to approach trauma care without a solid understanding of the impact disturbing experiences can
have on the brain and body is insufficient care at best and reckless at
worst. The body is deeply engaged in trauma, and it will "keep the
score." Susan Brison, a philosopher who survived a nearly fatal sexual
assault in southern France, captures how trauma impacts the whole
person and remains in the body: "I did not yet know how trauma not
only haunts the conscious and unconscious mind, but also remains
in the body, in each of the senses, ready to resurface whenever something triggers a reliving of the traumatic event."[9]

It is not just in the moment of threat that these functions we have
discussed in this chapter become activated. Unprocessed trauma or
distressing memories can get triggered in everyday life and the brain
and body will continue to react. The body responds to a threat or a
perceived threat in nearly equal ways. "We have learned that trauma
is not just an event that took place sometime in the past; it is also
the imprint left by that experience on mind, brain, and body. This
imprint has ongoing consequences for how the human organism
manages to survive in the present."[10]

As believers, we should embrace the brain/body connection. When
the brain is affected by emotional trauma, our mental judgment and
thinking is affected as well. Yet, despite traumatic events, we are still
instructed to live lives that are good and acceptable to God (Romans
12:1-2). We are to love and obey God in both our mind and body
(Mark 12:30). We are sanctified in both our mind and body (1 Thessalonians 5:23). This connection is God's design.

Author and pastor Matthew LaPine challenges counselors, pastors, and theologians alike to take up the task of becoming better equipped in this area:

> God formed us from the ground and enlivened us with his breath. We are not mere souls, but embodied beings. Our entire agency is qualified by physicality. If so, pastors and theologians need to develop a basic knowledge of how the body functions in emotional experience. For example, if we know how the sympathetic nervous system involves our body, we know why our anxious moods persist and so we choose more effective means of dealing with them. Understanding how neural pathways are strengthened helps us see how habits are formed and why they are durable. Our thoughts are not unencumbered by neurons. While Christian pastors and theologians are not therapists, there is no principled reason why they should ignore empirical research about the natural world, and especially about human beings. Theologians especially need to do some cross disciplinary work to assist pastors in this task.[11]

Reading this book is one step in that direction and will help you to recognize trauma and trauma responses. It is my hope you will gain more familiarity with the language associated with trauma care so you are better equipped to attend to those who have been through terrible experiences.

Where God's Word Fits

Post-traumatic stress disorder (PTSD) is the label the clinical mental health world uses to describe the symptoms of someone still suffering

from the impact of traumatic circumstances. I hope you are starting to see that trauma and post-traumatic stress are not topics only
for the clinical mental health world to address. But this raises questions. Does God's Word address the automatic responses of those
who have endured trauma? Where can we go in the Bible for direction on this? These questions are important to answer if we are to
care well for others.

Counselors, pastors, mentors, and friends may struggle to know
where to point traumatized individuals when these questions arise. To
remain biblically faithful while understanding trauma's impact will
require a holistic view of people, a view supported in Scripture. This
can be challenging if we have been taught that Scripture applies only
to areas of spiritual struggle. Yet the Bible is sufficient for addressing all areas of life, including complex issues like trauma. We draw
upon the clear teachings of God's Word to guide and address areas
where the text may not specifically mention words like *trauma*, seeking to apply its principles with wisdom and discernment. And we
must listen well to people to know how to point them toward the
hope found in God's Word. The observations below from psychologist and author Ed Welch are deeply instructive.

> The problem is that we tend to access Scripture by way
> of a concordance. For example, the words fear, anxiety,
> anger, and shame appear in Scripture, so we can quickly
> find relevant verses. But there is no concordance that
> lists PTSD, there is no verse that gives us specific lan-
> guage on what to do with trauma. This should concern
> us because it can look like the most pressing matter in a
> person's life is met by divine silence. We may then con-
> clude that Scripture is intended for other matters and
> we will look elsewhere for help and the church becomes

irrelevant in the search for help when it comes to trauma. An alternative is to listen even more carefully to the person who is suffering.[12]

Listening to a suffering person will not only provide you with more helpful categories with which to understand their difficulties, it will also give direction on how you can compassionately apply God's comfort and hope to their situation.

In fact, we can look to Scripture for examples of those who were deeply impacted by what the clinical world labels as PTSD. Trauma is indeed in the Bible. When we stop looking for specific labels and instead listen to stories, we will see God's Word is not silent when it comes to the experience of trauma. When the prophet Jeremiah realized the destruction of Jerusalem was imminent, the traumatic impact was evident in various ways in both his body and his soul. His words "Oh the walls of my heart! My heart is beating wildly" revealed a physical reaction to trauma that describes symptoms often associated with traumatization or a panic attack (Jeremiah 4:19). "Oh Lord, you have deceived me, and I was deceived; you are stronger than I, and you have prevailed" (20:7) speaks of the spiritual quandary trauma can thrust upon a person's faith. The trauma of the situation took an emotional toll on him, and he despaired of life itself. "Why did I come out of the womb to see toil and sorrow and spend my days in shame? Cursed be the day on which I was born" (20:14, 18) expresses the mental anguish he was under in reaction to traumatic circumstances. Jeremiah was no different than you or anyone else who experiences life-altering distress. When we slow down and listen more carefully, we will likely begin to see parallels between a person's story and the stories in Scripture. That should compel us to seek to better understand Scripture and the impact of trauma and what we can do to help.

How Trauma Hides

Trauma may be right in front of you, yet it can be hard to recognize. A man's seemingly unforgiving or distant disposition could be a self-protective traumatic response. A woman's chronic illness might be directly connected to living through an emotionally abusive and traumatizing situation. A church member's resistance to being involved in the life of the church may be related to a disturbing past full of abandonment and betrayal by those who should have loved and cared for them. Trauma burrows deep and can be hard to identify.

A lack of understanding can lead to further harm or re-traumatization, which we will explore in future chapters. Knowing what to look for can help you to become more sensitive to potential trauma responses. Below is a list of symptoms that may be the result of trauma:

- Anxiety, fear

- Sadness, hopelessness

- Shock, denial, disbelief

- Body aches, pains

- Anger, irritability, mood swings

- Withdrawal from others, isolation

- Difficulty concentrating, confusion

- Muscle tension

- Guilt, shame

- Racing heart

- Nightmares

- Fatigue, insomnia

- Easily startled, hypervigilant

- Intestinal issues

- Social awkwardness

- Mental health diagnoses such as OCD, ODD, or ADHD

- Depression

- Worry

I am sure as you read that list you could relate to many of the symptoms. You probably know others who also struggle with these symptoms as well. That is the point: Trauma hides behind commonly experienced symptoms. This is not to say if you see these symptoms, you must automatically assume trauma is the reason. Rather, if symptoms seem to be somewhat out of place or unexplainable, if it is difficult to identify the cause of the symptoms, or if emotional instability and relational difficulty accompany the symptoms, we should be mindful of the possibility trauma could be the explanation.

It's important to have this awareness to avoid the possibility of retraumatizing people or responding in a way that compounds their wound. Becoming aware of how trauma hides can help you to have a more compassionate understanding of a person and their situation. That is important because mislabeling trauma symptoms or assuming a person is "difficult" can also perpetuate stigma and judgment that adds to the person's suffering. It can also lead to misconceptions that the individual is intentionally difficult or flawed. This results in blame, ostracism, or the invalidation of their experiences. That's why it's essential for you to provide a supportive environment that opens the doors for conversations about the love and compassion of Christ and the perfect justice found in the God who sees, knows, and perfectly understands their suffering.

Differentiating Trauma from Upsetting Experiences

The experience of trauma is deeply personal, and people will respond to potentially traumatic situations differently. However, it is not as simple as thinking that what may be traumatic for one person may be tolerable for another. There are many things in life that are upsetting but would not be classified as traumatic. It is always wise to look at extenuating circumstances around events to understand the potential for deeper impact. Here are some examples of upsetting or disturbing situations that don't *necessarily* qualify as trauma. They are mentioned not to discredit anyone's experience, but rather, to help us avoid labeling something as trauma when it might not be.

- Relational difficulties in marriage or with family, friends, or co-workers. While these are emotionally painful and distressing, they typically do not meet the criteria for trauma except for when abuse is involved.

- Breakups or heartbreaks. Again, these experiences are painful but they do not usually meet the criteria for trauma.

- Financial troubles. This can be a source of tremendous stress on you and others in your family, but it is usually not considered traumatic.

- Feeling excluded or rejected by others. Social challenges cut deep, but as painful as they might be, they are generally not considered traumatic unless they include ongoing abuse or bullying.

- Major changes or job loss. Moving or losing a job ushers in major transitions that are not easy to navigate. They require adjustments that present challenges that can be unsettling but are not typically classified as a trauma.

- Minor illness or injury. Sickness and suffering physical harm are never remembered with fondness, but as recovery progresses, the distress of the situation is usually alleviated and the person can usually gain an appropriate perspective about what happened.

- Experiencing a temporary setback such as failing a class or not getting the desired job or promotion. As disappointing as these are, they do not classify as trauma.

- Feeling overwhelmed or stressed due to many responsibilities or demands. Whether these are professional responsibilities or relational demands, these situations can leave you feeling frazzled or even anxious, but they are not trauma-inducing.

Distinguishing the difference will help the sufferer and the caregiver to better know how to respond and what might be needed for the road ahead. As you have seen, becoming aware of the impact of trauma can expand your understanding of the scope of care. The care you offer traumatized people will be a slower and more holistic approach compared to the care you offer someone in a disappointing relationship or circumstance.

The situations above are not shared to discredit the difficulty they bring; certainly, counseling and care is a good idea. Rather, they are shared to clarify that circumstances that are upsetting are not automatically traumatic.

We want to remain balanced in our approach to becoming trauma aware. Not every distressing or upsetting event will result in traumatization. Making this distinction is necessary. Utilizing the Basic Trauma Questionnaire 15 (BTQ-15) found in Appendix A can be helpful. If you are still unsure, consult with others who have experience in working with trauma to help you.

PART 2

FROM AWARENESS TO ACTION

In this pivotal second part of *Trauma Aware*, we'll delve deeper into the profound journey of healing and support. While we will continue our focus on trauma awareness in the pages ahead, awareness alone is not enough to bring about healing and change. Rather, change begins in the realm of action. When our actions are fueled by the promises of God and the hope we have in Christ, the seeds of transformation can take root. We must let awareness serve as the compass that guides us on the path of empathy and understanding that results in concrete acts of loving and caring for those affected by trauma. It is through intentional actions that our awareness gains momentum toward making a genuine difference. In this section, we will bridge the gap between knowledge and practice. We will explore how to transform Christlike compassion into tangible acts of love toward those impacted by trauma.

CHAPTER 5

RECOGNIZING TRAUMA

A s we've learned, trauma can be caused by a single devastating event or a prolonged series of distressing experiences. Regardless of its cause, it can have a profound impact on a person's mental, physical, and even spiritual well-being. The symptoms of trauma can be as diverse as the circumstances that cause it. But symptoms are not only diverse, they're also often bewildering, manifesting in ways that can confuse the sufferer and the helper.

While there are many signs of traumatization, we are going to focus on six of the most commonly seen symptoms. Examining these six symptoms will provide a nuanced lens with which to explore trauma's impact, allowing for a comprehensive understanding of potential signs of traumatization. In addition, we will address these ideas in a way that not only helps you to identify but also remember these common signs. To do this, we are going to use a simple acrostic that spells TRAUMA. Each letter represents a negative symptom often experienced by those who are living with the effects of trauma. There are certainly other symptoms of trauma; however, these are the most common.

This acrostic will act as an easy-to-remember framework as we delve more deeply into trauma and address the multifaceted aspects of trauma-related challenges.

Triggers

Recurrent memories or dreams

Avoidance

Unwanted somatic responses

Mood disturbances, and

Arousal responses

As we work through each of these six symptoms represented by TRAUMA, each letter in the acrostic will be followed with actions you can engage in to support a sufferer. These suggested actions do not require you to have formal training in counseling. However, anytime a situation feels beyond your understanding of trauma care, your best support can be in helping the person find a trained counselor.

I have sought to make these action steps simple and self-explanatory. They are not exhaustive, but they will give you needed direction on how you can offer care that takes into consideration the impact trauma has had on the person.

One of the initial steps in assisting someone with these symptoms is recognizing they may not realize the symptom's link to their trauma, and therefore, they could resist your suggested connection. To alleviate any potential resistance, it is essential to communicate to trauma survivors that what they are experiencing makes sense in light of what they have suffered. They are not crazy, broken, or damaged goods. They are also not necessarily acting sinfully when they respond in various ways as a result of what they have been through. For example, a person may cope with discomfort related to traumatization by avoiding crowded events, having stricter boundaries around their personal space, always sitting in a seat that gives them a clear view of the exit, or by avoiding eye contact. Though such actions could have their roots in sin, we shouldn't conclude they are sinful—even if they are perceived as deviations from social norms. Your first step of action is to help the sufferer know what they are experiencing makes sense considering their circumstances. Trauma responses are normal reactions to abnormal situations. With that understood, let's look at the first of six common signs of traumatization and what you can do to help.

T–Triggers

Our first letter in the acronym is *T* and stands for triggers. We start here because triggers to past memories may be the most common symptom people think of when they consider traumatization. It is important to understand this symptom, so we will spend more time on this than any of the other symptoms.

A trigger is a response to a supercharged memory of past trauma stored deeply in our brains and nervous systems. When I refer to a memory being deeply stored, I am simply referring to the fact that the memory is not easily retrieved, discussed, or contemplated by the victim. In chapter 3, when we explored how trauma memories are stored in the brain, we learned those memories are packed with sensations and emotions from the distressing event. The fact that the memories are so charged with sensations can be one reason why trauma survivors often do not like to talk about their trauma. Though a memory may last only a brief second when triggered, the result is a sensory-packed response. Triggers cause a person to be overwhelmed with little to no warning. Triggers can cause anxiety, emotional distress, and even panic attacks as they link to a distressing memory.

Keep in mind that though a trigger is a *memory link*, the traumatized person may or may not realize or know the link. But a wise and caring friend or counselor can help make connections by asking careful and compassionate questions after the trigger subsides.

A Quick Look at Dissociation

The counseling session was not an easy one. Drew sat across from me and was staring out the window. He came to me to talk about his struggle with survivor's guilt. Though it had been years since the attack on the World Trade Center, he was still haunted by the events that took place that dreadful day. Being a New York City first responder who lived through the terrible events of September 11, 2001, also known as 9/11, he now lived with unwanted horrors. He knew he had done all he could that day, but the deaths of so many—including his close friends—left him feeling like maybe he could have done more. Maybe he did not sacrifice all he could have. As we processed things together, he paused a bit more and seemed to get lost in his thoughts.

Allowing Drew space to think, I waited patiently for him to continue sharing. Instead of talking, he stared out the window behind me. After a long silence, he apologized for losing his train of thought. I asked him where he went in his mind, and he replied, "I am sorry, I just spaced out. I find myself doing that from time to time when I feel overwhelmed. It also happens sometimes when things are slow at work and I am doing menial tasks. My mind goes on autopilot and I get lost in my thoughts." Drew was experiencing dissociation.

Survivors may not always realize when they are being triggered, and in some situations, triggers can cause a person to lose awareness of their surroundings or present situation. This is what's known as dissociation. When dissociation occurs, a person's thinking separates or disconnects from the present moment or surroundings. This can happen on a continuum and may be experienced as losing your train of thought or no longer tracking with a conversation. It can also become more intense. Acute situations of dissociation are less common but can include instances in which a person seems unreachable or has lost awareness or responsiveness. Normally, however, dissociation is hardly noticed. Dr. Bruce Perry explains dissociation in a helpful way.

> Dissociation is a complex mental capability that we use in everyday life; it involves disengaging from the external world and focusing on our inner world. When we daydream, when we allow our minds to wander, that's a form of dissociation. And like the arousal response the dissociative response is a continuum. With increasing stress or threat the dissociative response takes a person deeper and deeper into a protective mode.
>
> Whereas the physiology of the arousal responses is to optimize fight or flight, the physiology of dissociation helps us to rest, replenish, survive injury, and tolerate pain. Where arousal increases heart rate, dissociation decreases it. Where arousal sends blood to the muscles, dissociation keeps blood in the trunk to minimize blood loss in case of injury. Arousal releases adrenaline; dissociation releases the body's own painkillers, enkephalins and endorphins.[1]

Think of dissociation as a protective mechanism that our minds employ when faced with overwhelming or distressing situations. It's like a mental autopilot that kicks in to shield us from emotional or psychological harm. It can also kick in to give our brains and bodies a needed break. During dissociation, a person may feel as though they are watching themselves from a distance. This sensation is usually temporary and not something to be overly alarmed about. Most of the time, this feeling subsides on its own as a person reengages with the present moment, just as Drew did with me.

Dissociation is something everyone does. You have likely experienced dissociation yourself when you've driven on a familiar road. Consider your drive from work to home. During that drive, your brain might go on autopilot, enabling you to take the familiar path home while allowing you to mentally check out in such a way that you pass certain markers on your drive without noticing them.

Or maybe you've found yourself becoming so engrossed in the plot of a book or movie that you momentarily forget all that's happening around you. You detach from your immediate surroundings even though you are physically present. This is similar to what happens to people when they experience a trauma trigger. Their mind is coping with the distressing memory by "leaving." Again, this kind of dissociation is not normally something to be overly concerned about. However, if dissociation becomes frequent, distressing for an individual, or interferes with normal functioning, you may want to encourage them to seek guidance from a mental health professional.

Triggers and the Senses

Triggers can involve any of the five senses. When Branden was seven years old—and after his father had left home—his mother signed him up for a mentorship program. Her hope was to give Branden a positive male role model in the face of his father's abandonment. Branden enjoyed the outings he went on with his mentor until the day his mentor took him to see a film at the movie theater and began touching him inappropriately. This happened several more times before Branden got the courage to tell his mother what was happening. Many years later, he shared with his counselor that the smell of movie theater popcorn is a trigger that sends distressing feelings throughout his entire body.

The sense of smell is one of the primary ways people experience triggers. This has to do with the way a scent enters the brain—it bypasses the thalamus. "Your thalamus is your body's information relay station. All information from your body's senses (except smell) must be processed through your thalamus before being sent to your brain's cerebral cortex for interpretation."[2]

When the brain detects a smell, the signal goes directly to a region called the piriform cortex, which is in the limbic system. You might recall from chapter 3 the limbic system is the emotional center of the brain. Because of this, the smell can be emotionally associated with the person's experience, forming a memory link. Therefore, encountering a specific smell connected with a traumatic event can trigger an intense and visceral reaction.

People can also be triggered by the other senses. I spoke with one woman who had experienced significant trauma while growing up with her alcoholic father. She shared that, even now as an adult, the sight of specific liquor bottles she saw during her childhood would cause her to feel as though her body would freeze. This was the same feeling she would often get as a child when her dad would take his liquor bottles out of the cabinet above the refrigerator.

For someone who has lived through a hurricane or tornado, a sudden rise in humidity coupled with increasingly cloudy skies and wind can bring automatic sensations to their body that stir up emotional distress. This causes an urgent desire to find a safer location even if it is only a summer thunderstorm that's brewing.

And we have all heard of how the backfiring of a car, the popping of a balloon, or the accidental dropping of a dish can trigger combat veterans into a hypervigilant response. These are only a few examples of how triggers can be induced through our senses.

Places and locations can be triggers as well. The sight of a doctor's office, an interstate highway, an aunt or uncle's house, or a church building are all examples that have been mentioned by my coun-selees as places that have been triggering because traumatic situations occurred at those locations.

As we think about what helpers can do to support someone who is being triggered, it is important to keep in mind logic alone isn't enough to talk traumatized people out of their triggered response. This is because, as you recall from chapter 3, when a person is trig-gered, the part of the brain that engages rational thinking (prefrontal cortex) is being superseded by the limbic system. This means when your traumatized friend, counselee, or congregant is triggered, they can physically feel the way they did in the original situation. There-fore, it is more helpful to address the sensory link than to try to talk them out of what they are feeling. You do this by addressing the dis-tress in their body and helping them to calm down before you cau-tiously explore what caused the feelings they experienced.

If the person you are caring for exhibits a physical response to a trigger (being startled, breathing rapidly, clenching their fists or jaw, acting fidgety or restless, etc.), acknowledge the specific physi-cal reaction by noticing and then asking how they are doing. Sim-ilarly, if you notice signs of physical agitation, focus on employing techniques that promote physical calming so you can alleviate the agitation effectively. As a helper, remember deep breathing can help, as can body movement. Suggest the person walk with you or encour-age them to stretch their body by reaching their arms to the sky and standing as tall as they can. You can also encourage them to shake out their arms and legs. Or ask them to gently rub their arms with their hands. This gets the blood moving differently and can help them to calm down. Take slow, deep breaths with them and utilize what you learned in chapter 4.

You might be tempted to touch the person to help calm them down. Be sure to always ask permission before you touch someone, and share how you are going to touch them before you do so. A gentle and reassuring touch can be helpful, but it can also be distressing and uncomfortable if touch was a part of their traumatizing experience.

When a person is triggered and is responding in a hypersensitive way, their body is taking over because it believes it needs to be on high alert against a perceived threat. Addressing a physical response with encouragement to trust the Lord could be helpful, but more than likely, they might not be able to receive such advice until their nervous system calms down. Avoid making any assumptions or judgments regarding a person's spiritual condition based on their reaction. Please remember, for a person to feel overwhelmed by a trigger to the point they cannot receive spiritual direction in the moment does not mean they do not love or trust the Lord. A trigger is not a character flaw or a sin. It is a response to trauma.

We experience life with our senses. With trauma, memories can be linked to our senses in discomforting ways, causing the first symptom of trauma we have looked at, known as a trigger. But memory links are not always distressing. They can be pleasant too. You can likely think of times you have been reminded of a happy and enjoyable memory through a familiar scent or a visual reminder. In my case, the smell of Scotch tape can take me back to happy memories of wrapping Christmas gifts late at night on Christmas Eve and anticipating the joy I would see on the faces of my little children. I feel the reminders in my body in positive ways simply through that smell.

Just as my body responds to that and takes me back to Christmas, the same can be true with traumatic memories. However, when memories are negatively triggering, we can help. Below are three ways you can assist someone who experiences triggers related to trauma. And if you feel ill-equipped to use these tips (or any others in this book) or you encounter challenges, consider seeking support from a qualified mental health professional.

Awareness to Action

We have seen a person can experience strong emotional or physiological responses that are tied to their past experiences. Triggers are rarely predictable and often unavoidable and can activate the body's stress response. It is essential to always be ready to respond with empathy, support, and understanding. Below are three ways you can help a person who has experienced a trauma trigger:

1. **Create a safe place.** Wherever they are, seek to establish a safe and comfortable space where they feel supported. This includes offering your comforting presence and listening ear. Never force them into any action or conversation.

2. **Utilize a grounding exercise.** There are several exercises to choose from in the appendices of this book. When a person has experienced a trigger, exercises like deep breathing, breath prayers, mindfulness, or sensory awareness can be helpful toward alleviating the emotions and sensations that result from trauma's triggers.

3. **Stay present and pray with them.** If the person is open to it, offer to pray with them right then or pray for them silently. Remind them that God knows and understands their struggle. Encourage them that God does not judge them for being triggered and is with them, and you are with them as well. Stay with them until the response subsides. Your presence and support can provide a sense of calm. Remind them that even in times when they feel alone, God is always with them (Deuteronomy 31:6; Matthew 28:20; Hebrews 13:5).

R—Recurrent Memories or Dreams

The next letter in our TRAUMA acrostic is *R*, which stands for recurrent memories or dreams. These are often experienced as symptoms of trauma and refer to the persistent and intrusive recollection of distressing events or themes from the past. They are unwanted and reoccur regularly, usually as fragments or distortions of the traumatic event. The term *recurrent* is significant when discussing memories and dreams related to trauma because it emphasizes the repetitive nature of these experiences. These are not the occasional unpleasant thoughts or bad dreams we all have. Instead, they occur during waking hours as vivid, intrusive thoughts and can also manifest during sleep as repetitive or distressing dreams. They are regular even if their regularity is seasonal.

Your body remembers what time of year it is even if you don't. Every year late in the fall, one woman I counseled had persistent bad dreams that she was dying. Reviewing her history, we discovered the timing of the dreams aligned with the time her world was turned upside down when, after enduring a traumatic physical assault, she escaped from a highly abusive marriage.

A person's recurrent memories may come in the form of flashbacks. A flashback is a reliving of a traumatic event as if it were happening right then. They are often brief but provoke a lot of emotion. The memory and its associated feelings collide without any separation, merging instantly and inducing a physical response. As the memory and the feelings associated with it are smashed together, there is no space for logical processing to occur, and the somatic response can feel overwhelming. All of this happens within seconds. Flashbacks are vivid, almost always negative, and come on with little to no warning. Flashbacks are common when someone has experienced or witnessed a near-death experience. They can be distressing and overwhelming, causing significant emotional distress. They can also disrupt daily functioning, leading to difficulties in relationships, at work, and in one's overall well-being.

It is important to note flashbacks are common in near-death experiences and are most prevalent in the days right after the incident. They can also occur later in situations when trauma has not been processed and integrated into a person's understanding and system of belief.

Whether in the form of memories, dreams, or flashbacks, these recurrent experiences are all responses to a traumatic experience and reflect the brain's attempt to process and integrate the unresolved emotions and memories associated with the trauma. The brain experiences heightened activity from a flashback in a similar way it does during the traumatic event itself.[3] This is believed to arise from the intricate interplay between the various brain regions involved in memory consolidation, emotional regulation, and sleep processes. But ultimately, these unwanted recurrent memories or dreams serve as important cues that unresolved trauma may need to be addressed.

Awareness to Action

When a person experiences recurrent memories or dreams, you may feel uncertain of how to help. The key is to offer compassionate support. Below are a few ways to do that:

- **Validate their experience.** Assure them that what they are going through is understandable given their past trauma. Help them to grasp that these memories and dreams are their body's and brain's way of trying to process what they have been through.

- **Encourage the seeking of professional help.** As with any of the symptoms we will talk about in this chapter, seeking professional help is always an option worth exploring. When a person has recurring dreams and memories that are adding distress to their life, a qualified mental health professional may be an excellent resource of help. However, instead of simply giving them a referral, offer to help them find the best-suited counselor. Be willing to accompany them to their appointments if that would help them feel more comfortable. Offer consistent support and reassurance throughout the process, reminding them that they are not alone on this journey.

- **Share comforting Scripture passages.** When distressing memories flood a person's mind, it can be hard for them to think about anything else. Offering comforting Scripture passages can provide helpful mental redirection. After confirming Scripture was not used in abusive or manipulative ways, consider reading these passages aloud to your friend when you are together. Or send them via text messages, emails, or images that they can refer to when needed. Here are some suggested scriptures you can share:

  » Psalm 9:9: "The Lord is a stronghold for the oppressed, a stronghold in times of trouble."

  » Psalm 50:15: "Call upon me in the day of trouble; I will deliver you, and you shall glorify me."

  » Matthew 11:28-30: "Come to me, all who labor and are heavy laden, and I will give you rest. Take my yoke upon you, and learn from me, for I am gentle and lowly in heart, and you will find rest for your souls. For my yoke is easy, and my burden is light."

  » 2 Corinthians 9:8: "God is able to make all grace abound to you, so that having all sufficiency in all things at all times, you may abound in every good work."

A–Avoidance

The next symptom in our acrostic is avoidance. When it comes to psychological trauma, avoidance may be one of the most common symptoms manifest by individuals. This is understandable. When you have a painful memory or experience, you want nothing else but to relive that experience even if it is only in your mind. Instead, you want to avoid reminders of that experience or push away thoughts or feelings associated with it.

Avoidance is a defense mechanism aimed at protecting oneself from distressing emotions that might arise if you were to confront the trauma directly. Though it is common for individuals who have a diagnosis of PTSD to engage in avoidant behaviors, anyone who has gone through something distressing or traumatic may turn to avoidance to cope.

These behaviors can include avoiding places, people, or situations that remind the sufferer of the trauma. The person may also avoid discussing or thinking about the event altogether. You may already be deducing the impact this might have on their ability to heal. If a person is avoiding talking about the trauma, they will likely avoid questions you might ask about it. They will probably not want to answer how you can pray for them, or they may avoid your inquiries about how they are doing as it relates to the traumatic situation experienced.

They may also be very hesitant to engage in counseling because that means they must talk about the subject they're avoiding. When trauma survivors resort to avoidance, they can end up avoiding the very people who could help them.

It is important not to confuse avoidance with noncompliance or willful stubbornness; avoidance is a symptom of trauma. It is a way for individuals to protect themselves from distressing emotions, experiences, or memories. Because people who are traumatized don't want to re-experience their trauma, their avoidance can lead to prolonged suffering. They would love for their symptoms caused by the trauma to be gone, and avoidance is the means to make that happen. But, as we learned already, triggers are unexpected, unwanted visitors, which means they are often impossible to avoid.

Avoidance can have both short- and long-term effects on a person's emotional health. In the short term, avoiding reminders of the trauma may provide temporary relief from distress. However, in the long run, doing this can hinder the needed healing process by preventing the person from effectively recognizing the significance of what they have been through. This hinders the necessary integration of the traumatic experiences into their lives in a healthy manner.

By gradually facing the avoided memories, thoughts, and feelings in a safe and controlled environment, individuals can learn to process the trauma and reduce its negative impact on their lives. In clinical settings, therapeutic approaches like cognitive behavioral therapy (CBT), exposure therapy, and eye-movement desensitization and repossessing (EMDR) have been shown to be effective in helping some individuals confront and overcome the need to engage in avoidant behaviors associated with trauma. These methods can often provide needed symptom relief and enhance memory tolerance, which can lead to an openness toward processing and reframing the memory in light of God's character and promises. For more information about these or other clinical methods of trauma treatment, see Appendix E at the back of the book.

Awareness to Action

The symptom of avoidance can be challenging to deal with when you seek to help a person who has been through a traumatic experience. This is where compassion needs to be coupled with patience. As you take steps to help a person who is struggling with this symptom, be aware of the temptation to take their avoidance personally.

You may feel like they don't want your help or maybe don't want you around. The tips below will help you walk with someone struggling with the symptom of avoidance. As mentioned earlier, you do not need formal training to engage these tips; however, do not hesitate to refer a person to a qualified mental health professional to discuss these tips further.

1. **Provide psychoeducation.** What you have learned so far in this book and especially in this section can be helpful to the person you are caring for. Explain that avoidance is a common response for someone who seeks to protect themselves from overwhelming emotions. Gently help them understand while it feels better to avoid, essentially what is being avoided is help and healing. Explore with them the fact that many of the most effective trauma therapies include a careful and cautious engagement of the trauma story.

2. **Encourage gradual exposure.** Slowly and gently encourage the person to consider alternatives to avoidance by gradually engaging them in conversations about the traumatic situation. This must be done in a way that respects a pace tolerable to the person. Start by revisiting less-triggering aspects of the trauma and honor their courage when they engage the conversation. Be sure to emphasize God is with them through the process, providing them with strength and courage.

3. **Promote self-care practices.** Help the person with routines and practices that promote overall well-being. Rather than avoidance, encourage them to engage in activities they enjoy, such as exercise, spending time in nature,

reading, journaling, or engaging in hobbies. Highlight the importance of finding space to be with the Lord in prayer and reading the Scriptures. Encourage them to encounter God through nature or by attending to the needs he created them to have. Being with people can be another way of caring for themselves. Because avoidance tends to lead to isolation, encourage engagement in activities that they can enjoy doing with others.

U–Unwanted Somatic Responses

Earlier when we discussed triggers, we touched briefly on the experience of sensory reactions. We are going to expound on that a bit as we explore unwanted somatic responses, another common symptom of trauma. Before going any further, I want to share a term that will be important for you to know so you can better understand the symptom of unwanted somatic responses. The word is *somatization*, and it is defined by the *Oxford English Dictionary* as the production of recurrent and multiple medical symptoms with no discernible organic cause.[4] These are physical symptoms or sensations that occur in the body without clear causation or conscious control. This can result in having undiagnosable illness, pain, or symptoms.

When a person experiences a distressing or life-threatening event, it can have a profound effect on their mind and body. As they continue to experience the impact of unprocessed trauma, their body will continue to be exposed to the fight-or-flight response, which can result in the body becoming overwhelmed as it seeks to continually regulate its nervous system. Unwanted somatic responses are a symptom of unprocessed trauma. Some common unwanted somatic responses include rapid heart rate, muscle tension, headaches, difficulty concentrating, gut issues, nausea, rashes or hives, tightness in the chest, lightheadedness, difficulty breathing, and chronic pain.

Traumatic experiences dysregulate the body's stress-response system. In many cases, the trauma is endured and processed through various healthy coping measures or supportive structures in a person's life. In other situations, trauma is so extensive or continual that processing the event on their own is challenging and takes a toll on their overall well-being.

We saw the connection between trauma and unwanted physical responses when we looked at the body and trauma in chapter 4. A person experiences negative somatic symptoms when the body's efforts to regulate become taxed. Evidence of the continual dysregulation of the body's stress-response system indicates that negative physical symptoms and even neurological abnormalities can occur in people with PTSD.[5] People who have survived a traumatic event or series of events have often learned to survive by staying on high alert, but this is not without ramifications. As the famously titled book explains, the body does indeed keep the score.[6]

A Word About Children and Trauma

Unwanted somatic responses are often the most-missed symptom of trauma in children. It is often said kids are resilient because it seems they can be exposed to a life-changing crisis relatively unscathed while the adults in their lives are reeling from the event. Children will be playing with their toys, singing songs, and wanting to eat ice cream while the grownups who are with them are trying to wrap their minds around what just happened. While this book is not specifically about children and trauma, it is worth mentioning that unwanted somatic responses are a common way kids experience symptoms of traumatization. I will say a bit more about that later and offer some resources.

Children who complain of unexplainable tummy trouble, changes in bowels, or headaches may be experiencing these negative somatic symptoms due to trauma. They may not talk about what they are feeling, but attuned parents or caregivers may be clued in to the impact of trauma in these symptoms. Pay attention to how children play. Often, they will act out how they are experiencing life in their play. This can alert you to the need for supportive care. You can also look for changes in appetite due to unwanted somatic symptoms or changes in sleep patterns as certain memories come up in dreams. Emotional outbursts are often reactions to physical feelings of being overwhelmed.

While children are remarkably resilient, it is essential to acknowledge this discussion merely scratches the surface when it comes to noticing and responding to the effects of trauma in them. Further exploration into childhood emotional health is warranted when trauma has been a part of a child's story. A helpful resource for adults caring for children who have been through a traumatic event is a small book written by Darby Strickland, titled *When Children Experience Trauma: Help for Parents and Caregivers.* A couple other resources written for younger children who are experiencing emotional distress: *Something Scary Happened,* also by Strickland, and a book I wrote for children titled *Count Yourself Calm: Taking Big Feelings to a Big God.* For teens facing physical responses to trauma, I wrote *Teens and Anxiety: How Parents Can Help,* which offers practical advice for parents on managing anxiety symptoms similar to those of traumatization.

For both children and adults, trauma affects the body long after the traumatic event is over. If someone is dealing with negative physical issues, it is always good to explore these issues fully with a doctor. When there might be no medical explanation and the sufferers have been through something difficult and distressing, the symptoms could be a result of traumatization.

Awareness to Action

Enduring something traumatic is difficult enough on its own, and the unwanted somatic responses that can follow increase the impact of the suffering. Because somatic experiences are felt and noticed in the body, it is important to address the body as you seek to move from awareness to action. When you think someone may be dealing with symptoms of trauma, here are some techniques they can turn to for help.

1. **Deep breathing.** There is profound wisdom in the way that God interconnected the human body's systems. This is abundantly clear when we look at how modifying our breathing can calm and regulate our nervous system. This divine design is simple yet powerful. By regulating your breath, you set in motion a cascade effect of calming throughout the entire body. You can most effectively calm unwanted somatic responses by controlling your breathing. Rather than simply asking the struggling person to breathe deeply, do the deep breathing exercises together.

2. **Body scan.** A body scan is a way to bring attention to the body and its needs. It is so easy for us to be completely unaware of what our body is telling us. Unwanted somatic responses do not happen overnight. They usually start with small changes we pay no attention to, such as muscle tension, headaches, or stomach discomfort. Body-scan activities can be enormously effective in helping a person become more aware of their ability to give the body what it needs and can be instructive in how to relax. Revisit the body-scan awareness exercise in chapter 4, or Appendix H in the back of this book for additional examples of body-scan activities with more detail.

3. **Sensory distractions.** Suggest engaging in activities that divert attention away from the somatic response, such as squeezing a stress ball, holding a fidget toy, listening to soothing music, or using relaxing scents such as essential oils, teas, or whatever is calming for the person. Other sensory distractions that are helpful are stretching or moving the body.

M—Mood Changes

It is quite normal to have an emotional response to a distressing situation. Terrible circumstances affect how we feel. It makes sense to feel upset after encountering something distressful, just as it is normal for us to feel elated over exciting news or a positive event. Our moods are impacted by what we encounter, and often our moods unconsciously adjust to fit the occasion. However, people who have been traumatized can often struggle with mood changes or have difficulty controlling moods in everyday life.

They can experience extreme moods that bring on such strong emotions they feel like they are out of control or overreacting, or are perceived by others as being such. These heightened emotional states can also be accompanied by intense anxiety or anger. Trauma survivors can be perceived as making more of a situation than is appropriate or as expressing emotions that are not fitting for a given situation.

They can also experience moods in which their emotional response is flat or nonexistent. Sufferers can struggle with negative thoughts about themselves and hopelessness about their future. They may lose interest in things they once enjoyed. Trauma survivors may also have difficulty experiencing emotions all together, especially good emotions. Alexithymia is the inability to recognize or describe one's own emotions.[7] Alexithymia has been found to be present in people who have experienced repeated trauma or multiple traumatization.[8]

A flat response to life may also manifest in detachment from friends or family and an overall downturn in mood. This can look like the symptoms of depression, and it may actually be depression connected to a traumatic event.

Research has shown trauma can significantly impact a person's emotional well-being and mood. From being explosive to numb, a person's mood changes are a symptom of traumatization. Trauma survivors can appear apathetic and disinterested or overly distressed or upset with something or someone. These mood fluctuations can disrupt daily functioning, affect relationships, and discourage the sufferer, ultimately having a significant impact on the individual's emotional well-being.

Awareness to Action

Everyone's experience with trauma is unique, so it is essential to approach each situation with empathy, understanding, and respect. Caring for someone who is struggling with mood changes or who has difficulty controlling their mood can be challenging, but there are practical ways you can provide support and care. As you seek to do this, be sure to also care for yourself. Know your limits and take the opportunity to step away when you need to do so.

As you engage with someone who is struggling with mood changes due to trauma, here is what you can do to help.

1. **Offer options.** During emotional highs and lows, trauma survivors can find it difficult to think of any other course of action than what they feel in the moment. Offering alternative options of response can help to preempt impulsive and emotional actions fueled by negative moods. Possible options to offer in a calm and gracious manner might include counting to ten and taking a couple deep breaths

before responding to what is upsetting them. This might mean stepping away for a few minutes to gain perspective and avoid impulsive reactions. It might involve suggesting they take time to talk to someone in their support system before responding to what is upsetting them.

2. **Encourage journaling or tracking moods.** When someone feels unable to control or regulate their moods, they may find it helpful to journal or track their moods. The aim isn't to help them process their mood, though that can be helpful. Rather, tracking their mood may enable them to make helpful connections. Tracking moods in a journal or on a smartphone can help determine what might be connected to or associated with the mood swing. Encourage the person to write a brief descriptor of their mood each day. They may find it helpful to journal what they were doing before and after they noticed the mood. This information can reveal what might be contributing to the mood. Smartphone apps such as Daylio or Daybook can help with journaling moods on a regular basis. You can also find many mood-tracker journals for purchase online.

3. **Don't take it personally.** This might be one of the hardest but most essential ways you can help someone struggling with mood dysregulation due to trauma. Often the effects of the person's mood are felt most deeply by those who are seeking to care for them. It is important to understand their mood swings may stem from their internal struggles with unprocessed trauma rather than you and your care. Regardless of their moods, your care is vitally important for them, so avoid taking their emotional responses or states personally.

A–Arousal Responses

Arousal responses are associated with psychological trauma. As we saw in chapter 3, during a traumatic event, the fear center of the brain (the amygdala) becomes highly activated. This activation triggers the release of stress hormones such as adrenaline and cortisol into the bloodstream. These hormones are messengers from the brain to the body that help determine which of the fight-flight-freeze responses is most needed.

However, in the case of psychological trauma, the fear center of the brain can remain chronically stimulated even after the traumatic event has ended, and the result can be an exaggerated or disproportionate arousal response. These responses reflect the body's instinctual and automatic reactions to perceived threats or danger, even in situations where the danger has passed. Some examples of arousal responses associated with psychological trauma include:

Hyperarousal

This refers to a state of heightened alertness and vigilance. Individuals may experience irritability, be easily startled, be sensitive to sounds, and overall, have a sense of being on edge. Sensitivity to being touched can also be an arousal response. When normal, healthy touch (even causal touch) produces a visceral or adverse response, you may be seeing an arousal response associated with unprocessed trauma.

Hypervigilance

This involves a conscious or unconscious constant scanning of the environment for potential threats. People with trauma may have difficulty relaxing or letting their guard down even in safe situations. This is connected to the hyperarousal symptom mentioned above and how the body seeks to regulate itself. When the fear center of the brain is stimulated, the secretion of cortisol enables a person to act based on what they perceive. However, prolonged exposure to high levels of cortisol can have negative effects on a person's body and can cause them to become hypervigilant, which is an exhausting state to live in.

Risky Behaviors

Individuals who have endured psychological trauma may exhibit self-destructive actions to cope with overwhelming emotional distress. Self-harm activities such as cutting, burning, and scratching can result from arousal responses. Drug or alcohol use and abuse or engaging in dangerous activities or relationships can also be manifestations of arousal responses due to experiencing traumatic circumstances. These behaviors reflect attempts to regain control, numb negative feelings, or escape the reality of their situation.

Sleep Disturbances

Trauma often interferes with normal sleep patterns. Individuals may have difficulty falling asleep, experience nightmares, or wake up frequently throughout the night unable to go back to sleep. The prolonged activation of the fear center of the brain causes sleep to be difficult or disrupted.

Other indicators of an arousal response to trauma include irritability, outburst of anger or aggressive behavior, distrust, and sometimes paranoia. Living in a state of hyperarousal can produce chronic anxiety as a person is constantly on the lookout for what could go wrong.

Arousal symptoms can show up as risky or self-destructive behaviors that go beyond self-injury, as mentioned above, and extend to eating disorders, hypersexuality, and putting oneself in unsafe situations. Another common response to being traumatized is an extreme sense of guilt and shame, which can be compounded by the risky behaviors someone has engaged in to cope.

Essentially, arousal responses indicate the body did not get the message the war is over, so to speak. Instead, the person is living in a continued state of arousal to protect themselves from any potential harm. This feeling of needing to always be on guard is exhausting yet automatic at the same time.

Awareness to Action

Supporting individuals who are experiencing arousal symptoms can help them get to the root cause of those symptoms, and addressing their response is equally important. As you extend your support, you become a valuable complement to others in their circles of care, including any professionals. Below are ways you can be supportive and show care:

1. **Encourage care for their body.** Regular exercise helps promote a sense of calm and reduces the anxiety that comes from being hypervigilant. Help the person to engage in progressive muscle relaxation, breath prayers, spending time in nature, listening to worship music, or other activities that lead to relaxation. Remind the person about how Jesus cared for the bodily needs of others by healing them (Matthew 8:1-3), providing nourishment (Mark 8:1-3), and encouraging rest (Mark 6:31-32).

2. **Create a safe and supportive environment.** Feeling safe and secure is essential for the person who is experiencing arousal responses. Listening attentively with empathy and understanding helps to create a sense of security. Encourage them to share what they are experiencing and validate them as you are able. Remind them of God's care and presence and love for them (Psalms 36:5-7; 46:1; Isaiah 54:10; Lamentations 3:22-24; Romans 8:35-39; Ephesians

2:4-7; 1 John 4:9-10). Take the time to pray that God would allow them to feel the security of his presence.

3. **Explore expanding their community of support.** Encourage the person to reach out to trusted friends. Help them to identify individuals whom they consider to be safe and trustworthy. Suggest involvement in their faith community through the local church. Invite them to attend a small group, prayer gathering, or church service with you and introduce them to people who may become great additions to their community of support.

Once you are more able to recognize and understand the symptoms of trauma, you are better equipped to support and care for those who are on a journey of healing. It is essential to emphasize the profound truth that God loves and cares for those who are experiencing these symptoms. He does not judge them. Use the Scripture passages shared above or from the "Awareness to Action" part of the Recurrent Memories and Dreams sections to encourage them. Despite the pain and confusion trauma brings, we have a loving God who invites us to bring our wounds, our fears, our shattered pieces to him. He welcomes us with unfailing grace, compassion, and the power to redeem the most shattered parts of us. As you share these truths and Scripture, do so with sensitivity, understanding the sufferer may not be immediately responsive.

Trauma does not define a person. We must always hold in the forefront of our minds that a person's ability to find healing is not beyond the reach of God's help. However, God often uses the people around the sufferer to bring about change. Perhaps he uses a person who is well-trained in trauma care, such as a trauma counselor or psychologist. Or help could come from a medical doctor if the symptoms are affecting the person's physical health. Or maybe it might be a pastor or spiritual mentor that is most needed. Or maybe it is you.

> *Trauma does not define a person. We must always hold in the forefront of our minds that a person's ability to find healing is not beyond the reach of God's help.*

As we become more trauma aware, we position ourselves to exemplify God's care. Just as the Lord walks beside those who are navigating the treacherous terrain of trauma, we have the sacred privilege of coming alongside others to offer comfort and hope. We can show the Lord's compassion as we extend care and support to those who are wrestling with trauma symptoms.

As we close this chapter, my hope is you will always keep in mind healing is a process that unfolds differently for each person, and we must seek to cultivate an environment in which those affected by trauma feel safe to express themselves. They need to know they will be met with compassion and understanding rather than judgment and shame. Laying this foundation of compassion is essential before we consider what the next aspects of care may look like. When a person recognizes your commitment to their well-being, your influence in their life magnifies, and the opportunities to accompany them in their journey of healing and sanctification increase as well.

CHAPTER 6

STAGES OF RECOVERY

M ost trauma experts concur trauma healing or recovery typically involves distinct stages or phases, providing a structured framework for the journey toward wholeness and restoration. In *Trauma and Recovery*, a benchmark book for understanding trauma, author Judith Herman establishes a pathway to trauma recovery. She categorizes trauma care into three stages: safety, remembrance, and reconnection. She posits, "Recovery unfolds in three stages. The central task of the first stage is the establishment of safety. The central task of the second stage is remembrance and mourning. The central task of the third stage is reconnection with ordinary life."[1]

These three stages are interconnected and build off one another. Each stage is crucial in the process of integrating various aspects of trauma recovery into a person's life to move them toward establishing meaning to what happened to them without overwhelming or destabilizing them. Clinical trauma experts typically align with these three distinct stages when it comes to trauma recovery, although the specific titles used for these stages may vary based upon the modality or therapist's approach.

In recognizing these stages, you must embrace the fact trauma recovery and care is a process for which much patience is required. It is imperative not to rush through or bypass any stage of the recovery process. Each stage should be navigated cautiously so you can ensure the individual is well prepared to move on to the next stage. Both the caregiver and the one receiving care must go at a pace that builds trust, which, in turn, establishes safety and stability.

Trauma recovery instantiates the fact that God designed us to need others as we go through life. "Recovery can take place only within the context of relationships, it cannot occur in isolation."[2] The church, therefore, should be a primary place people can turn to for help when trauma is experienced. While others can offer support, the church holds out the Cure. We bring people to the One who says, "Fear not, for I am with you" (Isaiah 41:19); we take them to Jesus, who understands trauma because he himself endured it as well. When we create a safe relationship by being *with* those who are suffering, we embody Emmanuel, God *with* us. In doing this, our care aligns with how we were created: to be dependent on the Lord and one another. I once heard author and speaker Ann Voskamp say that Jesus offers us *witness* (he sees us) and *withness* (he is with us).[3] That captures what should be the goal of every helper.

However, we have an almost magnetic pull toward a fix-it mentality. Rather than taking the time to be present with people, seeking to establish a safe and trusting relationship with them, our tendency is to see a problem and focus on how to solve it. When this happens, we then start to see strugglers as projects rather than people. But this does not fit well with the stages of care that are essential to trauma recovery.

When we create a safe relationship by being with those who are suffering, we embody Emmanuel, God with us. In doing this, our care aligns with how we were created: to be dependent on the Lord and one another.

In the simplest terms, pragmatism takes a practical and matter-of-fact approach to solving problems and making decisions to achieve sensible outcomes. It focuses on finding solutions rather than exploring the underlying contributing circumstances and their implications. Pragmatism emphasizes desired outcomes and the best possible results, not on exploring the uniqueness of the details of a person's story.

Christians can be guilty of pragmatism when it comes to counseling and care. This is especially true in relation to people who have lived through trauma. A pragmatic approach may be rooted in good motives—that is, a desire to alleviate suffering and relieve emotional pain. But being pragmatic can cause us to skip certain essential stages in trauma recovery.

No matter how important it may seem to help a person move toward addressing their pain, you must resist the urge to rush the sufferer's progress. First, you must establish a sense of safety and stability. This is the initial and essential stage of trauma care.

Safety and stability focus on establishing a person's sense of security and well-being. It involves creating an environment in which the person feels protected physically, emotionally, psychologically, and spiritually. It will likely include the introduction and development of coping strategies and expanding their circle of support to include other trusted individuals or professionals. Doing this stage correctly provides a solid foundation for further healing to take place. It allows the individual to gain a sense of control over their lives, a sense that is lost in the moment of trauma. Making a person feel safe also reduces the possibility of that person becoming overwhelmed as they seek to process their trauma.

Stage One: Safety and Stabilization

For us as believers, establishing a traumatized person's safety should be a natural element of our care. As Christians, we find safety and security in our Lord. God is called our Rock, our Fortress, our Protector, our Provider, our Shelter, our Comforter, our Defender, and our Trustworthy Deliverer. All these names remind us first and foremost, we are safe with God. As the church seeks to provide care for those who have been traumatized, we must remember we image God best when safety is our constant priority.

Where to Begin?

So, what does it look like to establish safety with someone who has experienced psychological trauma? First, make sure they are physically safe. Are they currently in a situation where the threat of continued abuse or emotional or personal harm is present? If so, suggest protective options through resources or support systems. Support groups, prevention helplines, and safety hotlines can offer immediate assistance to individuals who are in distress and can be easily accessed in your area through an internet search. Tangible resources such as housing, transportation, and financial aid may also be needed in the process of establishing physical safety.

Action steps toward physical safety must be initiated by the individual who is seeking support. Your role is not to take control of the situation but to offer guidance and respect the agency of the person in need of care. Trauma, by nature, causes a sense of powerlessness, leaving the person to feel helpless about change or getting out of the terrible event or circumstances they have endured. Respecting a person's voice and giving them options in their care restores confidence, encourages resilience, and affirms to them you are a safe person.

The Next Steps

Once physical safety is established, you can focus on creating relational safety with the person. This is built as you prove to be trustworthy with their story and struggle. Active and empathetic listening and asking good questions are key in building a relationship of trust. We will explore both of these skills briefly, though much more can be learned in these two areas. They are essential for anyone in the role of helper.

Active listening includes but is not limited to the following:

- Attentive eye contact: When you are listening, show you are invested in the conversation by focusing on the one talking. Avoid distractions that might pull you away from the conversation unnecessarily. For example, put your phone out of sight.

- Avoid interrupting: There will be a time for you to ask questions and share, but good listening requires you to be quiet. Allow them to express themselves fully.

- Engage in nonverbal cues: Gestures, nods, and facial expressions are all ways you can convey you are understanding and following along as they talk.

- Resist mental judgment: Don't give in to the mental pull that assumes you know how the person felt or what they thought. Be mindful of the natural tendency toward your own biases and opinions.

- Provide limited but appropriate feedback: Giving appropriate feedback expresses your engagement and understanding. You can make comments that reflect back the feelings you hear from the other person through statements like, "I can see how much this has impacted you," "That sounds really hard," or "You have been through a lot of painful things."

Asking intentional and appropriate questions is another skill helpers must have to establish relational trust. Sometimes we ask questions merely to satisfy our curiosity. It is human nature to be curious. We have a natural desire to satisfy a lack of information or details. However, in trauma care, you want to avoid questions that are meant to satisfy your curiosity rather than show your love and care for the person. Instead, ask questions that indicate you are invested in the person's well-being. Explore the individual's thoughts, experiences, and feelings. Here are some examples of questions you might ask:

- Is there anything you want to share about what you have been through? Would you like to talk about it?

- How can I best support you right now?

- Are there any specific triggers or situations that make you feel uncomfortable or unsafe that you need me to be aware of?

- Are there any boundaries or limitations that you would like me to honor as we meet and talk?

- What are the helpful things you do when you feel overwhelmed?

- Is there someone else you trust who you would like present in our conversations?

- What is the most comfortable environment for safely talking about your situation?

- What form of communication are you most comfortable with between our times together?

Validate and listen attentively. Be careful to avoid asking questions at a hurried pace, which can end up pressuring the conversation. One of your goals in this stage is to answer the question, "What is it like to be you?" Do not assume you know, even if you may have experienced something similar.

Through asking questions, I learned from one of my counselees that for him to feel comfortable talking with me, it was essential the path to the door was not blocked as we met. If there was anything (a desk, a chair, or an end table) that stood between him and the door, he found it difficult to concentrate and deeply engage in the conversation. He could feel his stress level increase and his body would respond with visible agitation and unease. Once I knew this caused distress in our meetings, I made sure to keep the door easily accessible to him, and this caused him to be at ease in our meetings. My willingness to make this small adjustment contributed to establishing trust.

Strive to do all you can to genuinely understand where a person is in their healing journey right now. Do all you can to create a safe-enough space that encourages them to feel comfortable and confident as they open up and share their story with you. When you establish safety, you facilitate movement toward the processing of traumatic experiences.

In addition to empathetic listening and asking good questions, you will want to assist the person in building a supportive network. You should not be the only one caring for them. Explore who else might be good to include in their circle of care. This might be a counselor, a pastor, or a trusted friend or family member. It can also include professionals in the medical field. The best care often happens when there is a collective voice of people committed to playing a part in walking with an individual.

Another way to establish safety is to provide resources and offer guidance related to calming exercises or self-care practices. Take time to not only explore what to do, but how to do it. In other words, as mentioned in earlier chapters, don't just tell them to do a breathing exercise when they feel anxious; do those exercises with them. You are helping them learn to self-regulate when you engage these practices with them. Show them how, practice it, model it. The same is true for self-care. Don't simply tell them they need self-care; show them what that can look like. Include it in their homework if your relationship is such that homework might be given. For more information on biblical self-care, see the book *The Whole Life: 52 Weeks of Biblical Self-Care.*

The safety of a traumatized person needs to be our highest priority, and the best trauma care starts there. If you are walking with someone who has been impacted by trauma and you do not have a clear plan for establishing safety, I encourage you to start developing that now. Use the questions and suggestions above to help get you going. Talk to others who have more experience in trauma care and learn what they do to initiate and establish safety with those they care for. Approach all your conversations with trauma survivors with empathy and sensitivity. Go slowly and be prayerful as you offer care.

Stage Two: Processing
(Remembering and Mourning)

Remembering and mourning is the stage in which processing happens, so it is reasonable to call this the "processing" stage. There is a tendency for helpers to jump into this stage too quickly. Because it is the stage in which the trauma story is usually told, we can easily assume it is the first or most important part of trauma care. However, as we learned earlier, that is not the case. In many cases, safety and stabilization may be the most crucial stage for ensuring effective trauma care. When safety is established, remembering and mourning become natural next steps. It is in this stage the person begins to connect meaning to what they have been through and starts to process how to live going forward. As they remember and process, opportunities will arise for sharing biblical truth. Remembering who God is amid difficult and traumatic situations confirms the safety and help they have from God as his loved children. Here is a sampling of Scripture passages that might be helpful as you seek to walk with a person in remembering truth:

- Psalm 34:17: "The righteous cry out, and the LORD hears them; he delivers them from all their troubles" (NIV).

- Psalm 46:1: "God is our refuge and strength, an ever-present help in trouble" (NIV).

- Psalm 91:4: "He will cover you with his feathers, and under his wings you will find refuge; his faithfulness will be your shield and rampart" (NIV).

- Proverbs 18:10: "The name of the LORD is a fortified tower; the righteous run to it and are safe" (NIV).

- Isaiah 41:10: "So do not fear, for I am with you; do not be dismayed, for I am your God. I will strengthen you and help you; I will uphold you with my righteous right hand" (NIV).

- Matthew 28:20: "Behold I am with you always, to the end of the age."

- 2 Thessalonians 3:3: "The Lord is faithful, and he will strengthen you and protect you from the evil one" (NIV).

In this stage, helpers often feel the least equipped. Because of that, we are going to spend a good amount of time in this chapter and the next unpacking what you can do during this stage as a caregiver. For the traumatized person, this stage can include emotional expressions of fear, anger, grief, and loss. Their story may unfold for them in ways they might not have experienced before. Exploring what happened and how it affected them is a big part of this stage.

During this stage, the person also acknowledges and mourns any losses associated with the trauma experienced. This can include mourning the loss of safety, which is why establishing it beforehand is a priority. This can also include mourning a loss of trust. People who have endured traumatic situations in relationships may not trust others, and they may find it hard to trust themselves. As they reflect on and grieve the past, they may experience regret over how they trusted others or themselves. Self-doubt can continue long after the traumatic experience. They may also mourn a loss of freedom or identity. They may feel the person they were before the traumatic experience is not the person they are today, and this can cause grief. Emotions can often be raw and on the surface, or the person may feel flat or come across as blunt. These are normal expressions of grief.

An important aspect of this stage is that it provides opportunity to bring meaning to what happened. Developing a coherent understanding of the event and its impact is essential. Professors of psychology and authors on post-traumatic growth Lawrence G. Calhoun and Richard G. Tedeschi emphasize what must take place during this stage: "The traumatic events themselves and the impact of the events are scrutinized. The impact of the ways the survivor is coping with the events should also be carefully considered."[4]

Exploring the impact of the event also includes identifying what the trauma survivor believes the role of God's sovereignty, character, or provision is in their life. In this stage, you can help the person to incorporate biblical truth, personal growth, coping strategies, and resilience into their life post trauma. The integration of meaning will look different for each person, but essentially it will result in the person ascribing significance and purpose to the overall circumstance. The goal, as believers, is to gain a new and more accurate understanding of what happened to the person, which includes the reality that the Lord is at work in them and is committed to their growth and healing.

We do need to be mindful that the concept of God's sovereignty or other attributes can be a source of profound pain. While a solid faith can offer comfort and strength, it can also raise challenging questions. Why would God allow such suffering? Where was he when I needed protection? How do I reconcile the fact that justice has not been served? Navigating these kinds of questions is a delicate process and requires the ability and wisdom to hold on to unanswered questions with the intention of providing biblically faithful comfort. This requires patience and empathy toward the sufferer and faith and dependence on God. Trust that God is working as you seek to create space for the hard questions to be asked. Depend on him to help you know what to say and what not to say. Not all questions need answering.

Trust that God will reveal, in time, what the person most deeply needs. In the meantime, be willing to serve as a conduit of God's grace and compassion. Allow space for difficult conversations and unanswered questions while holding out the hope that God permits suffering for a while but will ultimately right every wrong, heal every wound, and bring redemption to the most profound pain.

> *Trust that God is working as you seek to create*
> *space for the hard questions to be asked. Depend*
> *on him to help you know what to say and what*
> *not to say. Not all questions need answering.*

Processing trauma is hard and courageous work for the one who is suffering. It is also hard and courageous work for the caregiver. It requires a dependence on God and a willingness to explore matters that do not have easy answers. With a dependence on the Spirit, though, this can be a time of great spiritual growth. As you move into the processing stage with someone, you will need to be able to recognize and understand how trauma impacts a person. We will explore this in greater detail in the next chapter.

Stage Three: Integration and Reconnection

The last stage comes after meaning has been determined during the processing stage. This meaning can now be integrated into how the person goes about living their everyday life, with the goal of diminishing the negative impact trauma has had. When meaning is established, it informs the thought processes and beliefs. The person begins to see that the Spirit helps them and intercedes for them when they have no words (Romans 8:26-27) and that God does indeed intend to work all things for the good (Romans 8:28) and the *good* is that, no matter what happens, God uses it to make us more like Jesus (Romans 8:29), thus restoring hope despite the pain, challenges, and wounds.

Calhoun and Tedeschi offer clarity on the clinical world's goal for this stage. "The therapeutic goal is to replace extreme strategies of avoidance with better self-protective strategies that allow trauma survivors to feel less vulnerable."[5] As believers, we can agree self-protection is a wise and needed step, but we were never meant to be our sole protector. Ultimately our protection comes from the Lord, and he also calls us to life in community, where others are a part of protective strategies that promote wholeness in the midst of community.

Below is a sampling of ways in which those impacted by trauma may begin to connect to their story in a healing way. When these are present, the integration stage is likely in process.

- **Learning healthy emotional expressions:** Rather than being overwhelmed by emotions, a person can identify, acknowledge, and respond to their feelings in a manner that does not distress them.

- **Recognizing their limits:** This is especially helpful when people must re-enter situations or relationships that have been a source of emotional trauma. The goal is not to avoid situations completely, but rather, to recognize when a break or change is needed.

- **Reconnecting with relationships:** Trauma causes people to isolate. When healing has begun, a person will begin to rebuild or re-enter supportive relationships that foster trust and connection.

- **Cultivating regular habits of self-care:** When a trauma sufferer begins to implement self-care habits, it can be a sign that emotional healing has begun. Establishing habits that involve exercise, nutrition, sleep, and the spiritual disciplines helps to promote whole-person wellness.

- **Nurturing spiritual growth:** When a person can deeply engage their faith once again, it is a sign trauma has been holistically integrated. The integration of the traumatic experience into their deepest beliefs is at the heart of all faith-based care. In many ways, this is the ultimate goal. When a person is able to engage with God and find comfort and hope in his Word, healing is happening.

This stage will include reconnecting and integrating with relationships and routines that were disrupted by the trauma. As a person begins to re-engage in life in a meaningful and healthy way, they experience post-traumatic growth and change. Some relationships may be forever changed due to trauma, but a person can learn to wisely understand and appreciate the need for these changes and embrace them as part of their healthy new normal.

As a person moves into this stage of integration and reconnection, care can involve exploring personal values and convictions, thus deepening a confident hope in the Lord. It can include developing a commitment to personal growth, taking the time to do some deeper processing through journaling, or telling their story. It may even include embracing what forgiveness looks like for their circumstance. Being connected to a community is incredibly valuable, and the church plays an important part here. Encourage engagement in small groups, Bible studies, or other community settings in the church where connections can be made. Because trauma care is complex and individuals process trauma differently, suggestions or interventions should be based on the unique needs and circumstances of each person. Great wisdom and discernment are needed by the one providing this support so the care can be tailored according to the needs of the person and their situation.

God's Nearness in Recovery

When it comes to recovering from psychological trauma, the right awareness and care of friends or professionals can help a person to rise above the pain and the wounds of the experience and become resilient. This resiliency comes from being tethered to a God who heals and sustains his people. This is where people begin to rebuild their lives and find purpose and hope for their future. This third stage in trauma recovery is where transformation takes place. It is also where maintenance takes place. The person has learned skills to cope and utilizes these skills more naturally. They are on the path to wholeness.

They not only know how to stay on that path through healthy habits, biblical thinking, and helpful processing, but they also know how to get back on the path should they fall off again as setbacks can happen. In this stage, thriving begins.

In all three stages, a dependence upon and the inclusion of biblical truth remains absolutely vital, as nothing offers more accurate and profound meaning to our lives and circumstances than Scripture itself. As individuals reconnect with God's Word, his work, and his character and integrate these in their lives, they experience the supernatural healing the Lord offers, even in the face of horrific and painful situations.

More Than Three Stages

A traumatized person's healing relies on the three stages of safety, processing, and integration, yet it is important to emphasize that it is not limited to them. There are various additional means the Lord uses to bring help and healing. This chapter is by no means exhaustive. Rather, it serves to give you an introduction to and an awareness of the stages recognized by most trauma care experts. Through the process of establishing safety, walking through processing, and working toward integration and reconnection, individuals can delve into the depths of their experience and gradually unravel the complexities of the emotional memories and responses tied to their trauma.

Knowing these three stages is a vital part of understanding what care is needed for a traumatized individual and where they are in the healing process. In the next chapter, we will go back to stage two: processing. We will look at a practical metaphor to guide us toward ways to help a person through this stage of trauma care and better position us to come alongside a person in their journey toward healing.

CHAPTER 7

STARTING BLOCKS OF CARE

When I was in high school, my sport was track and field. I was a sprinter, which meant practice consisted of plyometric techniques and drills designed to enhance running speed. These exercises helped to increase our muscle elasticity and improve our power. They were also done to enhance our concentration and performance during races—from the starting blocks to the finish line. One of these exercises was called *block starts*. The goal of this exercise was to train us to be ready to burst out of the blocks with as much power and force as possible without jumping the gun—that is, crossing the starting line before the starting gun is fired. If that happens, the runner is disqualified from the race.

To practice the block drills, we runners would carefully place one foot in the rear block and the other in the front block. Then we would position our hips as high as possible without falling forward. With hands shoulder-width apart and arms locked and steady, we carefully placed our fingers behind the chalk starting line, being meticulously attentive not to touch even the edge of that white line.

In this position and with our gaze fixed forward, we would tune our ears for one sound: the starting gun that would signal the race had begun. Our coach would slowly say, "Ready...set," and then he would pause for what at times felt like an eternity. He was training us to hold that position with diligent focus. He was teaching us to wait alertly. Good timing was essential.

Once the starting gun fired, we would explode out of the blocks. In these drills, we would not run far. The goal was simply to practice staying in the blocks and waiting for the gun to go off. We were trained to listen with acute focus for that signal. If we jumped the gun in practice we could try again, but jumping the gun in a race meant it was over for us. We were committed to waiting for the cue and would not leave those blocks until that cue was given.

Trauma care takes a similar commitment. There are starting blocks of care we will discuss in this chapter, and as with the blocks used in track, it is important we don't burst out of them too quickly. That is where stage one from the previous chapter is essential. Establishing safety must precede entering the starting blocks—especially if the person is still in the traumatizing situation. Because we must also not jump out of the starting blocks too early, this chapter will help you to stay in the blocks until the time is right.

The starting blocks of trauma care are summed up in two words: *empower* and *connect*. Learning how to time ourselves well will help us to establish the right footing as we prepare to care for someone in need of processing and integrating their traumatic past. If we jump the gun in trauma care, the opportunity to move forward with the person you are caring for may be lost.

Jumping the gun in trauma care happens when, without proper preparation, we launch into processing. This can cause a person to feel threatened or destabilized. The starting blocks of care will steady both the helper and the one being helped in the initial stages of trauma recovery.

Two Starting Blocks of Care

As we explore the two starting blocks of care, you will gain tangible direction based on biblical principles. You will expand your understanding of what challenges can come along the way and how to best navigate them. Your firm footing in these blocks will ready you and the trauma survivor for the path ahead.

Starting Block 1: Empower

The empowerment of individuals who have endured psychological trauma is of profound importance. The Bible advocates for the protection of the vulnerable and justice for the oppressed (Psalm 82:3; Proverbs 31:8-9). It gives voice to those who have endured unimaginable hardships. Empowering those who have been traumatized is not about encouraging unchecked dominance nor is it about revenge. Rather, to empower them is a way we, as helpers, do justice and love mercy (Micah 6:8).

Empowering the traumatized person involves defending the weak, upholding their cause, and rescuing them from their distress. It helps them regain their strength and dignity, and it promotes a stronger grasp on who they are as a child of God. In all of this, we are fulfilling the biblical mandate that we should protect the vulnerable: "Learn to do right; seek justice. Defend the oppressed. Take up the cause of the fatherless; plead the case of the widow" (Isaiah 1:17 NIV). Part of learning to do right is discovering how we can empower those who have been oppressed. As Psalm 82:3 says, "Defend the weak and the fatherless; uphold the cause of the poor and the oppressed" (NIV). It should be obvious, then, that Christians, more than others, have good reason to embrace the concept of empowerment as one of the starting blocks of trauma care.

So what does it look like to empower the person who has endured trauma? Empowering someone essentially allows the individual to regain a sense of control over their own life. Trauma often leaves a person feeling helpless and powerless. As you empower them, you help to counteract those feelings, which gives them a sense of autonomy. By providing support and resources, you enable a traumatized individual to develop coping skills and make positive changes in their life, which, in turn, helps them to regain confidence and counteract the feelings of shame and self-blame that often accompany trauma.

Part of empowering a person will include anchoring them to who God says they are. If they are a Christian, they have an identity that includes dignity. If they are not a Christian, they still bear the image of God and are worthy of dignity and you have an opportunity to invite them to be a part of God's royal family.

As children of the King, they are loved and cherished. They also have access to the Father and his gifts of strength and support. This truth, affirmed in Scripture, can bring courage as they seek to regain agency. This is especially helpful when trauma has resulted from being in abusive relationships, which can leave a person feeling that their voice does not matter.

Traumatic events are traumatizing because the person felt powerless against a circumstance or person. They not only felt their lack of power but also doubted their ability to do anything about the situation. With no way to escape and no way to change the situation, they can end up feeling that sense of powerlessness even after the traumatic circumstances have ended. Empowering them communicates to the individual their experiences are valid and deserving of support.

To better understand this first starting block of care, we are going to look at some practical ways you can empower a person who has gone through a psychologically traumatizing experience. Then we will explore a few cautions.

EMPOWER THROUGH DECISION-MAKING

Traumatized people are often reluctant to make decisions. This keeps them in a state of helplessness and promotes the continued activation of the fight, flight, or freeze response that they experienced in the trauma. When they were in the traumatic situation, they likely had no choice but to endure. They were unprepared or unaware and, most likely, their only option was simply to survive.

A needed first step toward empowering someone is to encourage them to make small decisions for themselves. While the decisions may be small, they are not insignificant. Every decision is important. Your goal is to help the person not default to doubt their judgment, or to conclude it is better to let others make decisions for them. This is even more important when abuse has been part of their trauma experience. Here are some examples of decisions that survivors can be encouraged to make for themselves:

- **Daily activities and routines.** Encourage them to see the various choices they have in their daily activities. This could involve deciding what time they want to wake up or go to bed and what activities they want to prioritize that day. It can include decisions about when they want to leave a family gathering or when they will respond to a text or phone call. It can also include decisions about what interests or hobbies they may want to pursue.

- **Setting personal boundaries.** Help the trauma survivor identify and communicate their personal boundaries. Encourage them to express what they are comfortable with or what makes them uncomfortable without having to justify their preferences. Do they want a hug, or would they rather shake hands or simply say hello as a greeting? They get to choose, and this can start with your relationship.

Allowing them to have a choice in what your relationship will look like fosters a sense of safety and shows you are prioritizing their well-being.

- **Selecting their support system.** It is important that a trauma survivor has a voice in deciding who they will share their experiences with. Support them in thinking through and choosing who they want to share their story with or who they want to reach out to for additional support they might need. This act of letting them select their support system can help empower them. It allows them to know they will be surrounded by people who they know will respect their boundaries and provide a safe space for healing.

EMPOWER THROUGH RELATIONSHIP

Another important way to empower a person is by recognizing and keeping a check on your power in the relationship. You are not there as the arbiter of their experience; rather, you are there to learn and understand, and to provide care and support and alternatives to their present suffering. Because they will already see you as an authority, offer your suggestions carefully and do so in a way that affirms their input. This can be done by providing more than one suggestion and encouraging them to choose what might be best. Foster a sense of ownership in the decision-making process by emphasizing the importance of their input.

Here are some examples of what this might look like: "Would you like to meet again this week, or would you feel more comfortable waiting a week or two before we meet again?" "Would you like to talk about your relationship with your mother today, or would you rather talk about how you're managing the stress in your life, or is there something else that's more important for us to talk about today?" Giving options diminishes your power to control what will be discussed and instead, emphasizes their voice and choice in the conversation.

Avoid doing anything that might look like an attempt to control their actions. Remind them you are just one voice God can use in this process, and they can share your suggestions with others for further input. Encourage them to talk with trusted family members, a doctor or counselor, or mentors or friends from their faith community. The bigger their circle of care, the better care and support they will receive. And from their perspective, this will also keep you from becoming the resident expert.

Encourage sufferers to invite others into the process of healing. Find out who else knows their story. If you are the only one, then slowly explore who else they can trust. Talk about how other trusted people might be brought into the process. Allow the sufferer to choose who that will be and how much of their story they will share.

EMPOWER THROUGH VALIDATION

Empowering a trauma survivor means you validate their experience. Affirm the situation was out of their control and that what they went through was hard. Validate how trapped or stuck they felt. Reassure them you want to be there for them and you know the process will take time.

Trauma can make sufferers doubt many things, including the validity of their own feelings. Acknowledge their emotions and express empathy without minimizing their experience. You can do this by saying things such as, "It is okay to express your emotions about what happened. I want you to know I am here to support you as you process this." Another option is to tie in the idea of relationship with your validation by saying something like, "Please know that it's okay to lean on others when you need to. Your experience may be too big for you alone. I am here to listen and help in any way I can."

EMPOWER THROUGH REMINDING

Another essential aspect of empowering a trauma survivor is to remind them of the power they do have. Help them see what they have survived thus far. Point out how they have endured things they may have once thought they couldn't. You can say things like, "You've already proven that you can overcome difficulty," or "Reaching out for help is another way you have shown your strength and desire to heal." Remind them they got through the event or circumstance, which says much about their capacity to endure. Also remind them of the power of God that is in them to strengthen them and give them the ability to think accurately about their situation. In 2 Timothy 1:7, we are told that God gives us a spirit not of fear, but of power and of love and of a sound mind. Assure them of the power that belongs to them as a child of God.

Remind them of the support system they have. Point out they are not alone on this journey. Remind them of the people who care about them, including you. Remind them of how God promises to never leave them.

Finally, remind them the goal is progress, not perfection. Healing is a process, and it is okay to have setbacks along the way. Help the trauma survivor recall the times they have made progress because they will forget. Point them to small victories and remind them every step forward, no matter how tiny, is a win! Encourage them toward self-compassion because they may find it easy to be critical of themselves when progress is hard to see.

WHAT EMPOWER DOES NOT MEAN

As a trauma survivor begins to see and embrace the power they do have, it's important you continue to offer options, alternatives, and considerations. Empowerment does not mean you support decisions that compromise safety to themselves or others. Instead, it means you seek to encourage them to balance autonomy with responsible and appropriate choices. Empowerment also does not mean undermining God's sovereign control. Rather, it acknowledges faith as a valuable aspect of their decision-making and encourages personal participation in the healing process. This can be incredibly helpful for a trauma survivor because they may not readily think of the various options they have. As you offer suggestions, always allow them to decide what they will do. If they are not ready to decide, then allow them space but assure them you will be with them to help think through the options. This is a necessary way to care for them, which takes patience on the part of the caregiver.

On occasion, circumstances may arise in which, for the safety of everyone involved, you need to make a decision for a person. Such situations should be more of an exception than the norm. You want to guard against overstepping appropriate boundaries and doing the work that is theirs and not yours.

There may be times when you need to make a decision because an individual is experiencing severe emotional distress and experts are needed to provide support or to assess the severity of the situation. You may decide emergency medical care is needed to ensure the safety of all involved. In cases where the traumatizing circumstances are ongoing, you may need to make the decision to involve appropriate authorities to ensure the safety of everyone. You honor God and the person you are helping when you wisely assert a needed course of action that is best for the well-being of the person and others. However, never make decisions in isolation. Rather, involve other trusted individuals. To avoid overstepping, make these decisions alongside the trauma victim whenever possible.

As mentioned earlier, to empower someone does not mean you're undermining God's sovereign control over that person's life. God determined it was good for each of us to have personal volition and power. Stepping toward what God has given by empowering someone does not mean you are denying God's ultimate power and control. Instead, it is recognizing that we image God through the power we possess.

Starting Block 2: Connect

Now let's look at the second essential starting block of trauma care: connect. Though we are looking at the starting blocks of care one at a time, avoid thinking of your efforts to empower and connect as two separate, constitutive steps. Instead, think of them as I did of my track drills. The different parts of the drills—from placing my feet in the blocks to properly positioning my hips, shoulders, and arms—were equally important as I prepared to run. I had to pay attention to each aspect of getting ready as I awaited the sound of the starting gun. This second block is just one part of helping an individual prepare to process their trauma. You are establishing readiness, care, and trust before beginning to process the trauma. Much of what happens in each starting block of care naturally takes place at the same time.

Therefore, in addition to ensuring the person has power and volition in their decisions or circumstances, we want to do all we can to connect with the person. As mentioned, these two starting blocks work together because as you empower, you are also connecting with a person, and vice versa.

Connection requires knowledge. You must know the person. You must be invested in understanding what life has been like for them. You must seek to empathetically connect and understand in a way that establishes rapport.

To connect with someone requires basic yet essential counseling skills. If you are a counselor, you likely utilize these skills on a regular basis. However, when working with people who have been through trauma, you must emphasize and execute these skills all the more. Whether you are a counselor or a friend, pastor, mentor, family member, or another part of someone's support team, this starting block is vital. Connection will not only help you provide trauma-informed care, it will also help you in all your relationships, as connection is essential to us all. As you offer trauma care, review this section regularly and consider which of the four aspects of connection you do well in, and which you need to grow in.

1. Connect Through Listening

Everyone knows listening is of supreme importance when it comes to connecting with someone relationally. This is paramount when caring for someone who has experienced psychological trauma. Listening well provides a safe and supportive environment in which people can share their experiences, emotions, and concerns. Diane Langberg describes this kind of listening as seeking to answer the question, What is it like to be you? She explains:

> Have you ever listened, trying to understand what it is like to be them rather than trying to correct them and make them like you? So often we listen just long enough to convince another to be more like us or to instruct them about how to "get over" whatever has happened. It is an egocentric approach. Jesus' presence with us was not and is not like that. He listened and responded to the individual. Have you ever been struck by the fact that he healed all blind people in unique ways?[1]

You may not have clinical expertise in therapeutic interventions, but by truly listening, you can offer space that allows a person to express their specific thoughts and feelings. When you are attentive to their unique experience, it fosters feelings of being understood and valued, and helps them feel less alone in their struggle.

You may not have clinical expertise in therapeutic interventions, but by truly listening, you can offer space that allows a person to express their specific thoughts and feelings.

Listening Well

Even if you consider yourself a pretty good listener, you can always improve. Take a minute to reflect on the questions below to help you gauge how well you listen:

1. Do you listen to understand or to respond?

2. Do you give your full attention when someone is talking?

3. Do you refrain from disputing or debating the person's view?

4. Are you able to show empathy or validate their feelings?

5. Are you willing to consider different perspectives or hear things that may not be fully accurate without acting on the urge to correct?

Do any of the questions above reveal areas in which you need to grow? As you read each question, were you able to affirm that it was true of you? If not, consider focusing on the areas in which you need to grow. Go a step further by asking someone close to you how they would answer the questions in relation to how well you listen. Be prayerful about areas in which you need to grow. As mentioned earlier, we can all grow in becoming better listeners. The pitfalls to listening are many, and we must seek to avoid them—especially when caring for people who have gone through trauma.

Obstacles to Listening

The questions above can be a valuable resource for improving your ability to tune in effectively to a person when they are speaking. Nevertheless, it is crucial to be aware of common pitfalls that can hinder your capacity to listen attentively. Identifying and addressing these obstacles will help you refine your listening skills and continue to develop your ability to hear and understand others. Below are five of the most common obstacles to listening well. They are modes of listening that do not have the goal of hearing and understanding in view.

1. **Preoccupied listening:** Being distracted by our own thoughts and concerns or by external factors can cause us to be physically present but mentally preoccupied. This leads to a lack of genuine attention to the speaker.

2. **Interruptive listening:** When you interject your own thoughts or opinions without allowing the person to fully express themselves, it disregards their need to be heard and will disrupt the flow of conversation. This will also cause a disconnect in the relationship. The person will sense you are more committed to sharing your thoughts than allowing them to finish their thoughts.

3. **Selective listening:** This happens when you focus on certain parts of the conversation that seem to align with your agenda. Or the opposite: You focus only on the parts you want to challenge because they deviate from your opinion. Selective

listening causes you to tune out or disregard information that might be essential for understanding a person's story.

4. **Evaluative listening:** This is when you find yourself focused more on judging what you are hearing, which will prevent you from truly understanding the person's experience. When you get distracted by evaluations based on your biases or preconceived notions, you fail to listen.

5. **Defensive listening:** This happens when you become sensitive to criticism or negative feedback or when you have a different opinion. However, being defensive leads to misunderstanding and strained communication. It also prevents you from considering the speaker's personal perspective on what happened and can lead to invalidating their experience.

Did any of the descriptions above fit ways you might have listened to someone recently? Did the word *guilty* run through your mind as you read about these kinds of obstacles? Have you been on the receiving end of any of these types of listening? How did that make you feel? I hope you caught the irony over the fact these five different kinds of listening are not at all true listening. It is so easy to think we are listening well when, in reality, we may be quite far from doing so.

Being trauma aware means becoming excellent listeners. Listening is essential in connecting with a person and can be the determining factor as to whether the one who is looking for support will be receptive to your care.

One final note on the topic of listening before we move to another way to connect: Be very careful about jumping to spiritual application too soon. This is especially true when what is needed most is a genuine listening friend. Adam McHugh, in his book *The Listening*

Life: Embracing Attentiveness in a World of Distraction, states it well, saying, "Listening to people in pain is about giving them room to grieve and weep and rage and doubt. We are not there to spiritualize their pain or theologize their experience. Our religious talk, preemptive assurance and breezy conversation take space when instead we want to give space."[2] There is a time and a place for spiritual conversations, but going there too quickly can trivialize their experience and inhibit the vital connection that a person who has experienced trauma so desperately needs. Avoid feeling rushed to give spiritual advice or direction. That is not listening; that is advising. Listening is a process, and it requires patience. Don't rush the process. Just when you think you have listened long enough, listen a little more.

To help prevent the occurrence of blind spots, which we all have, review the questions in the two sections above regularly. Listening is a skill we must continue to develop all our lives. Irrespective of our roles or professions, becoming better at listening will bring valuable benefits to every one of us. Psychology professor David Benner says that "a major obstacle to growth in our listening abilities is that most of us already think that we are good listeners."[3]

It can be helpful to ask those closest to you if they feel you are a good listener. Ask them how you can improve and receive the feedback with humility. Not only will listening help you to connect with the trauma-impacted people you are trying to care for, it will also help you in all your relationships.

2. CONNECT THROUGH ASKING

There is much wise instruction one forgets amid the many hours of lectures in grad school. But for me, there is one statement from one of those many lectures that would not fall into the bucket of forgotten wisdom: "When you assume, you don't ask."

These wise words were spoken by one of my seminary professors while I was getting my master's degree in counseling. He shared them during a class in which we were learning how to conduct clinical interviews with clients. We were being taught to appropriately organize and skillfully ask the questions needed to assess a person's readiness for counseling. Though the class was all about learning how to ask questions, we also learned how prone we are to avoid or miss the most important questions because of our natural assumptions. And when you assume, you don't ask.

Let's do a quick exercise. When given the following scenarios, counseling students affirmed each situation warranted counseling. With only the information given below, might you agree or disagree with their assessment? Would you suggest counseling, or would the loving involvement of friends or family be sufficient?

1. Sam is a seven-year-old who was an eyewitness to a tragic four-wheeler rollover on his family's farm, which resulted in the tragic death of the 13-year-old driver. Since the accident, Sam has been regularly startled by the sounds of vehicles and will run and hide and sometimes shakes with terror when a car is heard outside. He refuses to be left alone, requires reassurance when he leaves the house, and cries when encouraged to play outside alone.

2. Kristen is a single 25-year-old who has been known to regularly avoid events where food is present. She declines dinner party invitations, and co-workers notice she rarely, if ever, participates in office parties when food is present. She is thin and often excuses herself in settings or conversations where food becomes the focus.

3. Jeff and his wife and children recently moved to a new area. The move was prompted by an invitation for Jeff to pastor

a small, rural church that was starting to get off the ground. An all-hands-on-deck approach was necessary for meeting all the ministry needs and to get everything ready for Sunday mornings. Though Jeff loves the ministry, he has become overwhelmed by the ever-growing demands. Thankfully, the church hired a secretary for him, and she has been a huge help to him during the past few months. He depends on her for many of the weekly details and often affirms how he could not do this job without her help. Lately, he has been seen in public showing extra kindness toward her, like taking her out for coffee, and last week, a volunteer who happened to be at the church to prepare for Sunday saw him secretly leaving flowers in her office before she came in to work.

For each of the scenarios above, certainly more information is needed. But at first glance, how do these situations strike you? How do they make you feel? What thoughts come to your mind? Would you consider counseling to be a necessary path for any of them? If not counseling, maybe a serious conversation to help address their situation? Well, you might change your mind if you knew Sam is a seven-year-old golden retriever, Kristen is a devout vegan who does not like to draw attention to her strong convictions related to dietary choices, and Jeff's secretary is also his wife.

In each of the situations above, you probably would have sought out more information before making a judgment call. Yet as you were reading along, you were already forming assumptions. And, as my professor said, "When you assume, you don't ask." That exercise exposes how prone we all are to make quick assumptions. Not only can our assumptions potentially be wrong, but they can potentially be dangerous as well if they lead us to make decisions without knowing all the facts.

As you seek to connect with those who have endured trauma, you must be especially careful you do not assume you know how they felt in the situation they faced. When you hear of a young woman who was raped by a schoolmate when she invited him over to work on a class project, you may assume she was afraid or confused. Those are very possible responses, but unless she tells you, you do not know. As you talk with her, you learn she mostly feels anger when she reflects on what happened that night. He had slipped something into her iced tea, causing her to lose her capabilities and inhibitions. As she recalls the night, she is angry. A significant reason for her anger is that he later tried to convince her that she was consensual to the encounter. She was also angry because he began to spread lies about her in attempt to claim his innocence. Once she tells you all these details, you know what she feels. But until she tells you, be very cautious about making or expressing any assumptions about how she feels.

When you seek to care for those who have gone through traumatizing situations, do not assume—even though circumstances may seem to support your suspicions. Your assumptions will keep you from asking questions and will hinder the connection you are seeking to build with the person.

Asking appropriate questions will keep you firmly planted in the starting blocks of care and prepare you to run the distance with compassion and clarity. Asking good questions starts with avoiding assumptions, and to do that, you have to realize just how prone you are to assuming things. The next time a person tells you their story, even if it is not a traumatic story, beware of making assumptions, and instead, seek to ask good questions that help draw the person out. This approach will help to create a connection between you and to establish trust.

Asking good questions requires sensitivity, compassion, and empathy. Good questions help foster a supportive relationship between you and the one you are seeking to care for. As you ask good questions, you will want to remember to employ the good listening techniques you learned about above. Prioritize the survivor's pace, allow them to take as much time as needed when giving answers, and avoid interjecting your comments too soon. Below are some helpful questions you can ask:

- "How are you feeling today?" Start with how the person is right then and there. Explore how they feel about sitting down to talk with you and ask what you can do to make the conversation easier.

- "Is there anything specific you would like to share or talk about today related to your experience?" By saying this, you are empowering the person in conversation, which encourages trust in the relationship.

- "Are there any topics or triggers you want me to be aware of as we talk?" Respecting the person's boundaries and being sympathetic to their experience builds connection.

- "What coping strategies have you found helpful? What activities or practices help you to calm down?" The person's answer will not only inform you of what is helpful for them, but will also acknowledge their strengths and how they have endured thus far.

- "How can I best support you right now and create a safe environment for you in which to share?" This will demonstrate your commitment to their well-being and your willingness to provide supportive care based on their needs.

- "What counseling results would you need to experience for you to consider the process a success?" You may not be able to provide all the person is hoping for, but in asking this, you are showing interest in helping them to know progress.

The importance of asking good questions and avoiding assumptions cannot be overstated. Jesus himself exemplified curiosity, wisdom, and empathy in his own interactions with people, including those who had been through traumatic situations. He knew all about them, yet still took the time to ask questions and allow them to share what they wanted him to know. As we model Jesus' approach, we will show compassionate understanding and discernment.

Asking good questions also demonstrates respect for others' experience and fosters a deeper sense of connection. It shows your willingness to be humble and exhibit a spirit of care and understanding. Proverbs 18:15 reminds us to cultivate this kind of attitude: "An intelligent heart acquires knowledge, and the ear of the wise seeks knowledge."

3. Connect Through Validation

The next essential in caring for someone who has been through trauma is to validate their experience. This can be difficult to do because validation isn't always the same as agreement or affirmation. Helpers sometimes express concern that if they validate the trauma survivor's experience, there might not be room for other voices or perspectives that can be both helpful and healing. They want to make sure validating the person will not affirm their thinking in a way that keeps them stuck.

Validating someone means acknowledging their feelings and experience. It accepts what they are saying is what they are experiencing. Doing this fosters trust, reduces emotional distress, and encourages self-reflection. Agreement, on the other hand, means you share the same viewpoint, opinion, or stance. In validation you are seeking to understand and not judge the validity of the person's feelings or experience. Validating someone communicates their feelings are worthy of consideration and causes them to feel heard and understood.

Validation may be a new concept to you. You might have experienced it in your own life without knowing it, or you may struggle over how to correctly validate someone who is suffering. Here are some examples of validating responses:

- "It makes sense you would feel that way."

- "It is okay to be upset about this."

- "I can see how challenging this situation is for you."

- "It is normal to feel overwhelmed in light of what you have been through."

- "I hear what you are saying, and your emotions make sense to me in light of the circumstance."

- "Thank you for sharing with me. It takes a lot of courage to talk about this."

- "You are not alone; many people have similar feelings in situations like this."

- "Your perspective is important, and I want to understand it better."

- "It is okay to have mixed or fluctuating emotions about this because it is a complex situation."

Validation is about showing empathy and compassion without having to agree with a person's opinions, reactions, or choices. The statements above convey a willingness to understand and express support. They create a nonjudgmental space for the individual to process their thoughts and build a connection. This is why validating statements like these are part of the essential starting blocks of care.

Validation is about showing empathy and compassion without having to agree with a person's opinions, reactions, or choices.

---

4. Connect Through Slowing Down

Finally, in an effort to connect, you must go slow and create space so the person can share their experience without feeling rushed. This establishes emotional safety, something that is absent in traumatic situations. Going slowly allows the person to share at their own pace in the hopes of limiting the possibility of retraumatization. Going slowly builds both connection and trust, and lets the person know you will stay with them, listen to them, and care for them without pressure.

There are many ways you can create an unhurried environment when seeking to be a supportive friend or counselor. A good starting point is your presence. Not every moment requires words. As you help someone process their thoughts, you may need to become comfortable with offering silent support. Allow time for the person to contemplate and gather their thoughts. More importantly, notice anything you might be doing that might make a person feel rushed. The list below exposes several common ways you can become hurried in your care.

- **You jump into problem-solving.** If you find yourself jumping to solutions or advice right away, it may indicate you are moving too quickly.

- **You interrupt or finish the person's thoughts.** Slow down and let them complete their thoughts: Avoid assuming you know what they are going to say.

- **Changing the subject too soon.** Taking a new direction can sometimes be helpful when a person is getting overwhelmed in a conversation. However, redirecting a conversation before a person is ready to move on can come across as wanting to avoid the person's feelings. Use caution and be aware of your own discomfort, which could be driving your desire to change the subject.

- **Ignoring nonverbal cues.** Paying attention to a person's nonverbal cues is essential. Often sufferers will express distress through changes or shifts in their expressions, breathing, or posture. Ignoring these cues will likely rush the process and inhibit the building of trust.

Going slowly and creating space is vital so the survivor can process and integrate the traumatic experience, which often becomes fragmented and disorganized in the person's mind and memory. By going slowly, you create the space needed to allow them to process their thoughts and feelings more thoroughly. When this happens, they are given the opportunity to make sense of the trauma in ways that promote healing and even reframing. Going slowly also allows the caregiver to avoid triggering memories that cause unhelpful responses. Slowing down also encourages the engagement of healthy coping strategies that make support and care more effective.

The process of connecting by avoiding assumptions, asking good questions, validating the person's experience, and slowing down requires patience and sensitivity. It also calls for a dependence on the Holy Spirit for wisdom and grace, and will make a significant difference in the healing journey of a suffering person.

The Gift of Empowering and Connecting

I trust you now understand how empowering a person and connecting with them are the essential starting blocks in trauma care. If you jump the gun without spending the appropriate time in these blocks, you may forfeit the opportunity to walk with someone toward healing. When you seek to empower them and connect with them, you show an awareness of the acute reality of their situation. By empowering, you give a weary sufferer wings for a long, hard journey. And by connecting, you create a needed bond of trust. These are gifts to the one who is suffering, and they are ways you can join them in carrying their burden caused by trauma.

In chapter 2, you learned that in years past people didn't understand trauma and approached what they saw in traumatized people by asking, "What's wrong with you?" As scientific technology has allowed us to see the impact of trauma on the brain and the physical effects on a person, we began to ask a more helpful question: "What happened to you?" As the fields of psychology and counseling grow in understanding what is needed to care for trauma survivors, they are now asking, "Who was with you?" That is, who was there to help you through it all? Who walked with you in the aftermath? Who was caring for you? "Who was with you?" is a better question because we now understand that people become less traumatized by traumatic events when they have someone with them in the aftermath. As you place yourself in the starting blocks of care, you become that person. Your intentional presence and pace can be what God uses to offer much-needed hope to those impacted by trauma. Even more, you incarnate the faithful character of God. He is always with us. He never leaves us nor forsakes us. At its core, this stage is about being with people on the path toward peace, clarity, and hope.

With these two starting blocks of empowering and connecting in place, you are more assured of giving trauma survivors the help they need. In the next chapter, we will learn how to offer continued practical help by bringing God's comfort and truth to the situation in a way that provides healing balm to the traumatized.

CHAPTER 8

PEACE FOR THE TRAUMATIZED

J ake was a 21-year-old college student when he first started seeing me. He came to counseling reluctantly only after promising his parents to give it a try. Jake was struggling with anxiety and panic that was manifesting physically and inhibiting him from living the life he wanted. The symptoms had come on after an assault he experienced one night when he was jogging through his neighborhood. Jake lived in what was considered a safe, suburban college town, a place where people could walk freely without concern. This made Jake unprepared for what happened to him that dreadful summer evening.

As Jake jogged by a quiet, wood-lined park in his neighborhood, he saw a man sitting alone on a bench alongside the running path. Jake had never seen the man before, but thought nothing of it. As he neared the bench, the man stood up. Jake intended to continue jogging, but the man motioned to him and started to ask him a question. Jake paused to listen, and suddenly, the man grabbed him with great force. Jake was no match for this man's strength. Within seconds, he was being pulled into the woods. What happened next remains a blur of terrifying and humiliating minutes during which Jake was unsure if he would survive.

The man did not end Jake's life, but he did take much from it. Leaving Jake stunned and crumpled on the ground, the man ripped off Jake's fitness watch and walked briskly out of sight. Jake didn't know it then, but the wounds the man inflicted that evening were not only physical, they were also mental and deeply emotional. The police report affirmed the assault and the property the man had stolen, but what it could never document is how that event stole Jake's confidence and peace of mind. The report would never capture all the assault took from him and how deeply the wounds went.

Ever since that night, Jake has struggled to sleep and has had a hard time concentrating at school. He had to quit his job because it meant arriving home late in his neighborhood, which would send him into paralyzing panic.

Jake wondered if life would ever go back to the way it was before the attack. He felt like too much had been taken from him and was starting to believe he would never feel safe again. He told me he just wanted peace—peace in his mind and in this life. Peace is something every survivor of trauma desires to achieve.

Is peace possible when people experience terrifying, life-changing trauma? I can answer that question with a confident yes! This chapter will focus on how peace can be a reality for those who have been traumatized. In the same way we went over the common symptoms of trauma with the acrostic TRAUMA in chapter 5, we will now use the acrostic PEACE to look at how peace can become a reality to those who have been traumatized.

Patience
Education
Acknowledge
Counseling
Encourage

Below, we will explore ways to offer tangible help and support to sufferers of trauma that can bring peace again to their life.

P–Patience

I trust by now, you have learned that trauma has no quick fixes and cannot be addressed with hasty remedies. Instead, the way to healing is one of gentleness, humility, and caution.

Allow Ephesians 4:2 to be your guide and approach to care: "Be completely humble and gentle; be patient, bearing with one another in love" (NIV). Patience is essential when working with someone who has gone through emotional trauma because you may be tempted to move forward or move on before they are ready to do so. Patience is a fruit of the Spirit and requires you to lean not on your own understanding, but on God's wisdom. Let go of your timeline for healing and prioritize love and gentle care.

Patience plays a crucial role in establishing safety and trust. Your patience will create an environment for people to open up and move toward healing. Rushing the process or expressing impatience may inadvertently add to people's trauma and hinder their progress.

Your patience with the trauma survivor will help them feel heard; it will show that you value their story. When you move forward at an unhurried pace, they will see your willingness to stay the course with them. This is a direct reflection of the way the Lord deals with us. He is patient and kind (Psalm 145:8). He does not break a bruised reed (Isaiah 42:3). He does not get frustrated at the pace of our healing; rather, he understands our frame and frailty (Psalm 103:13-14). He is not in a hurry but is merciful, slow to anger, and rich in compassion (Exodus 34:6). These truths about the Lord's care for us provide solace during our own challenging moments. When we respond to someone's journey with patience and composure, we effectively convey the peace God offers. As a result, our interactions can help serve as a source of calm.

Demonstrating patience also allows for genuine connection. Jake was intensely reluctant to share any details about the assault with anyone. When he first came to see me, the only other people who knew everything that had happened to him were the officers who took the police report. Even his parents knew only part of the story, and when we first met—at the urging of his parents—he did not want to open up to a total stranger about what had happened.

Patience in that situation meant that for our first several sessions, I would not broach the subject of the assault unless he did. Instead, I learned about Jake's musical interests. We played songs in my office I had never heard before, and I learned what he liked about both the artist and the song. I discovered how Jake felt about his major, a degree his parents thought he should pursue but had minimal interest in. We talked about his hobbies, his girlfriend, the races he had run, and the video games he played. He told me how he had mastered solving the Rubik's Cube as a teen. The next session, I brought one in and watched him solve it quickly again and again. Despite how hard I would attempt to mix up the cube each time, he always solved it. This intentional pace and patience let him know I was not in a hurry, but I would be there when he was ready to share. At each session, I asked him questions about how he was doing, and at first he would talk in generalities, but as time passed, that changed.

Then one day in the middle of him quickly matching the colors on the Rubik's Cube, Jake opened up. This breakthrough came only after many long and seemingly unrelated talks and even some sessions during which little was said. In the end, he was able to find significant healing through counseling. Long after our sessions officially ended, he reached out to share with me that he was engaged to his girlfriend, and his life was filled with hope again. He shared appreciation for the unhurried pace that changed counseling from something he dreaded to a place where some of the most painful parts of life could be shared. He felt safe because we went slowly.

Trauma care is unhurried care. It is good for us to remember the command in 1 Thessalonians 5:14: "We urge you, brothers, admonish the idle, encourage the fainthearted, help the weak, *be patient with them all*" (emphasis added).

E–Education

When it comes to trauma, always take the stance of a ready learner. Don't assume that because you have read a book or two, attended a conference, or received a certificate of some kind that you are fully informed about trauma. In fact, this book is titled *Trauma Aware* to reflect the idea that awareness is not a final achievement but an ongoing process. It is a continuous journey and there is always room to deepen our understanding and further our awareness. You will have much to learn even after reading this book. James 3:13 says, "Who is wise and understanding among you? Let them show it by their good life, by deeds done in the humility that comes from wisdom" (NIV). Your pursuit of educated wisdom will be a blessing to those you walk with, but it is just that—a pursuit. There is always more to learn, and if you embrace that, your efforts to extend care will always be done with humility.

When I write, I sometimes go to different locations outside my house so I can get away from the distractions of home projects, unexpected conversations with family or neighbors, and my pillowy couch that can entice even the most nap-resistant.

While these other writing locales are usually a local coffee shop or café, today, it just so happens I am writing this part of this chapter while sitting in the Library of Congress in Washington, DC. I live less than 30 minutes from this gorgeous library, and although the chairs are hard and uncomfortable, the intention of those who are with me in the richly decorated reading room is clear: They are here to study, work, and learn.

There are plenty of tourists wandering the halls, but the reading room is where academics come to learn from books too old or too expensive to buy. I may not fit in with some of the law students and doctoral candidates here, but I know my ability to focus will be better here. This is a place of education. The books afford the knowledge needed for research and study. People sitting at the desks are fixed on what they are reading or writing.

Amidst the ornate and detailed domed ceiling; the eye-catching arched architecture; the sculptures of the great thinkers of literature, philosophy, and academia peering down at the visitors; and the sophisticated aura of the polished mahogany desks, I remain focused on putting words to the white space on my book pages. If I don't, I will certainly stand out. For a brief second my silly habit of popping my chewing gum suddenly reminds me of how easy it is to disrupt the decorum around me, and I quickly desist. The last thing I want is for the national librarian to tilt her head, furrow her brows, and lift her finger to her lips in a gesture that says, "You really should know better."

One of the ways you can help those who have been traumatized is to educate yourself. You don't have to come to the Library of Congress to inform yourself about trauma and traumatization. Instead, you only need to take on the disposition of those who go there to study. Approach trauma with the mindset of being educated. Become and remain a learner. Consider yourself a novice even if you have had training. Learn as much as you can—from books, from those trauma-trained, from lectures, and especially from survivors. You are learning by reading this book. But let this be the beginning or one part of your journey in learning.

But don't just educate yourself, educate those you are caring for. Trauma survivors can teach you a great deal about their specific experience that a book cannot, but they often have a limited understanding of trauma and its impact. They are often uncertain, scared, and confused about what they are experiencing. They frequently feel like something is wrong with them. They believe they are damaged. Considering what they have gone through, it can be profoundly helpful for them to hear that their responses to their experience are normal.

Author, neurologist, psychiatrist, and Holocaust survivor Viktor E. Frankl summed up post-trauma responses when, in his book *Man's Search for Meaning,* he said that "an abnormal reaction to an abnormal situation is normal behavior."[1] For trauma survivors, it is a relief to learn that their reaction—or even lack thereof—is common. This knowledge can bring so much peace of mind and assure them they have not lost their sanity. While education is not necessarily the solution to a given situation, it can bring a sense of calm to a person who feels like everything in their world is chaotic.

I encourage you to become well-informed about what happens in the brain and body when the fight, flight, or freeze response is activated so you can explain it to trauma survivors in an understandable way. Knowing how and why the sympathetic and parasympathetic nervous systems are activated is valuable insight. Practice explaining this information to someone else before you share it with someone you are caring for.

While education is not necessarily the solution to a given situation, it can bring a sense of calm to a person who feels like everything in their world is chaotic.

In the aftermath of profound experiences, survivors often find themselves grappling with a palpable sense of instability. This can cause the foundations of faith to crumble. Trauma distorts our theology. It raises questions and casts doubt on things we once held as true. Those who are dealing with trauma need education about these foundational truths. Therefore, another aspect of educating trauma survivors is to teach them—or, in some cases, remind them—about who God is and how he works according to his character. While we don't know God's plans for others or what he will do with their experiences, we can trust what we know about his unwavering faithfulness. Tell sufferers what is true about God, even if you think they already know. Remind them that God affirms there is coming a day when all evil will end and perfect justice will be delivered. All tears will be wiped away, and everything will be made right. This knowledge helps all of us know how to live and how to respond to the most difficult circumstances.

While insight and knowledge about God are not all that is necessary, they are helpful for calming distressed hearts that can so easily forget helpful truths, often when it is most needed. God can use you to help those who have been traumatized, and one way he does this is through you prayerfully and diligently learning all you can. So educate yourself and those you are caring for. It is perfectly fine to learn together, but you can initiate the research. Your efforts toward education will help bring peace.

A—Acknowledge

As a new counselor, I had the opportunity to observe counseling sessions with those who were far more seasoned than I was. These times of observation had a lasting impact on me. One encounter still stands out in my mind. As I sat in the counseling room, the counselor I was observing listened to a young woman share how she had wanted nothing more than to skip her counseling session that day. This woman had endured the unspeakable trauma of living in an abusive relationship and was beginning to process how it had affected her. That was why she wanted to avoid counseling—things were surfacing that tempted her to run from it all. She told her counselor all the reasons she had come up with to cancel the session. She said she had even hoped she would come down with a fever or a sore throat so she could honestly say she was sick. But despite her desire to cancel, she said she knew that going to the session was the best thing for her to do.

Her counselor listened intently, then said, "I truly admire your strength in showing up here today. You are handling this with incredible resilience, and you have once again done a hard but good thing by showing up. I am honored to get to be the one to support you in this journey. What would make today a little easier as we talk?" I was not expecting the counselor's response. Her words were heartfelt as she acknowledged the woman's challenges. Her response honored this woman's efforts in a difficult situation. And the question posed by her showed that she knew the process was hard and she was willing to do what she could to make it easier.

Acknowledging what the sufferer has been through gives honorable recognition to difficult circumstances. This is essential in your role as a helper. When someone shares their story of trauma with you, you are in one of the most fragile and sacred spaces of their life. You may be the first person they are opening up to. They are handing you something to be handled with care. Acknowledge how hard their experience has been and how real it is. Commend their bravery and how they have survived thus far. Doing this can be helpful and healing. In other cases, you are inviting them to explore their story through a clearer lens. This reality alone can be challenging. It may surprise you that sometimes people have not even recognized that what they've gone through meets the criteria of trauma and what they are experiencing is traumatization. Acknowledging the traumatizing impact of their circumstances can be a validating and helpful response.

Acknowledging the importance of a trauma survivor's story can bring peace as they begin to feel known, heard, and understood. Sometimes, for the first time, they are realizing that another person understands the significance of what they have been through. This acknowledgment can make them feel seen, something trauma survivors don't readily feel.

You may not have thought about this before, but the Lord acknowledges our story through the accounts of difficulty, hardship, and trauma portrayed in the Bible. Where Scripture gives voice to painful circumstances people faced, we see a sense of solidarity. In 2 Corinthians, the apostle Paul shares about the pressures he was under. These struggles were far beyond what he and his friends felt they had the ability to endure. He acknowledged that what they had been through had caused them to despair of life itself (2 Corinthians 1:8). He acknowledged not only his own suffering but also the hardships of those who were with him. In doing this, he said that life can be painful for all of us. This acknowledgment of pain followed by the hope that he held on to during the pain can bring peace to us, and reminds us that God is our refuge amid painful circumstances.

The acknowledgment that I observed as a counseling student in that session so long ago has stayed with me. This is not so much because the woman was honest about her desire to skip counseling, but rather, because of the gracious and attentive response of the counselor. Anytime you hear a trauma story, you are on holy ground. You are invited to bear witness to and acknowledge the horrors endured. Your acknowledgment of the difficulty and pain honors the person and helps to establish a safe relationship in which the survivor can experience the Lord's care through you.

Anytime you hear a trauma story, you are on holy ground. You are invited to bear witness to and acknowledge the horrors endured.

C–Counseling

The Boy, the Mole, the Fox and the Horse is a heartwarming story of four unexpected friends on a journey together. Their travels are not filled with epic adventure; rather, they are contemplative. During their travels, all the ordinary things they encounter are considered in a reflective way. This reflection brings some of the most profound life lessons to each of them. The boy, curious yet uncertain, asks the horse—a creature strong, wise, and gentle—a question, and receives a reply that is not only honest but deeply insightful.

"What is the bravest thing you've ever said?" asked the boy.

"Help," said the horse. "Asking for help isn't giving up, it's refusing to give up."[2]

The horse's initial response of a single word powerfully captures what the Bible seeks to teach regarding human nature. We all need help, and we should not view asking for help as failure, but rather, as an opportunity to invite others into our lives, which aligns with God's intention for us.

How God Uses Counseling

We are told in Galatians 6:2 to "carry each other's burdens" because in doing so we "fulfill the law of Christ" (NIV). When we carry one another's burdens, we come alongside each other as a community, as a body of believers, as a family of brothers and sisters. When we help one another, we are living exactly how the Lord designed us to go through life. Counseling is one way we can carry one another's burdens—it is the asking and receiving of help.

The church did not adopt the idea of counseling from the world. Rather, the world employs what the Bible has taught for ages. We are called to counsel one another (see Romans 15:14). Often, God uses counseling to bring clarity during times of confusion and uncertainty.

God uses counsel to help us understand our world. He counseled Adam and Eve in the garden in Genesis 2:16-17 on what to eat, what not to eat, and why. This counsel was essential for life. In Exodus 18:17-23, God used Jethro to counsel Moses on the need to delegate responsibility to other leaders. This helped align Moses with God's plan for governing the people of Israel. This counsel was essential for sustainable leadership. The Psalms and Proverbs are full of counsel for godly living. The book of Proverbs speaks directly about the need for counsel, stating that without it, plans fail (Proverbs 15:22) and nations fall (Proverbs 11:14). The instruction on the importance of counsel continues to be seen in the New Testament; much of what is written in the epistles is for our instruction or *counsel*. And in Acts 15:28, the elders and apostles came together to discuss and provide guidance or *counsel* to believers on various matters. Counsel is an essential resource for all of us in all of life.

Counseling frequently becomes a crucial necessity when someone undergoes a traumatic experience, as it helps them to process, understand, and make sense of what happened to them. However, some people need to be encouraged to consider counseling. They can feel uneasy about revisiting their traumatic past. Talk with them about the value of counseling. Explain that finding a counselor is not a one-size-fits-all situation, and they can take time to explore different options. Help them to know that counseling should go at their pace. Do what you can to answer their questions or calm any fears.

One of the best ways you can do this is by offering to go with them to their counseling sessions. This might mean simply driving them and waiting for them, or it may mean that you sit in on the sessions with them. Not only does that offer support in the room, but it also allows for better processing to have another person who hears and remembers what was talked about. Most counselors welcome having supportive friends or family sit in, but it is best to talk to the counselor first before joining a session.

Where Can Christians Go for Counseling?

Once a person decides to go to counseling, the question of where to go arises. Not all counseling is helpful, and as believers, we must be mindful to pursue counseling that aligns with the wisdom given to us from God's Word. Some churches have a counseling ministry or lay counselors who can support the pastor with the needs of the congregation.

However, not all churches have such ministries. If that is the case, there are several options. First, the pastor is a great option in any situation. A pastor who is willing to meet with a person who is struggling is a valuable option. A pastor will often bring others into the care as well. If the church utilizes smaller groups where congregants meet for life-on-life engagement, often a small group leader or a mature group member can be a great option for care. Other times, a well-vetted referral list is a helpful way to point people to expert counseling in their area. Christian counselors are often willing to meet with pastors and leaders to answer any questions about their services and to explain their model of counseling.

Having connections with Christian mental health workers is an asset worth developing so that you can wisely point people to good care options. However, if you think counseling might be good for someone who has experienced trauma, don't simply give them a name or point them to a website. Instead, invest in the process with them. Offer to go with them to their first appointment. You can wait in the lobby, or if they prefer and the counselor agrees, you can sit in on the session. Often the first couple of counseling sessions can be overwhelming, and having another set of ears and eyes can be helpful toward applying and processing what was shared.

While counseling is not the end-all-be-all solution, it is a means that God often uses to help people sort out their story and find direction for their future. The counsel of other believers can be a source of healing and a conduit of hope and peace along the way. But sometimes situations require more professional help. If you are uncertain about what a person needs, here are six questions that can help assess whether counseling may be a good option:

- Are my emotional struggles interfering with my daily life and responsibilities?

- Am I experiencing ongoing feelings of sadness or hopelessness related to my situation?

- Am I using harmful or unhealthy coping strategies?

- Are my relationships strained or affected by my emotional well-being?

- Do I feel stuck even after talking with trusted family, friends, pastors, or mentors?

- Do my friends or family believe I should seek counseling?

If a person answers yes to several of the questions above and they have already tried meeting with others on an informal basis, that is a good indicator that professional counseling could be a beneficial next step. I coauthored a small book with my colleague Kyle Johnston, titled *How to Get the Most Out of Your Counseling*, which is specifically designed to help assess if a person would benefit more from professional counseling. We offer a brief overview of not only how to maximize the counseling experience, but also how to know when counseling is the next best step. Consider sharing the book with the person you are supporting and talking over some of the suggestions offered. See Appendix D in the resource section at the end of the book for more tips on referring someone to counseling.

As believers, we prioritize our spiritual health. There are many resources available on how to attend to our spiritual life. It is also important to pay attention to our emotional health, and counseling is often a key element of that.

E—Encourage

We all need encouragement. Without it, we can lose sight of progress and quickly spiral downward into discouragement. Encouragement is so important that Scripture commands it: "Encourage one another and build each other up, just as in fact you are doing" (1 Thessalonians 5:11 NIV). This is not merely a suggestion; rather, we are instructed to do this, and Hebrews 3:13 further tells us to do it every day.

People who have been through trauma need encouragement all the more. As we have seen, trauma impacts how we interact with ourselves, God, and the world—and, as a result, discouragement is a deeply felt reality. There are many ways to support people, and below are three practical action steps you can take to provide encouragement. These action steps will not only encourage a person who is struggling, they will also help them move toward the peace they long for.

First, stay with them. You will likely be tempted to give up on the journey of caring for someone who has been traumatized. You might want to quit when the pace slows or when setbacks come. You may feel as though you have shared all that you can and have given your best counsel, and yet the person is still in process. You may become frustrated at the triggers that remain. Or perhaps you are wondering if the caution, avoidance, and hypervigilance that continues to characterize their interactions will ever go away. But don't give up. One of the most significant ways you can encourage a struggler is to let them know you are still with them. They may even pull away from you—this is a common response from those who have been traumatized—but do whatever you can to avoid being the one who does the pulling away.

Next, give them supportive input related to their progress. Growth and healing are sometimes hard for people to see in themselves. Point out the good ways you see the person changing. This will deeply encourage them. Here are four things you can do to make your encouragement have more impact:

- **Be specific.** When giving encouragement, point out specific actions or distinct qualities that you see in a person as they continue to work through their trauma story. You can say, "The way you handled that situation yesterday was not only evidence of your trust in the Lord, but your growing humility in asking for help."

- **Be sincere.** Sincerity and encouragement are about genuinely expressing your feelings and thoughts, showing that you truly mean what you say. You can do this by saying, "I am deeply impressed by how you have persevered and continue to work so hard on this. Your courage is inspiring to me."

- **Be supportive.** Supporting someone means you show you are available for them both emotionally and practically.

Support can be one of the most-needed expressions of encouragement. You can assure the person of your continued support by saying, "Processing all you have been through is a lot for anyone to handle, I want you to know I am here for you as you continue doing this hard work."

- **Be sensitive.** When you encourage someone, consider that sometimes their emotions will be tender and even kind words can be weighty to receive. You can express encouragement in a caring and empathetic manner by saying something along these lines: "I'm sensitive to how hard this has been for you. I want you to know the work you are doing is helping you to make progress toward managing the complex emotions that come with all you have been through."

Revisiting the times I had met with Jake may help in illustrating this point. During a counseling session, Jake managed to sit through the entire hour without his legs trembling, a significant milestone in his healing journey. I sincerely acknowledged the gravity of Jake's experience and his struggles, but then sought to be supportive by offering specific encouragement about something he might not have noticed himself. I attempted to do this with sensitivity by saying, "Today I noticed something that encouraged me. I'd like to share it with you, hoping it will encourage you too." I went on to tell him he appeared more relaxed during our time together that day compared to months earlier, when sitting through an entire session was profoundly difficult for him.

Jake was surprised when I mentioned this and shared that he had not noticed the change. But my pointing it out encouraged him. He hadn't noticed his progress in this area, but he affirmed that counseling had become a positive experience for him.

Encourage people by telling them when you see change, progress, and healing. Let them know when you see the fruit of the Spirit in their life. Highlight the ways they are depending on God or trusting him for all that remains unknown in their journey. Affirm God's work in their life and the courage they have shown thus far.

Finally, point out their resilience. Another way to encourage someone is to highlight their successes and how they have overcome challenges. This is more than just noticing progress—it involves pointing out how the trauma has been the impetus of growth. The clinical world recognizes this kind of progress as a positive outcome of a traumatic event. It is called post-traumatic growth, and it is a result of people having a network of friends and caregivers to support and encourage them along the way. Point out growth when you see it.

Christians have a deeper reason to encourage one another—our Lord commands it! Don't hesitate to tell trauma survivors of the ways you have seen them endure in times when they would rather give up and remind them of the strength they have in the Lord.

Look for ways to notice their flexibility. Point out where you see their endurance through difficulty. Help them to see how God has used what they have been through to make them stronger and how their faith is being galvanized into healthy thinking and responding. Their endurance can be a testament of God's faithfulness, showing that he provides his children incredible resilience in the face of troubles as they trust in him.

Those are some of the ways you can encourage someone who is working through their trauma. The word *encourage* means "to put courage into." However you decide to offer encouragement, know that to do so will put wind in a person's sails. They not only have more courage to face what is ahead, but they will also have more motivation as well.

Soon after I encouraged Jake, his parents reached out to share that he'd had some incredible breakthroughs that week, one of which was his willingness to open up to them. He told his parents more about what had happened to him and shared how talking through things in counseling had given him a greater grasp of God's love and care for him. Perhaps a little encouragement was all Jake needed to take the next step in bringing others into his healing process. Perhaps the encouragement was what solidified his faith a bit more so he could see how God was working through it all. Never underestimate the power of your encouraging words to augment the peace of God in a person's life.

The Peace in Presence

Each one these elements of care—patience, educate, acknowledge, counseling, and encourage—anchored to the grace of God, can be a means of helping a traumatized person experience true and lasting peace despite their situation.

It is not a matter of prescribing each element of this acrostic as a list to check off. Rather it is essential that each aspect is expressed in the context of your caring relationship. Research shows that one of the essentials that makes counseling effective is the therapeutic relationship.[3] This is one reason people can go through similar traumas and be impacted very differently. It is not only about what happened to them, but, as you have already read in Part 2, who was with them to help them as they went through the aftermath plays an important part in recovery and resiliency.

Your presence in the process can contribute significantly to the peace that they can experience. This makes sense when we think about why the Lord tells us not to be fearful. We can have peace and not be afraid because he says, "Fear not, for *I am with you*" (Isaiah 41:10, emphasis added). Therein lies tremendous peace.

A quick note before closing out this chapter: Let me speak to you, the helper. Everything you read in this chapter, you also need. As you walk with people who have been through the horrors of traumatic events or continue to live in terrible circumstances, it can affect you. Your heart and mind are not fortified with a trauma shield that protects you from the impact of the evils you hear about. You are permeable. You, too, need support. You need wisdom in knowing when to engage and when to step away. You need a balanced approach to caring for others and caring for yourself. In the resource section, you will find a Compassion Fatigue and Burnout Assessment I created to help caregivers reflect on their own well-being as they care for others (see Appendix C). I recommend you take the assessment and share the results with your own counselor or a trusted friend.

PART 3

AWARE OF THE INTERSECTION OF FAITH AND TRAUMA

As we approach the final chapters of this book, we turn now to what the Bible has to say about trauma and how the church can respond biblically. The Bible is the authoritative source that shapes and informs the core tenets of the Christian faith. It not only provides encouragement and inspiration but is also the comprehensive framework and guide for all of life. Scripture reveals the heart of God and helps us to wisely interpret all that we face in life. The church is the family of believers seeking to live according to the Bible with one another as a supportive and loving community, sharing life together through good and bad times. While the Bible and the church are truly wonderful gifts, trauma is seen in both.

The most traumatic event in human history, the death of the Son of God, was also the most hopeful event in human history. This reality affirms that not only are faith and trauma topics that believers should know about, they are also topics that should be discussed together. Faith and trauma are often thought of as being on two very different ends of the spectrum of human experience. To explain this spectrum, think of it like this: Often, faith is seen as being on one side, representing hope and victory in this world. And trauma is seen as being on the other side, representing the horror and destruction in this world. Someone might be experiencing a season of great faith, during which it would seem impossible to experience the gripping symptoms of traumatization at the same time. But unlike most things on opposite poles, faith and trauma can be brought together suddenly. Like oil and vinegar when shaken together aggressively, faith and trauma can comingle in lived experiences.

We must avoid the polarization of faith and trauma, which can lead to believers feeling ashamed, misunderstood, or as if their troubles are too much for the church and maybe even too much for God. Rather, a wise helper will understand the reality that faith and trauma can be experienced together. By providing compassionate support rooted in the hope of the gospel, and by acknowledging the painful experiences people endure, you can gently assist the traumatized in recognizing that the church and the Bible are not only relevant but crucial for their healing journey. One way to do that is to provide an understanding of how faith and trauma can come together in a restorative way.

You may be wondering why I put this section in the last part of this book. Shouldn't the conversation about biblical faith in trauma care be our starting point? There are two reasons for this placement.

First, establishing a solid understanding of trauma is essential to wisely applying biblical truth with compassion and understanding.

Without this knowledge, the helper may be uncertain whether trauma is what the person has experienced, and what kind of care is most needed.

We should refrain from hastily providing spiritual guidance without first grasping the burdens a person carries. As helpers, let us embody Proverbs 20:5 and become individuals who draw out the hearts of others with empathy and insight.

Second, as you have learned, trauma is a weighty subject. I wanted to conclude this book by exploring how faith in Jesus transforms horror into hope, leaving you in awe of the extraordinary ways in which God can turn brokenness into wholeness. Exploring the intersection of faith and trauma will help you to see that we experience divine comfort in the midst of our troubles. When we grasp the fact that we are never alone, then hope breaks through. Despite deep brokenness and sadness, God can make us whole. With that in mind, let's look at trauma in the Bible and trauma in the church.

CHAPTER 9

TRAUMA AND THE BIBLE

When you find yourself caring for someone who has faced a traumatic experience, you will likely recognize that such situations inherently require a sense of meaning. Meaning often comes in the answer to the biggest question: Why?

"Why did this happen to me?"

"Why couldn't I do anything to prevent it?"

"Why did I survive when others didn't?"

"Why is life so unfair?"

"Why is the world so unsafe?"

"Why didn't God prevent this?"

The Bible provides meaning by answering these and many other *why* questions. How does it do that? When we are faced with trauma in the context of the Christian faith, we can cling to this twofold truth, which stands firm: God is absolutely sovereign, and he intricately orchestrates all things toward goodness.

I recognize that this twofold truth may feel like a pat answer that oversimplifies a complex reality. But stay with me. The key is not to question or avoid these truths; instead, we must move into them slowly with compassionate wisdom. To rush to try to apply them can diminish the comfort they might bring. There are no quick fixes when it comes to trauma, but it is essential to know answers *do* exist, and those answers can be found in the Bible.

The ultimate answer comes in the twofold truth that God is in total control and is working all things for good. This may be hard to grasp in the aftermath of trauma, but the Bible invites us to consider a reality beyond our present circumstances or feelings. This may sound simple, but it is far from easy. Often, people must wrestle with God's Word before it becomes a comfort. As you care for people, be prepared to respond with compassion and grace to their wrestling.

It doesn't take long for traumatic events to show up in the Bible. There are stories of murder and rape in Genesis, the very first book of the Bible. Turn the pages to Exodus, the second book of the Bible, and you will see people facing life-threatening destruction from devastating floods, fire, hail, and plagues. It doesn't stop there. Rather than going through every book of the Old Testament to cite more examples, let me assure you that a quick skim shows it is filled with traumatizing circumstances such as forced migration, kidnapping, oppression, enslavement, murder, sexual assault, political corruption, and more. Even within the poetry of the psalms we hear the deep cries of those who have endured intense suffering and distress.

Often, people must wrestle with God's Word
before it becomes a comfort. As you care
for people, be prepared to respond with
compassion and grace to their wrestling.

Trauma makes an alarming entrance in the New Testament as well. Right from the start we see a young refugee couple desperately fleeing to protect the life of their little one when political infanticide is enacted in their town (Matthew 2:16). Keep reading, and you will encounter terrible suffering due to debilitating sickness, which, in that culture, often led to rejection and isolation. And if those aren't bad enough, people faced the intense shame and fear of being an outcast or even stoned to death if they were caught in sin. Paul describes encountering troubles so great that they caused him to despair of life itself (2 Corinthians 1:8).

Why is there so much trauma in the Bible? Is the purpose only to confirm that as sparks fly upward so man is born to trouble?[1] One reason is because we live in a fallen world, which makes trauma inevitable. Another is because the Bible speaks to all of life and gives us needed direction and hope in all that we face. And trauma certainly affirms our need for direction and hope, which can help us regain our footing and stability in life. This stabilization happens when a person finds meaning in what they went through. This meaning, in turn, will lead people to conclusions that enable them to make sense of what happened to them. Even those with a solid faith in God can find themselves wrestling with tempting conclusions that don't align with the character and nature of God.

Two Tempting Conclusions

When confronted with the agony of traumatic experiences, individuals often grapple with two tempting conclusions, each tethered to the delicate interplay of faith and the harshness of traumatic realities. The horrific pain of trauma can make it challenging to believe the Bible's assertions that God is always working things for the good of his children and is always in sovereign control. When this happens, two tempting conclusions or beliefs can arise. First, a person can be tempted to believe there is no good on the other side of a traumatic situation. This can come from the incorrect view that for things to be good, everything needs to be resolved and the suffering ended. The second tempting conclusion is to doubt whether God is in control, because if he is, he would have stopped the terrible situation from happening in the first place.

In the face of profound suffering, grappling with these two temptations can bring about a significant crisis. They have the potential to intensify the burden of the trauma and cast doubt upon sacred truth. Even so, the Bible affirms that all things are under divine control, and that ultimately, all things are orchestrated for good for God's children.

Applying the Bible Compassionately in the Face of Trauma

Because of the profound struggles individuals face in making sense of biblical truths amid deep suffering, when it comes to applying the Bible to trauma, it is crucial to do so with the utmost compassion, consideration, and sensitivity. Wisely engaging Scripture in your care for a person who has endured trauma involves a nuanced approach that recognizes the need for empathy, discernment, and a deep understanding of both the individual's experiences and the transformative power of God's Word. Unfortunately, this doesn't always happen, and the Bible can end up being used haphazardly. Much like someone passing out Band-Aids to those who need intensive care, God's Word can be handed out like a trifle to those suffering deeply.

To see this, let's look at a verse often shared to comfort those who have gone through painful situations. Romans 8:28 says, "We know that all things work together for the good of those who love God, who are called according to his purpose" (csb). If this verse has been quoted once, it has been quoted a thousand times to people enduring painfully hard circumstances. Is it helpful? Yes, of course.

It is helpful because it is from God's Word, and his Word is timeless and true. But sometimes the way the verse is presented can be quite unhelpful, maybe even hurtful.

Often, Romans 8:28 is shared with the hope it will provide help in the midst of a hopeless situation. But isolated from its context and shared outside of an understanding relationship, it can trivialize a person's circumstance and the hopeful truth of the verse can get lost. However, when shared in its fuller context and in a trusting relationship, it can be a tremendous help and comfort. For practical purposes, let's look at how this might work.

First, consider the fuller context. The book of Romans was written to believers for encouragement and guidance, and we see the pinnacle of this in chapter 8. This chapter is a hope-filled reminder of who we are: children of God, alive in Christ through the Spirit, no longer condemned, and inseparable from God and his protection. Knowing who we are fuels how we think and live. It is in this context that these verses appear. Take a few seconds to read the fuller context:

> [26]In the same way the Spirit also helps us in our weakness, because we do not know what to pray for as we should, but the Spirit himself intercedes for us with inexpressible groanings. [27]And he who searches our hearts knows the mind of the Spirit, because he intercedes for the saints according to the will of God. [28]*We know that all things work together for the good of those who love God, who are called according to his purpose.* [29]For those he foreknew he also predestined to be conformed to the image of his Son, so that he would be the firstborn among many brothers and sisters. [30]And those he predestined, he also called; and those he called, he also justified; and those he justified, he also glorified (csb, emphasis added).

Now let's unpack this passage together to gain a better understanding of why verse 28 is such a comfort. Notice that verse 28 appears between two important ideas. This verse hinges on understanding what comes before and after it. First, verses 26-27 tell us that we have a helper in everything we face. No matter how hard or how terrible the situation, we are not alone. The Spirit is with us, in us, and helping us.

The Spirit not only helps us to pray but also intercedes. When we have no words, he is pleading and petitioning for us. When the situation is so difficult that we cannot even pray, the Spirit prays for us. When we can barely lift our voice, the Spirit speaks for us. What a gift to know this truth when life is hard! The Spirit doesn't just intercede, he intercedes "according to the will of God." God has a plan and purpose for our life, and his purposes will be accomplished. We will also see in the next verse, verse 28, that his purposes for us are good.

But what is "the good" that the famously quoted verse 28 is talking about? To answer that question, we need verses 29-30. The good promised in these verses is not that the situation will dissipate, or that a person's wounds will be erased, but that what we are going through is conforming us, or changing us, into the image of Christ. Nothing else is as good as being made to look more and more like Jesus. Jesus was steady when life was unsteady. His responses to everything he faced was always honoring to God. He always responded with appropriate righteousness. Romans 8:29-30 tells us that the difficulties we face are used to transform us. When we endure deep suffering while trusting God and yielding to the work of the Spirit, we become more like Jesus.

Putting all these thoughts together, we come up with this: All things work together for the good because in everything we face, we have the Spirit interceding for us and causing us to become more and more like Christ. That is the good. The good is not that everything works out as we hope, but that in all things God is working, is with us, and is working in us.

If we want to better share biblical truth in ways that are helpful to a person, we must avoid using Scripture as an impersonal prescription. "Take two verses and call me in the morning" misses the role that relationship plays in engaging God's Word. We are to speak the truth to one another in love (Ephesians 4:15). To speak truth in love requires a relationship, and relationships take time to cultivate. People are not problems to be solved. They are not projects requiring assembling or adjusting. They are fellow human beings whom we are called to love.

Sharing Romans 8:28 without the verses before or after is like giving someone a peanut butter and jelly sandwich without the bread. It might be edible, but it will be messy. There is a better way to serve it up. First, Romans 8:28 is intended to be given with the bookends of instruction and hope on each side. Context is vital—this is true for all of God's Word. And second, when you share God's Word, do so in the context of relationship. Seek to know a person well enough to lovingly apply truth. Love someone well enough and long enough so that you can give them the timeless truths of God wisely and compassionately.

People are not problems to be solved.
They are not projects requiring assembling
or adjusting. They are fellow human
beings whom we are called to love.

The Meaning Trauma Demands

Scripture can bring meaning to people by answering the many *why* questions they have. But we must use God's Word with wisdom and compassion so that we navigate the truth with sensitivity. For now, let's look at how the Bible gives words to victims. As we delve into the pages of Scripture, we discover how its words become a refuge, giving voice to the experiences of those who have suffered, and in doing so, illuminating the path toward healing, hope, and restoration.

The Bible Gives Voice to
the Experience of Trauma

World-renowned trauma expert Diane Langberg explains the importance of giving voice to trauma: "The paradox is that in order to heal from such atrocities one must learn to speak the unspeakable. The indescribable must be described."[2]

Articulating trauma is crucial for several reasons. The opportunity for a survivor to express their experiences provides a sense of validation as the pain and suffering are shared with a listening friend. Helping a person find their voice enables more effective support and understanding, which fosters connection and trust between the survivor and those supporting them. Articulating trauma also enables survivors to take ownership of the pace and space in which they choose to share their story. Ultimately, by vocalizing their experiences, these individuals can actively engage in the process of healing, which helps to build resilience as they move toward a more hopeful future.

When we encounter deep suffering, we are invited
to use the very words of Scripture as our own.

Scripture does not dodge the fact that in this life people will endure horrible things. Rather, it gives voice to the sufferer's pain. Looking at the trauma in the Bible can provide needed words for those who carry the weight of having endured a traumatic circumstance. When we encounter deep suffering, we are invited to use the very words of Scripture as our own. Just as Jesus used the words of the psalms to articulate his own torment amid the crucifixion when he cried, "My God, my God, why have you forsaken me?" (Psalm 22:1), we, too, can let the words of Scripture articulate our pain and we can help others do the same. Consider the lines of Scripture below and how they articulate the experience of a traumatic interruption in life:

- "Fear and trembling come upon me, and horror overwhelms me" (Psalm 55:5).

- "I have forgotten what happiness is" (Lamentations 3:17).

- "The chords of death encompassed me" (Psalm 18:4).

- "I am in despair" (Psalm 69:20).

- "I am helpless" (Psalm 88:5).

Words like these are often the very words articulated by those whose lives have been affected by trauma. Consider the story of Kelly.

Kelly came to me to process the deep wounds caused by sexual abuse during her childhood, which she experienced from her brother. Kelly wanted to process what happened to her but found it difficult to put words to the pain she endured. The pain of the betrayal she felt from her older brother was as deep as the shame she carried from the abuse he inflicted. She loved her brother. She looked up to him. He was her hero. She believed he was her protector. But he told her she had to keep this secret. He told her really bad things would happen if she told on him. As terrible as the abuse was for her to endure, she was confused and didn't want to be the cause of losing her brother's friendship, so she kept silent.

Now as an adult, though many years have passed since the abuse, it is difficult for Kelly to put into words the pain regarding what happened to her. Then one day, she found her voice in a place she did not expect—in Scripture. She came to see me, and it was evident when she walked in that she had something she wanted to share. She went on to explain how she was reading the Bible and came upon Psalm 55, and it arrested her attention. Tears welled in her eyes as she told me about what she read. "These words are mine!," she said. They were exactly how she felt:

> Fear and trembling come upon me, and horror over-whelms me. And I say, "Oh that I had wings like a dove! I would fly away and be at rest; yes, I would wander far away; I would lodge in the wilderness...For it is not an enemy who taunts me—then I could bear it; it is not an adversary who deals insolently with me—then I could hide from him. But it is you, a man, my equal, my companion, my familiar friend" (Psalm 55:5-6, 12-13).

"He was my best friend and yet he hurt me more than any enemy could have. The Bible is telling my story!" Scripture gave voice to Kelly's experience, and this gave her comfort. The Bible understands the wounds caused by traumatic experiences and can give voice to those who experience deep pain.

God's Word is not only timely and true, it is also timeless. The Bible gives voice to the deepest cries of our hearts just as if it was written today. Its words aptly vocalize the struggle faced by those who have endured trauma. Let your care include assisting people in using Scripture to give voice to their pain. In the Bible, victims find words. God understands and compassionately gives voice to their suffering. And Scripture not only gives words that accurately express suffering, it also gives words that proclaim hope.

God's Word is not only timely and true, it is also timeless. The Bible gives voice to the deepest cries of our hearts just as if it was written today.

Trauma does not have the final word. When individuals who have endured profound suffering and pain cling to the unwavering love of the Father and the promises found in Scripture, they are helped. They find their help in the Lord and their comfort in his Word. Scripture becomes their anthem as they hold on to truth even while they wait for healing.

The traumatic stories found within the pages of the Bible remind us that our faith does not shield us from life's trials, but rather, it sustains us through them. Psalm 34:18 assures us that the Lord is near to the brokenhearted and saves those who are crushed in spirit. Even in the midst of traumatizing realities, we have the comfort that the Lord is near.

This does not dismiss the awful reality of the situation, but instead, it allows us to see that we can simultaneously experience both brokenness and belief, horror and help, and pain and promise. You can be a believer and yet be shaken by trauma. The heroes of the faith faced trauma and they expressed their anguish before the living God. We can follow their example. We can use their words for our own.

Assist trauma survivors in praying with the psalmists and echoing the cries of the saints of old. Remind them that God was faithful then and he remains faithful now. As you support them through their suffering and struggles, point them to places where the words of others, preserved by God in Scripture, can provide expressions of their own experiences. Here is a small sampling of comforting words from Scripture that express hope in God and confidence in his faithfulness even while facing profound suffering:

- "Do not fear or be in dread of them, for it is the LORD your God who goes with you. He will not leave you or forsake you" (Deuteronomy 31:6).

- "He will hide me in his shelter in the day of trouble" (Psalm 27:5).

- "God is our refuge and strength" (Psalm 46:1).

- "What can man do to me?" (Psalm 118:6).

- "I am yours; save me" (Psalm 119:94 CSB).

- "[Nothing] will be able to separate us from the love of God" (Romans 8:39).

One Bible teacher tells the story of how the words of Psalm 42 became his own in a season of great discouragement and depression. "Why are you cast down, O my soul, and why are you in turmoil within me? Hope in God; for I shall again praise him, my salvation and my God" (Psalm 42:11). As this teacher faced another day of despair, he found himself overwhelmed by his circumstances. The words of the psalm became the exact words to express his struggle. "Hope in God, John. Hope in God. You will again praise him. This miserable emotion will pass. This season will pass. Don't be downcast. Look to Jesus. The light will dawn."[3] When he was not able to feel or see hope, he spoke Scripture and held on to the promise that he would one day hope again.

I saw this happen in the life of a woman I counseled. I will call her Leah. She had been a faithful member of her church for many years, served in various ministries, and was well respected.

When the church hired someone to be the women's ministry director (I will call her Christine), Leah felt honored when the pastor asked if she could help Christine learn about the various women's ministries at the church. Leah had served in so many areas of the church for so long, and the pastor figured she would be a great resource for Christine. But Christine had her own insecurities and was unkind to Leah from the start. She made it clear that she didn't need Leah's help because she would be taking the ministries in a new direction. This was only the beginning of the hurtful interaction between Christine and Leah. Before long, Christine had excluded Leah from roles in which she had served and appointed new volunteers in her place. She then began to talk about Leah in disparaging ways. This influenced the way others thought of Leah, and soon, the church was no longer a safe place for her. The hurt was compounded when some of the things shared about her began to sway the pastor's view of Leah, and he wondered if she was indeed a problem.

Leah felt alone and without support, and was afraid of what Christine's influence could do to her remaining relationships at the church. Leah, though deeply afraid, decided she needed to confront the situation. She didn't know what Christine would say or do, and her fear caused her to doubt herself. Then one day she was reading Isaiah 41 and found incredible help in these words:

> Do not fear, for I am with you;
> do not be afraid, for I am your God.
> I will strengthen you; I will help you;
> I will hold on to you with my righteous right hand.
> Be sure that all who are enraged against you
> will be ashamed and disgraced;
> those who contend with you
> will become as nothing and will perish.
> You will look for those who contend with you,
> but you will not find them.
> Those who war against you
> will become absolutely nothing.

For I am the LORD your God,
who holds your right hand,
who says to you, "Do not fear,
I will help you" (Isaiah 41:10-13 CSB).

"He holds my hand! How much closer can he get than that? He will help me!" Leah exclaimed. The words were exactly what she needed during a deeply painful situation. She met with the pastor and shared what was happening, and as she did, she told me she kept rehearsing the words "He holds my hand" in her mind. The story took some painful turns before it was resolved, but through it all, the words of Isaiah 41 continued to help her. The phrase "He holds my hand" gave Leah stability on the days when she felt ready to give up.

God's Word provides great comfort in the midst of trying circumstances. However, we must be careful not to assume that what comforts us will comfort others. Allow the person you are caring for to interact with Scripture and explore how it impacts them. Ask them where they have found God's Word to be helpful in their circumstances. You can and should suggest Scripture that might be helpful, but do so as a suggestion, and encourage the person to explore Scripture on their own through daily reading and meditation.

You can also pray Scripture with them during your time together and model how God's Word can offer the very words needed to provide comfort and help. The words of Scripture are more powerful than our own, and we can trust that the Bible will be beneficial in a person's life—especially when shared within the context of a caring relationship.

The Bible's Guidance and
Example for Trauma Survivors

While it may seem paradoxical to find hope amid stories of forced migration, kidnapping, rape, plagues, and incest, the Bible's acknowledgment of these painful realities also offers guidance for our times of distress. The Bible not only offers profound insights into our challenges and gives voice to our traumatic experiences, but it also provides guidance needed for recovery. It is rich with messages of compassion, hope, and restoration. Embracing the wisdom and insights found in Scripture can help us foster hope in the lives of survivors, as well as ourselves.

We don't shy away from the wounded because God's Word doesn't shy away from them. But just because the Bible gives testimony to stories of trauma doesn't make the pain of the trauma dissipate. Instead, seeing trauma in the Bible encourages us to honor what happened to a person who has faced trauma. Hear their story while pointing them to the many stories in Scripture that resonate with their suffering. Hear their story while guiding them to our Savior, who was beaten, stricken, and afflicted, a man of sorrows and acquainted with grief (Isaiah 53:4).

Follow the Example of Jesus

Jesus not only endured trauma, but he also overcame it. He journeyed the terrible path of pain and death with unwavering trust in the Father. "Jesus endured the force of human horror in ways we cannot easily fathom. Yet, Jesus' measureless suffering was matched by his incessant trust in the goodness and love of his Father."[4] Despite the terror of it all, he knew there was healing ahead. And ultimately, that healing would be for us (Isaiah 53:5-6).

Jesus is the perfect high priest who can empathize with our pain (Hebrews 4:15) because he entered it. If your pain was caused by others sinning against you, he understands because he was sinned against. If your pain was caused by your own sin, when you confess, he covers it. As helpers, let us seek to point people to our sympathetic Savior. Let us never shrink away from the darkest places of people's stories.

You do not need to be a professional counselor to enter in; you do not need to be a trauma therapist to be empathetic to pain. You can lovingly walk with others and teach them of Jesus who loves them and understands their pain.

"There is no dark corner that Christ has not gone—both on his way to the cross and on his way to finding you."[5] And he did this empowered by the Holy Spirit and with an unwavering trust in the Father. Jesus is an example for us as we seek to care for the traumatized sufferer.

Jesus' example is also for the sufferer. He teaches us how we can endure the most horrible circumstances. His example provides a path through the darkness by encouraging an unwavering trust in the Father, who loves us. The darkest hour of human history, the cross of Jesus, stands as a powerful symbol of both suffering and victory. Our Savior endured unimaginable emotional and physical trauma, yet he fully entrusted his life to the Father. This trust was not disappointed, and he accomplished the will of God in and through suffering.

The Bible's Hope for Trauma

Trauma is never too big a subject for the Bible. There is no human experience too deep for the God's Word to reach. There is no circumstance too complex for Scripture to address. "God speaks to the depths of human suffering on almost every page of Scripture."[6] And trauma can take us to the lowest depths of suffering. Consider this explanation of trauma by Dr. Ed Welch, who sums up trauma as death coming near. "Death," he says, "has come close…and death does not travel alone, you will find that it has companions." He goes on to describe death's companions as wickedness done to you through the works of the flesh. "Trauma travels with wickedness as a kind of ambassador."[7]

Welch gives a vivid picture here that being unprotected and vulnerable when you should have been cared for can feel like death coming near. When you experience sexual abuse, explosive and unbridled anger, or neglect, you encounter the nearness of death and its wicked companions.

Finding Hope When Death Comes Near

Jason got as small as he possibly could under the coffee table. The space might not have been big enough for an 11-year-old to squeeze into, but in desperation, he hid himself out of sight while still keeping an eye on his mom and dad. It was then that he saw what he dreaded most. His father put the gun to his mother's head. He closed his eyes tight and turned away. He hoped that if he could shut his eyes tightly enough, this would all go away. His heart began to pound so hard it drowned out his father's raging. Then suddenly the pounding of his heart seemed to change. It was louder and out of sync. Boom, boom, boom! *What happened? Did he shoot her?* Boom, boom, boom! Jason then realized the sound wasn't from his heart or a gun. Someone was pounding on the door.

The police had been called, probably by a neighbor, and they were entering the house. Jason opened his eyes just in time to see two officers pounce on his father, who had dropped the gun at their command. The details of that night are now a bit blurry, but Jason does remember with clarity that he feared his mother would die that night, and maybe he would too. Death came close.

Though five years have passed, Jason still processes that night with both his counselor and his youth pastor. Though he and his mother are safe now, the impact of that evening remains. The nightmares still come. He feels more fearful and hypervigilant than his peers. The distrust he has of people, especially men in positions of power, is something he doesn't like. He can get angry with himself when these symptoms arise.

What hope is there for people like Jason and his mother when death has come so very near? Jason found hope, but not because his father was sent to jail. Nor was hope found in moving far from the place where death had come close. Instead, hope was found in knowing that God had saved him—not just from death that night, but from eternal death. He is learning, despite the trauma, that God's purposes will be accomplished. Jason is learning that wounds and healing can exist together to bring meaning and hope in life.

As we seek to help traumatized people, the goal is not to return to life as they knew it before the trauma. Instead, we are to help people see that there is no situation so dark that God cannot bring light into it. The Bible profoundly portrays that the human experience encompasses both triumphs and tribulations, and God is working in them all.

The darkest hour of human history, the cross of Jesus, stands as a powerful symbol of both suffering and victory. It was a day filled with atrocities, a day on which our Savior endured unimaginable emotional and physical trauma. Yet it was a day of great hope. Jesus overcame death!

Trauma is a result of the evil that presently reigns on the earth, but evil's reign is limited. There will come a day when all pain, sorrow, suffering, and trauma will end. When that day arrives, the author of trauma will receive the full the wrath of God (Revelation 20:10), and death, mourning, crying, and pain will come to an end (Revelation 21:4). Jesus will one day destroy both death and the one who has the power of death (1 Corinthians 15:26; Hebrews 2:14).

Remember, trauma does not get the last word. The last word has already been spoken, and it comes from our faithful God.

CHAPTER 10

TRAUMA AND THE CHURCH

As we continue to consider how faith and trauma intersect in people's lives, we must now turn to the church. How can fellow believers support one another well through deep suffering? It starts by recognizing the extent of the burdens that are being carried within congregations of gathered believers and learning how to help people take those burdens to a loving God even in the midst of their suffering.

On any given Sunday within the walls of your church, amidst the smiles, hugs, the Sunday outfits, and the exchange of cordial greetings, the seats are filled with a multitude of stories, some known, and others hidden, of individuals who have experienced deep, emotional trauma. Regardless of how healthy your church may seem, there are countless people silently grappling with the aftermath of various kinds of trauma. Trauma has become more and more prevalent, requiring the church to become more sensitively attuned to helping those who are struggling. One medically reviewed article exploring the statistics of psychological trauma leading to PTSD cited the following:[1]

- 70 percent of adults experience at least one traumatic event in their lifetime

- 20 percent of people who experience a traumatic event will develop PTSD

- About 13 million people have PTSD in a given year

- 1 in 13 people will develop PTSD at some point in their life

Though many who go through emotionally traumatic events or circumstances will not develop PTSD, they may still experience distress when recalling what caused their trauma. Others, because of these events, may grapple with a spectrum of emotional and psychological challenges—for example, anxiety, intrusive memories, and difficulties with feeling safe. Many of these have already been explored earlier in this book, and we've learned how they can extend into various facets of a person's life, influencing their emotional well-being, cognitive processes, and overall functioning.

There is no doubt that within our congregations a significant percentage of people have faced or are currently facing difficult situations such as abuse, loss, violence, or life-altering illnesses or accidents. While many may not become traumatized, they are indeed carrying heavy emotional burdens.

It is good for the church to learn what it might look like to have a sympathetic investment in understanding these struggles. The Bible calls us to be compassionate and supportive toward one another. If we are to carry one another's burdens, we must be willing to be open to learning about those burdens. When we do that, we create nurturing spaces where those who have experienced trauma are safe to share their pain and receive care. A trauma-aware church acknowledges the reality that trauma could be a part of people's stories and seeks to know how to respond with empathy and understanding, and point individuals to gospel hope and comfort. This is where the path to healing begins.

In addition to recognizing the pain within our pews, we must also reckon with the tragic reality that, in some cases, the church may have been the very cause of the trauma people have encountered. A survey of 1,581 adults found that "religious trauma is a chronic problem within the U.S. population." The results of the survey are disturbing and reveal, "It is likely that around one-third of U.S. adults have experienced religious trauma."[2]

Religious trauma was mentioned briefly in the early pages of this book, and now is a good time to define it more clearly. The Religious Trauma Institute defines this kind of trauma as "the physical, emotional, or psychological response to religious beliefs, practices, or structures that is experienced by an individual as overwhelming or disruptive and has lasting adverse effects on a person's physical, mental, social, emotional, or spiritual well-being."[3] Many refer to this as "church hurt." This problem is on the rise, and it is a major catalyst for people leaving the church and even the faith all together.

In addition to recognizing the pain within our pews, we must also reckon with the tragic reality that, in some cases, the church may have been the very cause of the trauma people have encountered.

For the church to be a place of respite for the traumatized, we must be willing to acknowledge that church hurt is at times an unfortunate part of people's story. That's why it's so essential to cultivate a culture of empathy, restoration, and unwavering support that demonstrates humility and displays Christlike love in action. To do this well, we must acknowledge a couple of uncomfortable realities.

Two Areas of Needed
Acknowledgment for Change

If you, like me, long for the church to be a place of comfort for those impacted by trauma, then we must explore two critical areas in which the church has historically fallen short. With deeper awareness of past shortcomings and with a humble desire for change, the church can become a place where people's burdens are carried, not increased.

First, we must address how the church has struggled to provide adequate support for individuals who have endured trauma. And second, there is a need to confront the unsettling reality that for some, the church has tragically ended up being the origin of trauma. When this happens, people will be reluctant to share their personal struggles, which is unfortunate because the church should be the first place those in need turn to for help. By humbly addressing these shortcomings, we have the potential to cultivate a more compassionate and gracious community.

In bringing this up, I'm not wanting to disparage the church in any way. I love the church; I am part of the church; it is my family. Rather, my goal is to provide guidance for necessary and constructive change so that we can figure out a way forward. Also, when I refer to the church, you may be wondering whether I mean the universal body of believers following Jesus, or specific groups of believers in local churches. What you read in this chapter can apply to both—I won't be making a distinction one way or the other.

Also, I want to recognize that even though the church has sometimes failed those who are dealing with trauma, at the same time, there are many churches that have been sanctuaries of help, providing support and comfort for those who need it. They have played a crucial role in walking alongside individuals, fostering transparency, and thoughtfully addressing the painful experiences people have faced.

Ultimately, my goal—which I assume is yours as well—is for

gospel-centered churches everywhere to always be where people turn when they need support in their healing journey. With that in mind, let's look at where the church has fallen short, and what we can do about it.

Acknowledgment #1: The Church Has Been Unsupportive of Those Deeply Suffering

The church hasn't always fallen short when it comes to offering support for those who endure profound struggles. Early church leaders provided the church with theologically rich direction on how to address the deepest troubles of the soul and body in books like Thomas Brooks's *Precious Remedies Against Satan's Devices* and William Bridge's *A Lifting Up for the Downcast*. These early resources give us a picture of how the church has spoken openly about the suffering people faced while pointing them to a God who comforts. Though these books do not use the same verbiage we use today, they aptly describe the impact of deep suffering, which at times mirrors what traumatized people experience. In giving voice to these sufferings, they also offer comforting wisdom.

For example, without making less of the struggles people faced, Brooks shared a list of various helps afforded to the believer, the Spirit being one of those helps. He encouraged the downcast by affirming that they were not alone. He assured them, "The Spirit of the Lord is your counselor, your comforter, your upholder, and your strengthener. It is the Spirit alone, who makes a man too great for Satan to conquer. 'Greater is he who is in you, than he who is in the world.' (1 John 4:4)."[4] Leaders like Brooks were able to aptly apply Scripture without oversimplifying a person's struggle. The legacy of such leaders can be recaptured so that we can graciously offer timeless hope for sufferers.

What stands out is that these church leaders did not simplistically reduce all of people's struggles to personal sin. Rather, they included sin (both personal as well as the sin of others) along with other contributing factors, such as physiology, temperament, relationships, and more. Timothy Keller, in his paper titled *Puritan Resources for Biblical Counseling*, captures the Puritans' approach to deep suffering:

> The Puritans had sophisticated diagnostic casebooks containing scores and even hundreds of different personal problems and spiritual conditions. John Owen was representative when he taught that every pastor must understand all the various cases of depression, fear, discouragement, and conflict that are found in the souls of men. This is necessary to aptly "fit medicines and remedies unto every sore distemper." Puritans were true physicians of the soul. Their study of the Scripture and the heart led them to make fine distinctions between conditions and to classify many types and sub-types of problems that require different treatments.[5]

When church leaders approach life's struggles with that kind of discernment and compassion, sufferers will be able to turn to the church for help in the midst of their pain. For more on similar past approaches to suffering, I recommend reading the entirety of Timothy Keller's paper quoted above.

AN UNHELPFUL SHIFT IN CHURCH CULTURE

But today, much has changed. In general, the church is no longer recognized as a significant voice when it comes to dealing with trauma. As more and more people struggle with mental health, the church talks less about these issues, leaving trauma to be addressed by the secular world.

What led to this shift in focus in the church? One possible factor is the subtle infiltration of self-righteousness, ironically driven by a call for godly living. The pursuit of godliness is a good thing, but when it is focused on external behavior, this becomes a slippery slope. I do not cast judgment on the church; the shift was likely intended for good. However, the unintended result was a shift from supporting those strugglers with compassion and grace to emphasizing behavior modification for the sake of personal holiness. And that, in turn, may have caused the church to veer toward a stance that pushed away—rather than embraced—those in need.

In addition, there has been a tendency today for people to elevate pastors and church leaders to an almost superhuman status, putting pressure on them to lead flawless lives untouched by the struggles of the world. Sadly, this has created a situation where both pastors and congregants feel compelled to conceal their struggles and give the impression that they have everything together.

Leaders like John Bunyan, who wrote about the terrible struggles faced in this life and the help that a Christian needs throughout this journey, are less common. We see less of the transparency evident in Charles Spurgeon, whose entire congregation knew his regular struggles with crippling depression. And those who write worship songs today don't seem to struggle like William Cowper, the man who wrote famous hymns but whose profound torments of the soul caused him to want to die. Rather, to live up to the expectations of those who look up to them, many of today's pastors and leaders present themselves as if they have everything together, and in many cases, those in the church follow suit. And the church ends up resembling a community country club, where people display their best and hide the rest.

Self-righteousness and high expectations aren't the only reasons for this shift. Another significant reason is the church's limited understanding of trauma. The modern church has only begun to recognize the need to be able to provide counseling in general and has not yet been positioned to delve into more specialized endeavors like trauma counseling—a conversation that's still evolving and is one of the reasons why I wrote this book. How can we bridge this gap and foster a more supportive environment for trauma survivors within our faith communities?

THE NEEDED CHANGE: HOW THE CHURCH CAN BECOME A SUPPORTIVE REFUGE

One solution is to encourage pastors and leaders to increase their awareness of the need for counseling in their congregations and to receive some level of training. It is not uncommon for church leaders to have very little background in counseling. Even pastors whose jobs require them to spend significant hours in counseling others have often taken only one or two counseling classes during seminary, and much of what they learned was theoretical rather than practical. Churches should encourage and provide continued counseling training for their pastors and leaders. One way to do this is to purchase this book and similar ones for their staff. Read them together and discuss what is learned.

Most churches do not have any staff trained in biblical counseling and often must refer members of their congregation out to ministries, private practitioners, or counseling centers. What if churches began hiring staff who are not only theologically trained but also specifically trained in counseling? This would help reduce the need for people to look outside the church for help. Having a trained counselor on a church ministry staff would create an avenue of support for pastors and leaders as they care for congregants.

Another solution is to talk about trauma and mental health from the pulpit, in small groups, and in one-on-one relationships. Offer classes that help inform others. Talk about the painful realities of abuse and address how they affect a person. Encourage people in the church to read books on topics related to mental health and trauma. Even the simple act of acknowledging the presence of painful struggles in people's lives goes a long way. Share your own story. You can do this in general and appropriate ways that communicate to people that the church is a place where they can be open about their pain.

To give you an example of how this might look, one Sunday in our church, our pastor shared how he and his wife went through a deeply challenging time after the birth of their third child. During that time, his wife was struggling with depression, and he was feeling exhausted and overwhelmed. In a moving act of transparency, he invited his wife to join him in telling their story to the church. This was a tender and honest moment for the church to be a part of, and it communicated that we are all people who are prone to struggles. He encouraged the members of our congregation not to struggle alone.

In the weeks that followed, many people shared how meaningful that moment had been for them. They spoke about various difficulties they, too, had faced or were currently facing. As a result, many reached out for help and received the support they needed. This highlights the crucial need for churches to be open and transparent about trauma and related issues, fostering an environment where people feel supported and understood.

Acknowledgment #2: How the Church Has Caused Harm

Regrettably, there have been times when we, as a church, have been the cause of a person's trauma—whether direct harm from abuse, cover-ups, or spiritual mistreatment, or indirect harm through complicity.

In recent decades, cases of sexual abuse and clergy misconduct have brought to light a stark reality: The church, which should be a place where the hurting find refuge, has been a source of harm for many.

In some cases, before many of these past atrocities came to light, the victims were often encouraged to believe that they were the problem, which only worsened the trauma they experienced.

The church has also been the breeding ground for ecumenical conflicts, racial and social discrimination, financial misconduct, disputes, divisions, and controversies—all of which leave behind wounded people trying to make sense of the disillusionment, betrayal, and emotional wounding they experience.

Headlines have exposed the painful reality that trauma can come from within the four walls of our most sacred places. And in some instances, the victim's trauma is compounded by unjust scorn or blame. Acknowledging that there have been times when the church, rather than being a place where the vulnerable felt loved, became a place where people felt preyed upon, is not about wallowing in shame. Instead, it can be a step toward meaningful change.

We can celebrate positive steps that have taken place both in broader contexts as church denominations publicly admitted harm done, and in smaller contexts as local churches confessed where they have failed to support survivors or have neglected to help trauma survivors feel safe.

How can we, as a community, address these painful realities and work toward healing and restoration for all? For the church to become a safe place for the traumatized, we must humbly acknowledge these past failures and seek to rectify them through genuine repentance and transformation. The path forward is one where we not only acknowledge failures but move forward toward change with humility and compassion.

The Needed Change: Becoming a Church That Does No Harm

The first step toward becoming a trauma-safe church is to accept that the church is a community of imperfect individuals relying on a perfect God, and to communicate that in our life together. A church that desires to be a safe place for all people is willing to acknowledge and discuss challenges and shortcomings. Creating a safe place can also include talking about the troubles that we face that cause deep suffering in our lives. Pastors and leaders do well to address matters like abuse, divorce, childhood trauma, and other situations that are traumatic. This approach creates a culture of honest vulnerability and reinforces a commitment to being supportive to all. We must cultivate empathy and a genuine desire to walk alongside those who have experienced trauma. As we have seen in the previous chapters, listening without judgment, offering support, and welcoming the stories of sufferers are essential in the healing process.

Ultimately, the church should be known by its love for others. We love because we have been loved by a gracious God who understands our stories and cares for us every step of the way. Our love serves as a testament to the love we have received from God. Despite past shortcomings, the church has the potential to become a place people turn to for finding hope in their hurt. As we rely on God, we can create an environment in which the traumatized find acceptance and support as the love of Christ cultivates seeds of restoration and renewal.

Creating a Trauma-Safe Church

Becoming a church that is trauma aware leads to a church becoming trauma safe. By this I mean that the church becomes a safe place for a person to share their story and receive help and support. It starts by being a listener and a learner. "Trauma-safe churches are churches who liberally witness the stories of survivors and are not threatened by their testimonies."[6] We must become willing to enter the discomfort of stories of horror, especially when those stories include how the church was complicit in or the direct cause of the trauma. We must be open to the complex relationship that a person might have with the church. We must be willing to acknowledge that individuals may have experienced emotional and psychological harm that has had a spiritual impact and may require time before trust can be built again.

A church that is trauma aware also embraces the biblical command to support and encourage one another (Galatians 6:2). Love and compassion are our motivating virtues for creating an environment that is safe for the vulnerable and wounded (Matthew 22:39). For this to happen, we must be invested in listening and learning more than directing and correcting (James 1:19).

Action Steps for the Church

Presently, the church stands at a turning point where the narrative of pain and alienation can be transformed into a story of healing and redemption. The path forward involves rediscovering a more honest understanding of who makes up the church—believers who wound and are wounded, yet who humbly seek and find forgiveness and grace. The church is the place where faith in a God who redeems can guide us through the darkest of times. By embracing a culture of humility, empathy, understanding, and love, the church can be a place where people find hope as they see that when faith meets trauma it doesn't have to snuff out belief, but rather, it can fuel stronger faith. As they experience a community of believers who are willing to be transparent about deep hurts and honest about trusting in a faithful God, they will find encouragement. When they hear the words of Scripture echoing their own cries, they will be validated. When they see others clinging to their faith in the midst of trials, their own grip on faith will grow tighter.

If that is where your church longs to be, if that is the desire of your heart as a helper, here are four specific ways a church can bring comfort to sufferers. Review these with your leadership and pray for the Lord to make your church not only trauma aware but trauma safe.

1. **Speak of human suffering.** As we have seen, the Bible does not shy away from portraying the harsh realities of human suffering. Scripture validates the emotional pain and anguish that trauma survivors endure (Jeremiah 4:19; Psalms 73:21-22; 109:22). Individuals will find comfort in knowing that their experiences are articulated and understood on the pages of Scripture. Acknowledging others' suffering also opens the opportunity for guidance from the Scripture as we help people see that they can take the most painful parts of their story to the God of all comfort. It also communicates that they are not alone.

2. **Affirm God's presence amid suffering.** The Bible emphasizes God's compassionate nature and how he promises to be with us in times of distress (Psalms 9:9-10; 23:4; 31:7-8; Isaiah 46:1; 49:14). These promises and assurances remind us that even during the darkest moments, God's presence is a comfort and solace. We may not feel that God is present, and even that is normal to feel and voice. Jesus himself felt that as he called out from the cross, "My God, my God, why have you forsaken me?" (Mark 15:34 NIV). Give space for this and continue to point the person to the Lord's promises to be faithful and just. It may seem as though he is slow, or not there, but he is. He will not overlook the evil and injustice done to someone. He promises to be the protector and avenger of his children.

3. **Remind people that restoration and redemption are assured.** The Bible is filled with stories of redemption and restoration,

in which brokenness is transformed into wholeness. These stories illustrate how God can bring healing and hope to those who have experienced suffering, including trauma. These stories are gospel reminders that one day, all things will be made new (Isaiah 43:19; Revelation 21:5), and we must continue to proclaim this truth to all—especially to those whose lives have been impacted by trauma. The Bible reminds us that God can bring beauty out of ashes and glory out of disgrace (Isaiah 61:3). The stories in the Bible serve as a reminder that because of Jesus, there is a future joy beyond pain (Joel 2:25-32; Revelation 21:4).

4. **Encourage people toward compassionate action.** The presence of trauma in the Bible encourages us to respond with compassion and empathy toward those who are suffering. As Christians, we are called to extend love and support to those who have endured trauma, just as Jesus demonstrated in his interactions. He did not shy away from people who had horrifying histories (Matthew 8:28-34; Mark 2:13-15; Luke 8:1-2). His compassion drew them to him (Matthew 9:36-38). "Trauma-safe churches are not afraid to witness such stories of trauma survivors. This is because there can be no trauma healing without telling the truth."[7] Our willingness to care for the sufferer can be a means of leading people to a path of healing and the Healer himself. It is not unlike Jesus to heal someone based on the faith of friends (Mark 2:1-5).

Traumatized people need people. They need others who will wisely support and care for them as they process what happened. They need others who will remind them of the truth that God loves them and cares for them. They need a safe place where their story can be shared. They need the church.

Again, Dr. Diane Langberg charges those who minister to people to remember that

> you have by the virtue of your calling, been invited to enter into atrocity in the name of Jesus Christ. Such an invitation is really nothing other than a call to follow in the footsteps of our Lord, who entered into the terrible atrocity of this fallen world and endured the unspeakable. He who did so for our sakes has called us to do the same for those who are suffering.[8]

CHAPTER 11

TRAUMA AND THEOLOGY

In attempting to write a theology of anything, I readily admit that, while R.C. Sproul,[1] Jen Wilkin, and J.T. English[2] say we're all theologians, I make no profession to claim the expertise or accolades of the well-studied biblical scholar. My theological understanding is shaped by diligent personal Bible study, years of listening to sermons, great conversations with smarter-than-me brothers and sisters in Christ, as well as engagement with scholarly and theological works.

This chapter is my humble attempt to provide theological insight on the topic of trauma in two specific areas. But before we begin, when it comes to theology, we all have blind spots or gaps. The very nature of blind spots means we just don't see them. Undoubtedly, there will be those who choose to focus solely on these gaps. I extend a warm welcome to any friendly conversation to discuss those gaps over a cup of coffee—or preferably, good tacos. I find it more helpful to navigate this journey of faith together as fellow brothers and sisters rather than antagonists and critics. And if we don't agree on theology, at least we can agree on coffee or tacos.

Even as I acknowledge these potential gaps in my theology, what better way to put them on display than by attempting to write on the subject? My hope is that you will read this chapter not so much in search of theological acumen, but to better understand our loving and gracious God. Let us shift our focus from the horrors of this world and look to the beauty of Jesus and the life that is to come for all who call him Lord.

We will look at two areas where trauma and theology intersect. There certainly could be more, but for the sake of keeping things practical and concise, this chapter will discuss (1) a theology of post-traumatic growth, and (2) a theology of remembering, because both topics are especially relevant to trauma care, and both must be viewed through a theological lens.

Exploring these two areas will help to construct a theological understanding of trauma. Much of what will be laid out is directed toward caring for Christians who are seeking to live a life in accordance with the Bible. I anticipate the question, What if the person is not a Christian? If that is the case, then you have a wonderful opportunity to introduce them to God, who has compassion and invites them into his care. His grace and love are available to them in Christ. Bring to them the same truths you would to a person who is a Christian, only bring them as an invitation. It is amazing how much trauma opens the door for gospel conversations.

A Theology of Post-Traumatic Growth

A solid theological framework is essential for cultivating a redemptive perspective of the past and the future. With this framework, a person can rebuild after trauma and be encouraged toward change. As a person reframes their narrative, they pave the way toward positive transformation and a renewed sense of hope that is anchored to God and his Word.

After working to help a person calm their physical responses to unwanted memories and the triggers of trauma (which we addressed earlier), that person is more ready to begin doing this theological work. The goal of this work is for the person to discover meaning beyond the traumatic event and learn how to integrate that meaning into their life. Positive transformation happens within a theological framework presented in a way that does not overwhelm, but instead, fosters a redemptive perspective. The mental health world calls this positive transformation *post-traumatic growth*. Psychologists Lawrence Calhoun and Richard Tedeschi are pioneers in the development of research and theory of post-traumatic growth, and they define it as "the experience of positive change that the individual experiences as a result of the struggle with a traumatic event."[3] They identify a set of elements that are common indicators of post-traumatic growth, though they avoid giving a general summary of each element because individuals will experience these elements in unique ways. These elements of growth that can come out of a traumatic experience are personal strength, relating to others, new possibilities, appreciation of life, and spirituality.

Calhoun and Tedeschi posit that these five elements fall into three categories that encompass the growth experience. The categories include *a changed sense of oneself*, *a changed sense of relationships with others*, and *a changed philosophy of life*.[4] While those categories can be helpful, they lack the needed connection to orient us to God. Using the theological lens of God's Word, those categories can take on deeper and eternal purposes. A theological framework brings God's sovereign plan to the forefront of every situation. And that plan, despite how we perceive it, will always be for our flourishing. With this theological reframe, trauma can not only lead to post-traumatic growth, but also to *post-traumatic spiritual growth*.

Post-Traumatic Spiritual Growth

I want to suggest that post-traumatic spiritual growth has its own three categories that encompass the growth experience. These categories include *an established sense of one's identity in Christ, an established sense of the need for community rooted in Christ's love*, and *an established biblical worldview anchored in the narrative of the gospel*. All three contribute to a person's transformation toward Christlikeness. When this happens, applied theology is taking place, and one's faith in and relationship with God grows deeper. Let's explore these three areas and see what it means to view trauma through a theological lens that can lead to growth.

An Established Sense of One's Identity in Christ

In contemporary society, the pursuit of identity has become an increasingly prevalent preoccupation. The passionate quest to establish and prove who we are becomes the focus of our lives and is matched only by the desire to ensure that others recognize and accept our achieved identity. However, as the late Timothy Keller astutely expressed, "Identity is received not achieved."[5] This truth is essentially relevant when trauma becomes a disrupting force in a person's life, taking a lethal aim at the very core of who we are.

In the midst of this struggle, it is crucial to be grounded in the foundational truth that we are all made in the image of God (Genesis 1:27), and as his beloved children (John 1:12; 2 Corinthians 6:18; 1 John 3:1), we have an identity that is secure and eternal (Colossians 3:3; 1 Peter 1:3-5). This stabilizing reality stands in stark contrast to the tumultuous assault that trauma can inflict on our understanding of our identity. The pivotal question arises: If identity is received, what or who is the source from which we are receiving it? The world would say it is yourself. But the reality of traumatization and the resulting alteration of self shows that we are not a strong enough source to keep our identity secure. Instead, the answer lies at the heart of the Christian faith: God is the giver and keeper of your identity. In his love, which was demonstrated through the sending of his Son, we become the righteousness of God (2 Corinthians 5:21), and nothing can separate us from this identity (Romans 8:31-39).

Because of this new identity we have in Christ, God fully accepts us and loves us. We are his children. No matter what happened to us, what we have done, what has been done to us, or what we have been through, nothing can change what God says about us. We are his, and he will keep us.

The verses in the paragraphs above are the ballast that will keep a heart steady when the storms of life come. Read them to those you walk with. Let them serve as anchors for your own heart. Isaiah 43:1-5 is a great reminder that you are loved, chosen, and precious to God even when trauma has been a part of your story. Remember, in Christ, you are God's beloved child. Our minds easily forget these truths or tell us a different story. The eloquent words of Dietrich Bonhoeffer capture the tension we can experience in our minds: "Who am I? They mock me, these lonely questions of mine. Whoever I am, thou knowest, O God, I am thine."[6] A deep understanding of one's identity in Christ is the catalyst that will usher in spiritual growth and keep us steady even in the traumas of this life.

An Established Need for Biblical Community Rooted in Christ's Love

Understanding our need to have our identity established in who God says we are is essential for flourishing and well-being. Out of that flows another need: the need for biblical community.

Community is not a human construct. Rather, it is God's idea, and it is inextricably tied to eternity. Community always existed and always will. It transcends the constraints of time. For human beings, life's journey not only commences and concludes within the realm of community, it will also continue in the life to come. Community is God's plan for people. In the first book of the Bible, we see the divine community of the Father, Son, and Holy Spirit (Genesis 1:1-2, 26) existing together and preparing to add to their community by creating man. The first declaration of something not being good in creation was in reference to the aloneness of man. In Genesis 2:18, God said, "It is not good that man should be alone; I will make him a helper fit for him." Initially, man had no one like him to live in community with, and that was not good. But this was corrected with the creation of Eve, at which time human community began. In response, man uttered a heartfelt and poetic reply to what Eve's presence assured (see Genesis 2:18-23).

> *For human beings, life's journey not only commences and concludes within the realm of community, it will also continue in the life to come. Community is God's plan for people.*

A look at the final book of the Bible reveals that eternity to come will also be marked by community. In the new heaven and the new earth, God will live with and among his people. "I heard a loud voice from the throne saying, 'Look! God's dwelling place is now among the people, and he will dwell with them. They will be his people, and God himself will be with them and be their God'" (Revelation 21:3 NIV). A look at the plural pronouns in this passage—and their antecedent—attests to the fact that we will live together as a community with God for all eternity. Is it any wonder why Jesus says there are many rooms in his Father's house? God intends to fill those rooms with lots and lots of people (John 14:2).

Throughout the entire Bible, we see the express purpose for this life together. Kline Snodgrass, in his excellent book titled *Who God Says You Are: A Christian Understanding of Identity*, explains it this way: "If indeed we are created in the image of God, we will never understand what it is to be a person apart from our relation to God, a very personal God. We become ourselves most of all in relation with God, but relation with God is impossible apart from relation with other people. Life is caught up in the twin love commands, love of God and love of neighbor as oneself."[7] Essentially, it is impossible to live and grow as a Christian (to love God *and* love others) apart from community. But how does this all relate to growth and healing after trauma?

Christian growth is intrinsically connected to a deep understanding of the need for community rooted in Christ's love. Hebrews 10:24-25 urges believers to consider how to stir one another to love and good works, emphasizing the role of mutual encouragement within the community. Additionally, 1 Corinthians 12:12-27 beautifully portrays the interconnectedness of believers as the body of Christ, highlighting the indispensable nature of each member. When a person has a traumatic experience, they need people with whom to process it. They need others to comfort them. Often, the reason that two people can go through the same event yet have different experiences and effects has to do with whether someone was with them in the processing of it all. People need support, encouragement, and love as they walk through trauma.

The Bible talks frequently about the need we have for support, encouragement, love, and help from one another. Community is a vital part of maturing in our faith after we endure trauma. Here are other passages in which the Bible mentions the importance of community:

- Proverbs 27:17: "Iron sharpens iron, and one man sharpens another." The analogy of iron sharpening iron underscores the mutual influence and encouragement that occurs within a supportive community. We lift up and sharpen each other through shared experiences, wisdom, and faith.

- Matthew 18:20: "Where two or three are gathered in my name, there am I among them." This emphasizes the significance of prayer and fellowship with those who share our faith. Not only is it not good to be alone in our struggles, but we have the assurance that Christ is intimately present in our community support and prayer.

- Romans 15:5-7: "May the God of endurance and encouragement grant you to live in such harmony with one another, in accord with Christ Jesus, that together you may with one voice glorify the God and Father of our Lord Jesus Christ. Therefore welcome one another as Christ has welcomed you, for the glory of God." This passage reminds us that living in harmony creates a spirit of welcome that permits us to share what we have faced and receive encouragement in our time of need. This welcoming environment strengthens us as we seek to live a life that aligns with Christ's example.

- 1 Thessalonians 5:14: "We urge you, brothers, admonish the idle, encourage the fainthearted, help the weak, be patient with them all." This passage provides a blueprint for compassionate and supportive interactions with one another. We are exhorted to foster an environment in which believers can navigate and overcome trials together, finding strength in one another's patient care and direction.

- 1 John 4:11: "Beloved, if God so loved us, we also ought to love one another." Our love for one another becomes a catalyst for mutual care and compassion, which, in turn, builds all of us up toward spiritual maturity.

It is clear from Scripture that we affect one another. As a person heals from trauma, it is helpful for them to be surrounded by a community of people who encourage them to persevere in accordance with Scripture. The secular culture offers community that can cast doubt on the faithfulness of God as it points people to find strength in themselves alone. We should caution traumatized people to be mindful of those who might pull them away from the truths of Scripture as they process what they have been through.

Someone once said, "You are the average of the five people you spend most of your time with."[8] Some argue that this statement is too simplistic. They say that you are more than the sum of the people you are with, *and* you're also the sum of those you are not physically with. This includes the people whose writing you read, whom you follow on social media, whom you listen to regularly on podcasts, or whose shows you watch. We shape one another. Because of that, we need to be attentive and intentional about who we spend our time with. The belief systems of the people you surround yourself with will rub off on you. This is why the Bible is so vocal about the need for us to be surrounded by other believers.

When someone experiences trauma, they can become more susceptible to the influence of others. That's why biblical community is essential. The passages above, along with the message of the whole Bible, affirm the transformative power of Christ-centered community in our spiritual journey. "The people you are with will shape you, and you will shape them. Your identity is at stake. Make wise choices."[9]

*We shape one another. Because of that, we need to
be attentive and intentional about who we spend
our time with. The belief systems of the people
you surround yourself with will rub off on you.*

An Established Biblical Worldview Anchored in the Narrative of the Gospel

The importance of cultivating a sense of one's identity in Christ and grasping an understanding of the indispensable role of biblical community is underscored by the need for a firm biblical foundation. This foundation ensures a person's progress is guided by the transformative power of God's eternal truth rather than by their experiences. A biblical foundation is the key to developing a biblical worldview, which then becomes the framework a person can use to rebuild their life after trauma. It is on this firm foundation that the impetus for growth in Christ can be manifest even through great trials.

Lest you think a worldview is something only Christians think about when it comes to trauma care, consider once again psychologists Lawrence Calhoun and Richard Tedeschi:

> A very important factor influencing the possibility that growth will be experienced is the individual's assumptive world, the general set of beliefs a person has about the universe, how it works, and the individual's place in it. *As we view them, traumatic events are those that have a seismic impact on the individual's assumptive world.* Just like an earthquake can shake, damage, or destroy physical structures, traumatic events have the same kind of impact on the schemas and beliefs people use to help them understand and organize their experience.

They go on to talk about the importance of "reviewing and examining core beliefs as a key catalyst for the possibility of post traumatic growth."[10]

People need a worldview that will withstand the blows of the terrible realities they may face. They need wisdom that is deeper and wiser than what this world has to offer. Growth comes out of trauma when the framework that is holding up a person's meaning of life is stable enough to answer the questions that trauma raises. The Bible alone can do just that, and it is the source of all that comprises the Christian's worldview. R.C. Sproul reveals many of the questions a worldview must answer.

> A Christian life-and-worldview seeks to establish the rules of thinking, the rules of determining how we know what is true.
>
> Who in the world is speaking the truth? Who do you trust? Who's telling the truth? How do you know? That's a question of epistemology.
>
> Ultimately, what is the truth; what is it? A question of *is*-ness. What is real, ultimately? That's a metaphysical question.
>
> "Who is the truth?" is a theological question.
>
> "How does the truth relate of me and define me?" is an anthropological question.
>
> And how the truth commands me is an ethical question.
>
> These are the elements of a Christian life-and-worldview. Ignore one of them, and you will have a distorted view of the world and of your own life.[11]

All the questions Dr. Sproul highlights are answered in the Bible, and the answers revolve around the message of the gospel of Jesus Christ. Romans 12:2 challenges believers not to be conformed to the pattern of the world, but to be transformed by the renewing of their minds. We must not allow the culture, or our experience, to determine our worldview. It is essential to establish a worldview that is biblical.

> *Growth comes out of trauma when the framework that is holding up a person's meaning of life is stable enough to answer the questions that trauma raises.*

A theology of post-traumatic growth must address *an established sense of one's identity in Christ, an established sense of the need for community rooted in Christ's love,* and *an established biblical worldview anchored in the narrative of the gospel.* I will also point you to a couple of resources and encourage you to go further.

First, a resource on the general topic of understanding the importance of worldview is *The Consequence of Ideas* by R.C. Sproul. This book explains how Western philosophy has shaped many people's worldview and how we need to make sure our worldview is built on the truths of Scripture. Second, a resource on understanding the importance of worldview specifically when it comes to offering counsel to others is *Equipped to Counsel* by John Henderson. This biblical counseling training text has an excellent four-chapter module dedicated to counseling and worldview.

When it comes to identity, community, and worldview, we must be committed to helping people to grow deep roots in the unchanging truths of God's Word. Christlike transformation is augmented as attention is given to these three areas, which, in turn, leads to a deepening of one's faith. In the next section, we will pause and examine how theological truths apply to trauma, particularly in how people remember or think about the traumatic event.

A Theology of Remembering

"I wish you could erase my memory." These were the words spoken to me by Lucy, a 19-year-old college sophomore who came to see me knowing she still had work to do to address the trauma of her past. Lucy was trafficked when she was just 11. She had spent more than three years in the sex-trafficking industry before being rescued in a sting operation by special operations officers.

The first couple years after her rescue were confusing and painful to her. She had been so brainwashed by her pimp that she did not clearly understand what had happened. Her mind had been so manipulated that she saw her perpetrators as family and wanted to be reunited with them. She dealt with intense bouts of rage, and when she wasn't angry, she was depressed. She pushed back at the limitations and changes in her life due to being placed in a witness protection program for the duration of the trial related to her case. Her parents were able to find a therapist who was a Christian and well trained in trauma recovery. Thankfully, Lucy willingly engaged in therapy, and this—plus the unwavering love and prayers of her parents—began to soften her heart and correct her thinking.

Eventually, Lucy began to process and make sense of what she had been through. In her senior year of high school, she attended a youth camp. She had no idea how much that camp would change her life. What could a church camp possibly offer someone who has been through such life-altering atrocities? Apparently, it could offer a lot—specifically, the gospel. Through talks and small group sessions, Lucy was able, for the first time, to truly understand that Jesus loved her and that she could have a new life in Christ. She prayed and asked God to help her live in the light of the truth of who God made her to be, rather than living in the light of all that had happened to her. At camp, Lucy experienced incredible hope and peace for the first time since her rescue.

In the months after camp, Lucy continued to grow in her relationship with the Lord. She was faithfully discipled by a mentor who served in the high school ministry at her church. This, coupled with her Christian counseling, helped Lucy make incredible progress, and her thinking became more and more directed by the Spirit and Scripture rather than by her feelings and fears about the past. She decided to get baptized and continued to depend deeply on the Lord. Scripture gave her hope for her future, and her church was a supportive community.

Over the years, Lucy continued to process what had happened, and what God was doing in her life. She was a testimony of how God's care and faithfulness heals even though wounds were still etched in her memory. I, too, wished I could help her to forget the horrors that she had endured. But as you just read, trauma can lead to growth. The way we remember plays a significant role in that growth.

The concept of remembering and the purpose of our memories are key aspects of trauma care in the clinical world. I want to explore one particular theory and offer another theological reframe.

Adaptive Information Processing

We explored what the clinical world refers to as *post-traumatic growth* and how, as believers, that growth can extend deeper to what I refer to as *post-traumatic spiritual growth*. This theological reframe underscores the potential for richer meaning and deeper growth to occur even as we encounter the terrible realities of trauma. And this is exactly what Lucy experienced.

Adaptive information processing (AIP) is a clinical theory in trauma care that describes how the brain organizes and processes memories to promote healing and reduce emotional distress. This theory is related to the purpose of memory. Essentially it explains that memories—specifically those created as we go through traumatic events—serve a purpose. In normal situations, memories and their meanings are both processed and integrated into our lives, causing healthy adaptive responses. We will see, however, that with trauma this process is disrupted, and memories can be stored in a more isolated rather than integrated way.

The AIP theory explains that our brains adapt based on the situations we experience. Essentially this means that as we go through experiences, our brains take in everything about the situations, including the sensory information—sight, smell, taste, sound, touch—gathered during the experience. That data is then encoded in our brains as memories, which we will then use as we engage future situations. Think of it as a filing system in your brain. Much like files on a computer, when organized properly, they can be out of sight but retrieved as needed. Experiences happen, your brain learns, and what is learned is organized and filed away for future use. The next time you experience something similar, your brain pulls that memory—with the sensory information—and adapts your behavior accordingly, based on what was learned.

A common example is helpful. A child who is told by their parent not to touch a hot stove will remember what was said. But when that child decides to touch it anyway and experiences the pain of being burned, the memory is stored with more intensity. In the future, the child will choose to make a more adaptive action based on what was remembered, which now includes sensory information. The child's brain will use that information for the rest of their life and cause them to use caution when reaching out to test and see whether a stove is safe to touch.

Or have you ever seen a child at a birthday party grab and tightly squeeze a balloon in the middle of a group of children? The other children who see what is happening will cover their ears in anticipation of the loud pop. Why? Because they have all been startled and unsettled by the sudden pop of a balloon. Without any thought, their brains have provided adaptive information that causes them to respond in a way that protects them from the negative experience they've encountered before.

This theory describes the organizational quality of our brain and goes on to explain that, in trauma, this organizational system gets glitchy. Trauma corrupts the filing system and organizes the files differently, along with the sensory experiences. The painful sensory information heightens the significance of the memory. When this happens, the memory and the sensations related to it can be recalled when situations have similar connections to that memory but are not threatening. The person's response is comparable to the reaction they had in the painful or traumatic experience. The acronym discussed in chapter 5 mentions examples of these types of reactions.

The AIP theory can be helpful for understanding how trauma disrupts the organizational filing system in our brains. It explains how trauma isolates memories from adaptive information and instead causes reactionary responses that then contribute to the formation of actions and beliefs based on the traumatic experience. For example, a woman who survived a rape may know that it was not her fault, but she may also carry significant feelings of fear and shame leading her to believe that had she only been more vigilant or made different choices it would not have happened. She may have physical manifestations of panic even when there is no threat. She may experience distress anytime she is around anyone who resembles her attacker. Because the traumatic memories are not integrated or resolved, the brain—seeking to keep the person safe—recalls the sensory information of a traumatic experience at a time when there is no threatening situation. This can cause people to feel stuck in a state of overreaction. They then can begin developing incorrect beliefs about themselves and the world which hinders growth and causes reoccurring distress.

Trauma counselors who embrace the AIP model posit that with intentional work, trauma survivors can learn to access and embrace adaptive information hardwired in their brains. They conclude that accessing this information will lead to better beliefs about life—beliefs such as I am safe, I am strong, I have survived worse, I can get through this, etc.

Why mention another clinical theory? Just as the clinical idea of post-traumatic growth, while helpful, is lacking in deeper application, so too, the AIP theory lacks depth that a theological framework can provide.

Redemptive Information Processing

To me, and I hope to you as well, a look at the adaptive information processing theory reveals that we have a God-given, dynamic ability to process, learn from, and store experiences. We take in, save, and access what we have learned to use it when it is needed most. This helps not only in making sense of our world, but also aids in keeping us safe. It influences how we live and is what contributes to the forming of core beliefs we have about life.

However, we need more than just *adaptive* information. We need guidance from God through his Spirit, his Word, and the wisdom of other believers. It is this information that must shape and direct our thoughts and actions. The most-needed and beneficial information does not come from lived experiences per se, as helpful as those can be. Rather, the most-needed and beneficial information comes from God.

Rather than adaptive information processing, we need redemptive information processing. This is an approach I teach to counseling students to help them in reframing a clinical method in order to emphasize a biblical approach to trauma care. Redemptive information is truth about God and his ability to redeem all things, including our past. We must be shaped by eternal truth and allow that to be what forms our beliefs about the world and our experiences. This is especially true as we face traumatic situations. As you care for believers, encourage them to hold tightly to redemptive information. Truths such as *God is with me, God will help me,* or *God is my strength* are examples of the redemptive information that are essential to a trauma survivor's processing. We will revisit this idea with practical applications later in this chapter.

One reason redemptive information processing is needed is because a person's memories of trauma can be incredibly painful and disruptive and lead to incorrect beliefs about themselves and the world. As helpers, it is vital for us to understand the significant role that memories can have in the suffering people experience after a traumatic event.

The Pain of Remembering

One of the hardest realities about experiencing something traumatic is that you cannot simply forget what happened. As we saw in chapter 5, when we talked about triggers, memories connect us to the past not only in our minds but also in our bodies, leaving us to wrestle with what to do with these haunting reminders. Richard J. McNally observes,

> *Psychophysiological reactivity* refers to the fact that survivors often react physically as well as psychologically when confronted with reminders of the trauma. That is, while feeling fear, they may sweat, tremble, and experience their

heart pounding. One former marine who had nearly been sliced in half by enemy machine gun fire in Vietnam reported that the sound of a car backfiring always sent him ducking for cover. Not only did the backfire incite intense fear, but it made his heart pound violently and his body shake all over.[12]

McNally continues:

> For people with post-traumatic stress disorder, remembering trauma feels like reliving it. Traumatic events from the past are recalled with such vivid and emotional intensity that it seems as if the trauma were happening all over again...*Intrusive recollections* are disturbing thoughts and images of the event that come to mind even when a person does not want to think about it.[13]

Miroslav Volf, in his book *The End of Memory*, aptly describes the struggle with memories:

> [W]e do not have complete control over our memories. Sometimes they simply pop into our minds without the involvement of our will in any significant way. At other times we deliberately store memories in our minds, from which we retrieve them in the work of recollection. Yet there are some memories that our minds refuse either to commit into storage or retrieve from it, no matter how hard we try, remembering often happens *to* us rather than *by* us.[14]

Historic figures in secular psychology acknowledge the challenges associated with memories. Sigmund Freud and his mentor, Josef

Breuer, worked together on an in-depth study of what was referred to then as hysteria. At the beginning of the book, you learned that in early psychological studies, hysteria was the label given to what would now be referred to as trauma. Underscoring how remembering can cause deep suffering, Judith Herman shared this about their work: "Breuer and Freud, in an immortal summation, wrote that 'hysterics suffer mainly from reminiscences.'"[15] Memories are a powerful factor in the experience of trauma.

Are we then victims of these memories and the experiences they bring? What theological perspective can address this complex reality? On this topic, I offer two areas of direction. Both are aspects of redemptive information processing, and both are anchored to an understanding of who God is and the precious promises we have from him. The first is to remember truthfully, and the second is to imagine hopefully.

Remember Truthfully

As mentioned earlier, assigning meaning to traumatic events occurs through the proper processing of memories, thereby reducing present-day negative impacts on the person's life. This does not mean, as Lucy wished, that the memories are erased. Instead, the memories are integrated into the individual's worldview in a way that offers meaning, causing the reminders to no longer be disruptive to daily life. In the words of Viktor E. Frankl, "In some way, suffering ceases to be suffering at the moment it finds a meaning."[16] When meaning is ascribed, beliefs are established. These are the goals of trauma work.

Unfortunately, one of the painful realities about going through something traumatic is that the horrors of the situation cause a person to question what they once believed to be true. This is especially true when trauma is ongoing. Truth becomes skewed by what they endured and what they learned when they were enduring it. If only the experience was a dream they could awaken from, they could shake it off, compared to the reality of what they experience in real life. But the traumatic experience was terrible and true. What does one do with the terrible truth? The painful truth? The fear-inducing truth? The real wrongs that have been done? Can theology help in the process of remembering truthfully when the truth is so painful? Not only can theology help, but theology is the essential guide for reorienting a person.

God does not expect us to forget. He is all about remembering. We see in the Bible that the word *remember* or variants of it appear hundreds of times. God created us with the capacity to remember and instructs us to remember. His intention was not that we would only remember the good and try to forget the bad. Instead, we are to remember his faithfulness—especially even as we recall the difficult times of our lives. We must allow God's Word to instruct us on how to remember truthfully.

Deuteronomy 5:15 says, "Remember that you were slaves in Egypt *and* that the LORD your God brought you out of there with a mighty hand and an outstretched arm" (NIV, emphasis added). The painful and hurtful memories of slavery were not to be forgotten; rather, they were to be remembered alongside the whole truth. The Israelites were slaves *and* God rescued them. He was working on their behalf and took note of the pain they were enduring. But he did not want them to forget that they were slaves because if they forgot, they would likely also forget that he had heard their cry and rescued them.

In the book of Joshua, we see the people of God finally enter the Promised Land after 40 years of living in the desert. Joshua 4:5-7 specifically calls them to remember:

Joshua said to them, "Pass on before the ark of the Lord your God into the midst of the Jordan and take up each of you a stone upon his shoulder, according to the number of the tribes of the people of Israel, that this may be a sign among you. When your children ask in time to come, 'What do those stones mean to you?' then you shall tell them that the waters of the Jordan were cut off before the ark of the covenant of the Lord. When it passed over the Jordan, the waters of the Jordan were cut off. So, these stones shall be to the people of Israel a *memorial forever*" (emphasis added).

The purpose of a memorial is to remember.

But what were they to remember? Yes, they were to remember that the Lord parted the river, and they were also to remember all that was connected to that moment. The parting of the Jordan River was the climactical ending to 40 years of wilderness living. You can read the book of Numbers to see all that the people endured in the wilderness. Before the wilderness, they were slaves in Egypt living under significant oppression. You can read the book of Exodus to learn more about what their life as slaves was like. They were not only to remember their entrance into the Promised Land, but also the wilderness wanderings. They were not only to remember their deliverance from the tyranny of Pharoah, but also that they had once been slaves.

This means that while they would recount the painful reality of their past circumstances, they would also remember that God was working to help them, free them, protect them, and redeem them. God was faithful even through the most painful trials. That was the truth they were to remember: God was working, and he would be faithful. This is the truth we must help others apply. When we remember truthfully, we remember more fully.

Flawed Memories

We don't need scientific proof or statistics to convince us that our memories are not always dependable. If you don't believe me, try to recall what you ate for lunch three days ago. When I thought about that for a while, I could not recall what I had eaten a mere 72 hours ago. Unless you eat the same thing for lunch every day or that lunch happened to be a special occasion, you will likely also struggle to remember. That is not the way it is with all memories, but this simple exercise does show that memory retrieval is not as simple as it may seem.

Not only are we often unable to retrieve memories, but we aren't always accurate in our memory recall. If you interview five different people who witnessed a hostile argument between two individuals, you will get five different versions of the same story. There will be similarities in the accounts, but there will also be differences as to what they remember. Then if you were to interview the two people who were arguing, you would get different details about what happened. With remembering comes the challenge to remember accurately. Our memories are not the event itself; rather, they are our interpretation of the event, along with all the emotions and experiences of how it impacted us.

What Else Is True?

Our memories need to be informed. This is not to say that someone's experience was not as bad as they may remember or that it was not traumatizing. To remember truthfully is to use our memories the way God intended. We must apply the unchanging truths of who God is and what he promises to our memories. As we walk with those who have a traumatic past, we can point them to the timeless truths of Scripture to remind them of what is true even as they face difficulties.

An exercise I share in my book *I'm Stressed: A Path from Pressure to Peace* applies here. It is a practical way to engage redemptive information processing as you use it to help someone remember truth in a more redemptive way. When a person can only call to mind a terrible truth, use the acronym AWE to help guide the person toward remembering more truthfully. The acronym stands for And What Else. Yes, it is true the traumatic event or circumstance happened. And what else is true? That is, what else is true about the situation, about God, or about the person you are helping? As Christians, there is so much more that is true even while we experience trauma. Here are some examples. Read these truths slowly, thinking about each one:

- *You are a loved child of God.* "To all who did receive him, who believed in his name, he gave the right to become children of God" (John 1:12).

- *God is your protector and your refuge.* "He will cover you with his feathers, and under his wings you will find refuge; his faithfulness will be your shield and rampart. You will not fear the terror of night, nor the arrow that flies by day, nor the pestilence that stalks in the darkness, nor the plague that destroys at midday" (Psalm 91:4-6 NIV).

- *God is faithful and will judge rightly those who have harmed you.* "The LORD passed before [Moses] and proclaimed, 'The LORD, the LORD, a God merciful and gracious, slow to anger, and abounding in steadfast love and faithfulness, keeping steadfast love for thousands, forgiving iniquity and transgression and sin, but who will by no means clear the guilty, visiting the iniquity of the fathers on the children and the children's children, to the third and fourth generation'" (Exodus 34:6-7).

- *Nothing will separate you from God's love.* "Who shall separate us from the love of Christ? Shall trouble or hardship or persecution or famine or nakedness or danger or sword? As it is written: 'For your sake we face death all day long; we are considered as sheep to be slaughtered.' No, in all these things we are more than conquerors through him who loved us. For I am convinced that neither death nor life, neither angels nor demons, neither the present nor the future, nor any powers, neither height nor depth, nor anything else in all creation, will be able to separate us from the love of God that is in Christ Jesus our Lord" (Romans 8:35-39 NIV).

When you take the time to explore what else is true, you can help a person remember a truth that can easily be forgotten in an awful situation. This is a way to apply theology to a traumatic circumstance. Apply what God and Scripture say about what is true. When we seek to help people remember truthfully, we are also helping them to hold on to hope.

One example of this is when Scripture instructs us to remember the trauma of the cross. This remembering calls us to reflect on the substitutionary atonement that Jesus accomplished through his death—he died in our place. Remembering this also reminds us that death has been defeated. This remembering is an invitation to hope.

> He took bread, and when he had given thanks, he broke it and gave it to them, saying, "This is my body, which is given for you. Do this in remembrance of me"...For as often as you eat this bread and drink the cup, you proclaim the Lord's death until he comes (Luke 22:19; 1 Corinthians 11:26).

When we remember the Lord's death, we are also proclaiming that he will come again. We are not only remembering the pain and darkness of the cross, but also the hope of the promise it ensures. He will be faithful to come back and put all things right. He will put an end to all evil. He will restore and heal fully. This leads to the second concept as we explore a theological understanding of trauma: We must help people to imagine hopefully.

Imagine Hopefully

We lived in Southern California when our children were young, and despite being only about an hour's drive from Disneyland, we did not take them there often. The main reason was the expense. Not only would we—a family of five—have to spend a fortune on tickets, but after entering the park, we would have to spend a big chunk of our grocery budget on a few baskets of Mickey-shaped chicken nuggets and a 12-inch churro (I must confess, though, that the churros at Disneyland are the best!). Though we did not go often, I remember the first time we took the kids to the park. They knew about Disneyland from their friends, but they had not yet seen it themselves. Part of what made that first trip so special was not just going to the park, but the anticipation beforehand as they imagined what it would be like. They thought about what was to come, and those imaginings brought them enormous joy.

When it comes to processing trauma, remembering and imagining are important. Remembering and imagining are mirror opposites. Let me explain: Essentially, they are opposites, yet they share the same characteristics. When we remember, we are transported to the past. When we imagine, we are transported to the future. When we remember, we are considering the experiences, both good and bad, that have shaped us. This introspective journey allows us to learn from the past, fostering growth and understanding. But when we imagine, we ponder the possibilities of the future and consider their potential outcomes. Often, when we imagine, we anticipate what was promised to us. Together, remembering and imagining form a dynamic interplay that helps a person to rightly and theologically process the trauma they have endured.

We looked at how remembering truthfully about who God is can lead to growth after trauma. We will now look briefly at the role of imagination as it pertains to a theological approach to trauma, and see why this is important when we care for someone.

The Bible and Our Imagination

Much about the Christian faith requires our imagination. The Bible is not a picture book, but it does provide enough details that our minds and hearts are able to envision the accounts it describes. Read the book of Genesis, and you will find yourself mentally transported to a garden. Later, you'll read about Egypt, where you'll encounter the reign of pharaohs and the horrors of plagues. Keep reading, and you'll get a picture of a rock that gives water, a furnace that scorches those who come near it (yet men are thrown into it unscathed). Keep going, and you'll spend a night in a den of lions! Move on to the New Testament, and your imagination will help you to "see" a manger scene, a storm calmed by a word, limbs being restored, pigs becoming possessed by demons, and dead bodies coming to life.

We are also given the opportunity to imagine the beauty of where we will spend eternity. We read the details given in Scripture and picture it in our imaginations.

As we read God's Word, our imagination brings it to life, and this helps the truth to go deeper. As each story is played out over and over in our minds, its truths are solidified in our hearts. And our anticipation builds for the day when we can see the fulfillment of certain truths with our eyes. Our imaginings do more than fill us with anticipation, they shape us and influence our present-day choices and actions.

The Bible uses the word *hope* to describe what we long for. Romans 8:24-25 says, "In this hope we were saved. Now hope that is seen is not hope. For who hopes for what he sees? But if we hope for what we do not see, we wait for it with patience." Caring for those who have been traumatized involves engaging their imagination in the direction of hope. While the truth of a person's trauma is not able to be erased, we can help a person call to mind the promises of God so they can imagine hopefully the fulfillment of those promises. This is another way to apply redemptive information processing. Below are verses you can use to encourage sufferers to imagine, call to mind, and think about truths that bring hope:

- Psalm 9:18: "The needy shall not always be forgotten, and the hope of the poor shall not perish forever."

- Psalm 10:17-18: "O LORD, you hear the desire of the afflicted; you will strengthen their heart; you will incline your ear to do justice to the fatherless and the oppressed, so that man who is of the earth may strike terror no more."

- Psalm 71:5: "For you, O LORD, are my hope, my trust, O LORD, from my youth."

- Isaiah 25:8: "He will swallow up death forever; and the Lord GOD will wipe away tears from all faces, and the reproach of his people he will take away from all the earth, for the LORD has spoken. It will be said on that day, 'Behold, this is our God, we have waited for him, that he might save us.

This is the LORD; we have waited for him; let us be glad and rejoice in his salvation.'"

- Lamentations 3:21-23: "This I call to mind, and therefore I have hope. The steadfast love of the LORD never ceases; his mercies never come to an end; they are new every morning; great is your faithfulness."

- Romans 15:4: "For whatever was written in former days was written for our instruction, that through endurance and through the encouragement of the Scripture we might have hope."

Making It Practical

While it is helpful to simply share these verses with people, often a better option is to help them practically engage with Scripture passages through various exercises. When Scripture gets practical through active engagement, it leads to growth. Through the following suggestions, you can help a person establish a firm foundation that will help them to remember truthfully and imagine with hope. Try these exercises yourself first, then consider sharing them with those you are walking with.

Daily Affirmation

- Help the person choose a verse that resonates with the truth they need most.

- Encourage the person to repeat the verse as a daily affirmation that enables them to start their day anchored to the truth. Have them write out the verse as a prayer that they keep with them.

Journaling Scripture

- Encourage the use of a journal to assist the person in reflecting on emotions and experiences that need God's Word applied to them.

- Have the person write a Scripture passage as a journal entry, and to use that as an inspiration for their journaling. As they think about the passage, they can respond to it in the form of prayer to God. For example, using Psalm 23 as an entry could look like this:

  Lord, you are my shepherd, and you say I lack nothing. I feel the weight of my need today, so help me to remember that you have provided everything I need. You lead me into green pastures. I know that wherever you are taking me, it is a place where I can grow and flourish. Help me to be able to rest like someone sitting beside still waters. May your peace restore my soul.

Scripture Art

- If the person you are walking with is creative, you could have them come up with visual representations of the Scripture passage they want to call to mind. These visual representations can then be put in places where they will serve as reminders of God's promises and love.

- The person can create small cards or a digital image of the verse that they can carry with them or use as a screensaver on a phone or laptop.

As we wrap up this chapter, I hope you have come to better understand that the journey toward healing from trauma is not only about overcoming the immediate impact of the event. Rather, healing includes discovering deeper meaning that transcends the experience itself and connects a person to a loving and compassionate God who will help and comfort them in the moment and give them hope for the future.

Integrating this meaning into one's life requires a framework that goes beyond psychological methods or theories. What is needed is a theological framework established in the truth of Scripture and experienced in a relationship with God. This provides a redemptive perspective to even the most traumatic realities.

As you help people grasp the crucial role of understanding one's identity in Christ, recognizing the importance of a supportive Christian community, and establishing a biblical worldview, you are helping them to move toward post-traumatic spiritual growth.

Redemptive information processing helps you to then apply biblical truth to memories and imagination, transforming them into avenues for healing and restoration. You will find various resources in the appendices to help you do this practically. Through these combined efforts, individuals not only begin to process their trauma more holistically, they cultivate a profound sense of purpose amid their healing journey, and the wounds of trauma become part of a larger narrative of redemption and hope.

A HOPEFUL CONCLUSION:

THE LAST WORD

It is my prayer that even though you're almost done reading *Trauma Aware,* you will continue to learn about this subject. I hope that your awareness of how trauma impacts individuals will continue to grow, and that you'll seek to expand your ability to offer thoughtful and compassionate care. I trust you found this book to be more than simply information, but an invitation to continue onward in the journey of expressing sympathetic concern while offering helpful strategies and practical interventions.

Exploring what it means to help those who have experienced trauma is to make an intentional choice to equip yourself with the tools needed to walk alongside the wounded. It is an invitation to love your neighbor and to share the love of Jesus with those who are hurting. As you reflect on the insights you've gained, I trust you will consider the reading of this book to be time well spent, and to be a valuable investment in your ability to care for those whom God has brought or will bring into your life.

Trauma care is always a work in progress. It is a journey that cannot be rushed. The people you are caring for are not the only ones the Lord is working on. He is also transforming you as you learn to graciously listen to and understand a person's story. As you trust the Lord for wisdom about how to offer care, you will continue to grow in this process. You will not always know what to say or what to do, but the Lord will always be ready to help you. Don't be surprised when the very truths you offer to someone who is struggling are the truths you need in your own life. It is good to be reminded that we are on this journey together, and, as one person observed, we are simply "one beggar telling another beggar where to find bread."[1]

Walking with those who have been through trauma is to be done with continual prayer, seeking the Lord for the help you need both for yourself and for the person you are caring for. Your dependence on the Lord gives you something no book, no skill, no clinical method, and no expert counselor can supply to you. You'll find a wellspring of grace as you lean on the help of a loving and compassionate God who not only understands the depths of our pain but actively engages in our healing. As you journey alongside those who have experienced trauma, remember that the word *trauma* originates from the Greek term translated "wound." Hold fast to this promise and let your heart be encouraged: "He heals the brokenhearted and binds up their wounds" (Psalm 147:3). If this book has made you become more aware of anything, I hope it has confirmed to you that trauma does not have the last word.

TRAUMA TOOLS AND RESOURCES

Welcome to the resource portion of this book. It was my aim that after reading this book, you will not only be trauma aware but also have practical help in caring for others. This section is where you will find that help. The practical tools, informative assessments, and additional resources are designed to continue to support you as you care for others.

BASIC TRAUMA QUESTIONNAIRE 15 (BTQ-15)

It is common for helpers who are not clinically trained counselors to have questions about whether a person's experience is trauma related. The Basic Trauma Questionnaire 15 (BTQ-15) is a tool you can use to recognize potential trauma indicators, and it may help you to determine whether professional care is a good next step.

Basic Trauma Questionnaire 15 (BTQ-15)
Created by Eliza Huie, LPC
(INSTRUCTIONS FOR HELPERS)

The following assessment can help you consider whether trauma might be contributing to a person's challenges or distress. The instructions here are for the helper only and not to be included in the assessment. It is best to have the person fill out the assessment while meeting with you, and to allow time for discussion afterward.

One of the best ways to learn whether a person is experiencing traumatization is by getting to know them and building a trusting relationship. However, there may be times when you are called to help someone with whom you have not yet had the chance to establish that depth of relationship. Other times, you may feel the need to explore with someone whether trauma is negatively impacting their life, but you're unsure about how to do so. In these circumstances and others, an assessment may be valuable for both the helper and the one being helped. The BTQ-15 is a resource that seeks to evaluate a person's emotional well-being, relational stability, coping mechanisms, traumatic experiences, and daily functioning.

Please approach this assessment with sensitivity. The set of questions below should not be considered a diagnostic tool. This is not a substitute for a professional mental health evaluation. Rather, it is a means to help identify whether traumatization may be a factor in a person's experience.

Print the assessment portion only and ask the person to answer questions 1-14 based on the past 1-3 months. Question 15 should be answered based on the entirety of their life as best as they can recall. Any score of 1-4 on question 15 should be explored further in the context of a caring conversation.

After the assessment is completed, tally the final score and find the range below. Again, consider this assessment to be a means of gaining awareness of a person's situation so you can come alongside them with empathy and compassion. Keep in mind the scoring is subjective, and the results should be used with caution.

Scoring
0-20: Low concern
21-40: Moderate concern
41-60: High concern

A downloadable version is available at
www.elizahuie.com/digital-resources

No matter what the score, your care is an important part of a person's healing journey. However, if a person scores in the moderate- to high-concern range, it is wise to consider seeking professional help from a mental health expert or counselor to ensure appropriate care.

Basic Trauma Questionnaire 15 (BTQ-15)

1. How would you rate your overall emotional state?

0: Very positive
1: Positive
2: Neutral
3: Negative
4: Very negative

SCORE: _____

2. Have you experienced changes in mood or extreme emotions?

0: No changes in mood or emotions
1: Mild changes in mood or emotions
2: Occasional moderate changes in mood or emotions
3: Frequent changes in mood or emotions
4: Severe changes in mood or emotions

SCORE: _____

3. Are you experiencing negative physical symptoms, such as unexplained pain, headaches, upset stomach, sleep disruptions, etc.?

0: No physical symptoms
1: Mild physical symptoms
2: Moderate physical symptoms

3: Significant physical symptoms

4: Intense physical symptoms

SCORE: _____

4. Do you find yourself feeling irritable, on guard, or easily startled under normal circumstances?

0: Never feel this way

1: Rarely ever feel this way

2: Occasionally feel this way

3: Frequently feel this way

4: Very regularly feel this way

SCORE: _____

5. Do you avoid certain people, situations, or places that bring up unwanted memories, thoughts, or feelings?

0: Never find myself avoiding

1: Rarely find myself avoiding

2: Occasionally find myself avoiding

3: Frequently find myself avoiding

4: Very regularly find myself avoiding

SCORE: _____

6. Do you feel supported and understood by those around you?

0: Very supported and understood

1: Moderately supported and understood

2: Neutral

3: Not very supported or understood

4: Not supported or understood at all

SCORE: _____

7. In general, how trusting are you of the people in your life?

   0: Very trusting
   1: Mostly trusting
   2: Mixed trust and distrust
   3: Not very trusting
   4: Distrusting of most or all

   SCORE: _____

8. Do activities or hobbies bring you joy and relaxation?

   0: Many activities bring joy and relaxation
   1: Some activities bring joy and relaxation
   2: Few activities bring joy and relaxation
   3: Rarely find activities bring joy and relaxation
   4: No joy and relaxation in activities

   SCORE: _____

9. Do you feel emotionally numb to your life or detached from life?

   0: Never feel numb or detached
   1: Rarely ever numb or detached
   2: Occasionally numb or detached
   3: Frequently numb or detached
   4: Very regularly numb or detached

   SCORE: _____

10. Lately, have you noticed any changes in your ability to cope?

    0: No changes
    1: Positive changes

2: Mixed changes

3: Negative changes

4: Very negative changes

SCORE: _____

11. Do certain situations or memories trigger intense emotional reactions?

0: No triggers

1: Mild triggers

2: Moderate triggers

3: Strong triggers

4: Very strong triggers

SCORE: _____

12. Do you find it challenging to concentrate or make decisions?

0: No challenges

1: Mild challenges

2: Moderate challenges

3: Significant challenges

4: Severe challenges

SCORE: _____

13. How much do intrusive symptoms (such as intense emotional or physical reactions, negative thinking, unpredictable mood shifts, hopelessness, etc.) impact your everyday life?

0: No impact on my everyday life

1: Mild impact on my everyday life

2: Occasional impact on my everyday life

3: Significant impact on my everyday life

4: Severe impact on my everyday life

SCORE: _____

14. How often do you experience feelings of guilt or shame with regard to things that have happened in your life?

    0: Never
    1: Rarely
    2: Occasionally
    3: Frequently
    4: Almost always

    SCORE: _____

15. Do you believe you have experienced one or more traumatic events at any time in your life?

    0: No traumatic events
    1: One traumatic event
    2: Two traumatic events
    3: Several traumatic events
    4: Many traumatic events

    SCORE: _____

Add the scores from the questions above.

TOTAL SCORE: _____

APPENDIX B

ADVERSE CHILDHOOD EXPERIENCES (ACE) ASSESSMENT

The ACE assessment is a tool that can be used to evaluate the extent of traumatic experiences an individual may have encountered during their childhood. It includes a series of questions related to various adverse events—such as abuse, neglect, and household dysfunction—to assess the potential impact of early-life stressors on an individual's overall well-being and health outcomes later in life. The purpose of this assessment is to identify whether a person is at higher risk for toxic stress.

The ACE assessment is an awareness tool; the results are not determinative of one's future. The person who fills out this assessment can use the information to engage in deeper conversation with a helper or counselor who can provide support toward processing one's experiences.

Prior to your eighteenth birthday:

1. Did a parent or other adult in the household often or very often swear at you, insult you, put you down, or humiliate

you? Or act in a way that made you afraid that you were in danger of being physically hurt?

2. Did a parent or other adult in the household often or very often push, grab, slap, or throw something at you? Or ever hit you so hard that you were left with marks or were injured?

3. Did an adult or person at least five years older than you ever touch or fondle you or have you touch their body in a sexual way? Or attempt or actually have oral, anal, or vaginal intercourse with you?

4. Did you often or very often feel that no one in your family loved you or thought you were important or special? Or that members of your family didn't look out for each other, feel close to each other, or support each other?

5. Did you often or very often feel that you didn't have enough to eat, had to wear dirty clothes, and had no one to protect you? Or your parents were too drunk or too high to take care of you or take you to the doctor when you needed health care?

6. Were your parents ever separated or divorced?

7. Was your mother or stepmother often or very often pushed, grabbed, slapped, or have things thrown at her? Or sometimes, often, or very often kicked, bitten, hit with a fist, or hit with something hard? Or ever repeatedly hit over a period of at least a few minutes or threatened with a gun or knife?

8. Did you live with anyone who was a problem drinker or alcoholic, or who used street drugs?

9. Did you live with a household member who was depressed or mentally ill, or did a household member attempt suicide?

10. Did a household member go to prison?

For more information on the ACE assessment
and for a downloadable version, visit:
https://www.acesaware.org/

Whenever you use any assessment tool, keep in mind that the Lord can use the most difficult circumstances in our lives for our good. Not only does God bottle up our tears, but he turns them into something beautiful. Read Isaiah 61 in full and be reminded that God takes ashes and turns them into beauty (verse 3). There is nothing so broken that he cannot rebuild, restore, and renew it (verse 4). Let these truths encourage you as you engage with any assessment results.

COMPASSION FATIGUE AND BURNOUT ASSESSMENT

I n any helping role, there is a risk of developing compassion fatigue or burnout due to exposure to vicarious trauma. While compassion fatigue and burnout are likely familiar terms, vicarious trauma specifically refers to the stress from repeated exposure to distressing events or the traumatic experiences of others. This can significantly impact a helper's physical, psychological, emotional, professional, and spiritual well-being. Below is an assessment I created to enable helpers to become aware of how compassion fatigue may be impacting them.

Compassion Fatigue and Burnout Self-Assessment
Created by Eliza Huie, LPC

Read through the following symptoms and check any that you have experienced in recent days or months. You do not need to experience them consistently to mark them; simply indicate those you have experienced recently.

Physical symptoms

☐ I seem to have an increased sense of susceptibility to illness (i.e., colds, flu, infections, etc.).

☐ I have an increased sense of feeling tired or fatigued during my day.

☐ I have been feeling keyed up and nervous.

☐ I am doing less than my regular amount of exercise.

☐ Normal sleep has been more difficult for me.

☐ I have noticed symptoms of stress (i.e., muscle tension, headaches, racing heart, etc.).

Psychological symptoms

☐ I have noticed that I avoid feelings by numbing, shutting down, or distracting myself.

☐ I have noticed myself being more cynical and pessimistic.

☐ I have had bad dreams related to work or ministry.

☐ I have had a decreased interest and enjoyment in activities that I normally enjoy.

☐ I have had difficulty in making decisions and doubted myself more than I used to.

☐ I am second-guessing my ability or calling to care for others.

Emotional symptoms

☐ I have felt overwhelmed or emotional more often in the past weeks.

☐ I do not look forward to meeting with those I am helping and am relieved when a cancellation happens.

☐ I have been increasingly irritable toward my colleagues or those I serve or care for.

☐ I feel guilty or slightly responsible when things go bad for those I am helping.

☐ I have been feeling flat, depressed, or hopeless at times.

☐ I feel less empathetic toward and more detached from those I am helping.

Professional symptoms

☐ I have been unable to get work, or things related to work, out of my head.

☐ My productivity at work has diminished.

☐ I find myself distracted during the workday.

☐ I have felt like quitting my job or ministry more than once.

☐ I am told by others close to me that I overwork or am overworked.

☐ I am less excited about the future of my role at work or in ministry.

Spiritual symptoms

☐ I am spending less time in the Word and prayer. When I do, it feels flat or mechanical.

☐ I have been avoiding spending time with my church family and friends.

☐ I have feelings of doubt or cynicism about things related to my faith.

☐ I find it difficult to trust others in my faith community.

☐ God's Word doesn't seem to relieve or lessen my feelings of discouragement.

☐ I don't pray for those I am helping, but I talk about them often.

How did you do? You may find that in some categories you are excelling, while in others, the number of checked statements may come as a surprise. Even if your results are positive, consider sharing your assessment with a trusted friend or colleague. Discuss the results together and ask for input. But most importantly, take heed of what the assessment reveals. If you are in a caregiving role, consider reviewing and reassessing yourself occasionally to ensure ongoing self-care and support.

A downloadable version is available at
www.elizahuie.com/digital-resources

For more information on dealing with compassion fatigue, see *Facing Forward, Professional Resilience: Prevention and Resolution of Burnout, Toxic Stress and Compassion Fatigue* by J. Eric Gentry and Jeffrey Jim Dietz.

For more information on helpful practices of biblical self-care, see *The Whole Life: 52 Weeks of Biblical Self-Care* by Eliza Huie and Esther Smith.

REFERRING TO COUNSELING

Counseling in the context of trauma can be sought on a spectrum. On one hand, there are professionals with specialized training in trauma recovery who are equipped to provide expert guidance. On the other hand, individuals who have experienced trauma can find valuable support from trusted friends, mentors, or pastors who offer a caring and empathetic presence and helpful wisdom. The key is to choose a level of counseling that aligns with a person's needs and preferences, and fosters an environment conducive to healing and growth.

A Guide to Counseling

In chapter 8, you were given six questions people can ask to assess whether counseling may be a good option. As you care for someone, you may find that the answers to those questions indicate counseling to be a good option. So, what do you do next? The conversation about seeking counsel can be sensitive. Below is a script you may find helpful as you prepare to talk with someone who may be hesitant to pursue counseling. Use this as a guide for engaging in such a conversation with someone you are caring for.

How to Refer

Pastor/Friend: As I've walked with you, I have seen how what you have gone through has had an impact on you. I genuinely care about your well-being and want to continue to do all I can to care for you. For your best, I wonder if it might be helpful to have another voice speaking into this complex situation, someone with more specific counseling expertise.

Person: I'm not sure. I mean, I'm trying to handle it, you know.

Pastor/Friend: I hear you and I see the efforts you are making, but sometimes expanding your support system can make a significant difference. God can use many people and voices to bring his care and wisdom to us. Professional counseling may be a helpful part of this. Think of it as having an expert guide on a journey. A counselor can offer insights and direction that friends or other companions don't have the expertise to offer.

Person: I don't know. Doing that feels like such a big step.

Pastor/Friend: I understand it might seem that way. That's completely normal. How about this: Would you consider exploring some counseling options together? I can help you find a professional who aligns with your faith and your needs. You can meet them for an initial session to see whether it feels like a good fit. There's no pressure here, just an opportunity for further support and understanding. If it is helpful, I would be willing to go to the first session with you. Or maybe you have another trusted companion you would like to have go with you.

Person: I appreciate that. I guess I could give it a try.

Pastor/Friend: Taking this step is a testament to your strength and courage. Remember, you're not alone in this, and seeking help is a brave and positive choice. I want you to know that suggesting counseling doesn't mean I'm stepping back from caring for you. I'm here to support you every step of the way. I'm committed to coming alongside you, whether through talks, prayer, or any other way that is helpful.

CLINICAL APPROACHES TO TRAUMA CARE

The clinical term for counseling is *psychotherapy,* and it essentially employs conversations to help individuals explore and understand their thoughts, emotions, and behaviors. Sometimes this is called *talk therapy.* Most counseling falls under this category. However, there are more specific types of psychotherapy that can be employed when someone has gone through trauma. Below is a sampling of some of the more common methods of care that may be used by a trained therapist to help specifically with psychological traumatization. The sharing of these therapeutic approaches is not an endorsement of the methods; rather, I offer them as brief descriptions of common clinical approaches to trauma care.

Cognitive Behavioral Therapy (CBT)

Emotional challenges that accompany traumatization often stem from flawed or unproductive thought patterns. They can also result from learned behaviors related to how emotional distress was approached in the person's family of origin. Cognitive behavioral therapy (CBT) is considered helpful for increasing an individual's tolerance to distress, which can lead to an increased capacity to engage more problems more effectively. This can lead to better coping mechanisms and symptom alleviation, and enhance a person's overall well-being. Cognitive behavioral therapy is considered highly effective in working through symptoms of traumatization. Some Christian counselors trained in CBT will incorporate biblical wisdom and spiritual truths into the CBT framework to foster a more holistic approach.

Cognitive Processing Therapy (CPT)

Cognitive processing therapy (CPT) is a type of cognitive behavioral therapy used to treat trauma-related conditions. CPT focuses on the connections between thoughts, feelings, behavior, and bodily sensations. CPT is an evidence-based therapy, which means that rigorous scientific research has proven it to be effective.

> CPT provides a way to understand why recovery from traumatic events is difficult and how symptoms affect daily life. The focus is on identifying how traumatic experiences change thoughts and beliefs, and how thoughts influence a person's current feelings and behaviors. An important part of the treatment is addressing ways of thinking that might keep an individual "stuck" and get in the way of recovery.[1]

Exposure Therapy

Exposure Therapy is a type of intervention for individuals dealing with significant symptoms often associated with trauma. This approach addresses avoidance, which is a common response to situations, thoughts, or memories related to a traumatic event or circumstance. There are various types of exposure therapies, and they should be practiced by a trained professional. Essentially, exposure therapy allows for processing post-traumatic stress in real time as the person is exposed to the stressor in titrated amounts in a therapeutic setting. Various skills are used to help a person regulate their distress and lessen the intensity of their response to the stressor. Calling to mind the promises of God or applying hopeful biblical truths during exposure therapy can make deeper connections of hope and offer more meaningful help to the person.

Eye Movement Desensitization and Reprocessing (EMDR)

EMDR is an evidence-based therapy that focuses on memory processing and somatic responses connected to traumatic experiences. I like to think of EMDR as a type of exposure therapy that uses bilateral stimulation. The exposure happens in mentally returning to a distressing memory and the associated images, sensations, and emotions tied to it. This is coupled with bilateral stimulation. Bilateral stimulation (BLS) is a noninvasive neurological stimulation that produces alternate activation of both the right and left hemispheres of the brain. This alternating activation, when combined with the revisiting or *reprocessing* of the memory, has been proven to significantly reduce the stress and symptoms of traumatizing events or circumstances. You can learn more about BLS in Appendix F.

EMDR is practiced by counselors who are trained in the protocol. While there is strong evidence-based research supporting the efficacy of EMDR for treating PTSD, it has also been shown to help in treating people dealing with significant anxiety, phobias, chronic pain, and more. Despite this being a helpful therapeutic approach for many struggles, it does have limits. Adaptive information processing (AIP) mentioned in chapter 11 is a core tenet of EMDR therapy. As mentioned in that chapter, the idea of AIP falls short of what we can offer those impacted by trauma. As a counselor trained in EMDR, I see great value in incorporating gospel truth in the processing protocol. One way to do that is through the use of redemptive information processing, which was also discussed in chapter 11. Another helpful adjustment to this therapeutic approach is to incorporate biblical truth over what is called the *positive cognition* in the protocol. Rather than exploring positive thinking, a theological worldview can be employed. These are valuable adaptations to EMDR for the believer who may desire to engage in this therapeutic approach.

Stress Inoculation Training (SIT)

This is essentially talk therapy with a focus on addressing new ways of coping with symptoms of distress. Stress inoculation training (SIT) includes learning strategies for problem solving, coping, practicing relaxation (including breathing and mindfulness), and challenging negative thinking all while the counselor tracks stress levels. All of these can be learned in a way that connects to biblical truths or hopeful promises from Scripture. The skills learned are not only helpful for processing traumatic events but can also be incorporated into other stressful situations. The process culminates in the counselor and client planning for how to better manage future stressful situations.

Because traumatized people often have high levels of stress, SIT focuses on skills to help individuals react differently to stressful situations and to manage their symptoms. The therapist helps the person consider how various situations, thoughts, and behaviors could be making it hard for them to deal with trauma symptoms and learn helpful ways of coping in order to manage those symptoms. (For more information, see https://www.ptsd.va.gov/understand_tx/stress_inoculation_training.asp.)

Medication

At times, counseling and other therapeutic approaches may not be sufficient on their own. The symptoms of traumatization can become so disruptive to a person's life that they cause participation in regular activities to be overwhelming. In addition, sometimes the mental and emotional engagement needed for counseling can be difficult for individuals to achieve or sustain. In other cases, traumatization can cause significant or ongoing depression or suicidal ideation. In such situations, psychiatric medication may be considered to help those who are grappling with emotional trauma. When someone is overwhelmed by intense symptoms—such as severe anxiety, depression, significant troubles with sleep, or mood disturbances—medication may help stabilize their emotional state so that they can better engage in the counseling process.

Research has revealed that medication alone is rarely a comprehensive solution, and when medication is used in conjunction with therapeutic approaches, the efficacy of symptom relief increases. The decision to incorporate medication into treatment should be made collaboratively between the individual, their counselor, and a prescribing healthcare professional, while considering the specific symptoms and needs of the person seeking help. Ultimately, the choice to take psychiatric medication is a matter of Christian liberty and wisdom.

APPENDIX F

RELAXATION TECHNIQUES AND CALMING STRATEGIES

Recognizing the intricate connection between the mind and body is crucial in caring for individuals who are grappling with psychological trauma. The importance of this has been addressed throughout this book. Below are several techniques and strategies, along with explanations for how to engage them. Employing these methods can allow for more holistic care.

Bilateral Stimulation (BLS)

This therapeutic technique was mentioned in previous chapters in connection with the topic of body scans and Appendix E in relation to EMDR. Bilateral stimulation (BLS) is a therapeutic technique used to engage both hemispheres of the brain through rhythmic, repetitive movements or sensory input. This therapeutic technique has been proven to be particularly beneficial for individuals dealing with emotional trauma, as it helps promote relaxation during the processing of distressing memories. Essentially, BLS is the engaging of a back-and-forth motion, such as eye movements, auditory sounds, or physical tapping. This rhythmic movement supports the brain in processing challenging experiences more effectively. This technique aligns with evidence-based practices, providing a structured yet uniquely personalized approach to trauma care. BLS can be paired with Scripture to create a helpful exercise for both physical and spiritual care.

BLS with Scripture

You can find a body-scan exercise with bilateral stimulation paired with Scripture at this link: https://www.youtube.com/watch?v= P7H4wCTa5Hs.

BLS Finger Tapping

This is a technique for applying BLS as a means of calming a person who is experiencing the negative impact of trauma in their body. This simple exercise causes the activation of certain parts of the brain that go into low activity when a person is experiencing distress. If a person is feeling dysregulated or notices they are stressed or anxious, this activity can help to regulate the nervous system. It can also be paired with a mindful focus exercise, as described.

Practice doing these on your own before sharing them with someone you are caring for. If you are reading this as someone who has experienced traumatization, consider sharing these exercises with a helper or friend and doing them together. However, the instructions below are written in a way that you can do these exercises on your own as well.

Preparation

- Find a comfortable and quiet place to sit.
- Take a few deep breaths to calm yourself.

Finger-Tapping Technique

- Position your hands comfortably hip-width apart with palms open. You can place the back of your hands on your knees or at your sides.

- Begin with your right hand. Tap or touch your thumb to your index or ring finger gently in a pulsing action. You can also bring your ring and index fingers together and tap them to your thumb at the same time. Tap about 7 to 10 times at a comfortable pace. Then pause.

- Switch to your left hand and repeat the same motion. Gently tap or touch your thumb and index, ring finger, or both fingers for about 7 to 10 times at a comfortable pace.

- Next repeat that same tapping motion, except alternate the tapping from the right hand to the left hand, creating a back-and-forth tapping rhythm.

- Continue the alternate tapping motion from your right and left hands at a comfortable pace—not too slow, but not too fast.

Add in Your Breath

- Slowly and comfortably take a couple deep breaths while you continue tapping. Relax with each breath.

- Continue your breathing at a natural pace with an occasional deeper breath when you are most comfortable.

Mindful Focus (Optional variation if desired.)

- Bring a peaceful or calming memory to your mind. This can be a place where you feel at rest, a sweet or meaningful memory, a word or phrase that gives you peace, or a Scripture passage that brings you hope.

- Hold that peaceful thought in your mind while you continue tapping and breathing slowly.

- If your mind drifts, bring it back to the peaceful thought or the tapping.

Concluding the Exercise

- After a few minutes, pause the tapping and take a deep breath.

- Take note of any shifts in how you feel. Do you feel more relaxed? Are your thoughts a bit more settled? If so, you can conclude the exercise. If not, pause for a minute and repeat again.

Remember, this exercise is meant to be gentle and self-paced. If at any point you feel uncomfortable or triggered, feel free to stop or modify the tapping and try one of the other exercises listed in this section of this book.

BLS Butterfly Hug

The butterfly hug is another BLS technique. This exercise follows the same instructions as the BLS finger-tapping exercise with alterations for the hug position.

Preparation

- Find a comfortable and quiet place to sit.

- Take a few deep breaths to calm yourself.

Butterfly Hug Tapping Technique

- Cross your arms over your chest so your hands rest near or on your shoulders (whichever is most comfortable).

- Your right hand should be on your left shoulder, and your left hand on your right shoulder, creating a crisscross or butterfly hug.

- Begin a gentle tapping motion with your fingertips on your shoulders—first with one hand, and then the other.

- As you do this rhythmic and alternating tapping, find a steady and comfortable pace that is not rushed.

- Continue the alternating tapping motion from one hand to the other at a comfortable pace—not too slow and not too fast.

Add in Your Breath

- Slowly and comfortably take deep breaths as you tap. Relax with each breath.

- Continue your breathing at a natural pace with an occasional deeper breath when you are most comfortable.

Mindful Focus

- Bring a peaceful or calming memory to your mind. This can be a place where you feel at rest, a sweet or meaningful memory, a word or phrase that gives you peace, or a Scripture passage that brings you hope.

- Hold that peaceful thought in your mind while you continue tapping and breathing slowly.

- If your mind drifts, bring it back to the peaceful thought or the tapping.

Concluding the Exercise

- After a few minutes, pause the tapping and take a deep breath.

Take note of any shifts in how you feel. Do you feel more relaxed? Are your thoughts a bit more settled? If so, you can conclude the exercise. If not, pause for a minute and repeat again.

BREATHING TECHNIQUES

B ecause breathing techniques can have a profound impact on supporting individuals who are navigating various challenges, here are some additional practical exercises. Throughout the book I emphasized the significant role these techniques play in attending to the negative symptoms of traumatization. Below are additional examples with clear instructions for how to implement them.

Box Breathing

You read about box breathing in chapter 4. Here is a bit more information about this helpful and accessible exercise for individuals who are navigating emotional trauma. As a reminder, this breathing technique involves inhaling, holding the breath, exhaling, and holding the breath again, while counting to four at each step. Box breathing reduces the physiological impact of stress and calms the body. While it's not a substitute for comprehensive trauma care, box breathing can serve as a grounding practice, fostering a sense of control and stability in the face of emotional challenges.

Pairing box breathing with Scripture allows the person to meditate on God's Word while calming and regulating the autonomic nervous system. The Scripture passages are to be recited in the mind as you do the box breathing. Below are some examples of box breathing exercises paired with Scripture passages.

Psalm 27:1

Breathe in: The Lord is my light and my salvation;

Hold: whom shall I fear?

Breathe out: The Lord is the stronghold of my life;

Hold: of whom shall I be afraid?

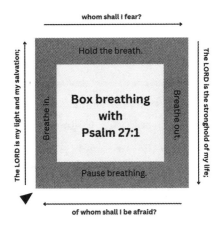

Jeremiah 17:7 *(NIV)*

Breathe in: Blessed is the one
Hold: who trusts in the LORD,
Breathe out: whose confidence is
Hold: in him.

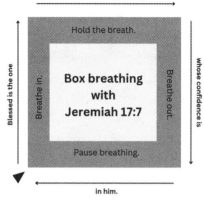

Proverbs 3:5 *(NIV)*

Breathe in: Trust in the LORD
Hold: with all your heart
Breathe out: and lean not on
Hold: your own understanding.

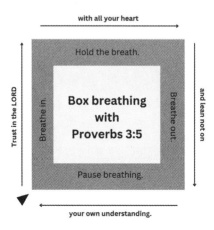

Breath Prayers

Below are several examples of prayers that can be practiced by those who are struggling with anger, fear, sadness, and shame. Encourage the person to create their own breath prayer by using a passage of Scripture that is meaningful to them in their healing journey.

Anger

BASED ON PROVERBS 15:1

Breathe in: A soft answer...

Breath out: ...turns away wrath.

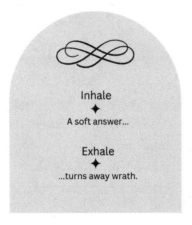

Inhale
✦
A soft answer...

Exhale
✦
...turns away wrath.

BASED ON COLOSSIANS 3:15

Breathe in: Let the peace of Christ…
Breath out: …rule in my heart.

Inhale
✦
Let the peace of Christ...

Exhale
✦
...rule in my heart.

BASED ON 2 TIMOTHY 2:22

Breathe in: Let me flee unhelpful passions…
Breath out: …help me pursue faith, love, and peace.

Inhale
✦
Let me flee unhelpful passions...

Exhale
✦
...help me pursue faith, love, and peace.

Fear
BASED ON PSALM 118:6-7
Breathe in: The Lord is with me...
Breath out: ...I will not be afraid.

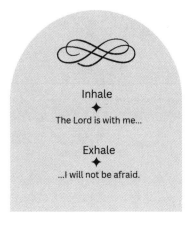

Inhale
✦
The Lord is with me...

Exhale
✦
...I will not be afraid.

BASED ON 1 PETER 5:7
Breathe in: Lord, I give you my cares...
Breath out: ...for you care for me.

Inhale
✦
Lord, I give you my cares...

Exhale
✦
...for you care for me.

BASED ON DEUTERONOMY 31:6
Breathe in: God is with me…
Breath out: …he will never forsake me.

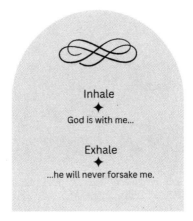

Sadness
BASED ON PSALM 27:14
Breathe in: Be brave and courageous…
Breath out: …wait patiently for the Lord.

BASED ON PSALM 91:2
Breathe in: God is my refuge…
Breath out: …my place of safety.

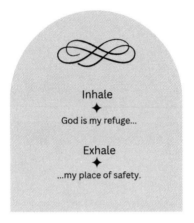

BASED ON PSALM 3:3
Breathe in: Lord, you are my shield…
Breath out: …you lift my head.

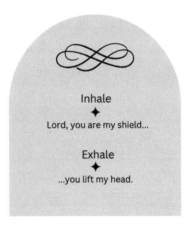

Shame
BASED ON PSALM 71:1
Breathe in: I take refuge in you, God…
Breath out: …you take away my shame.

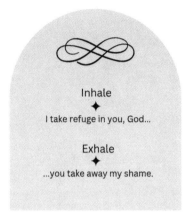

Inhale
✦
I take refuge in you, God...

Exhale
✦
...you take away my shame.

BASED ON ISAIAH 54:4
Breathe in: You take away my disgrace...
Breath out: …I no longer live in shame.

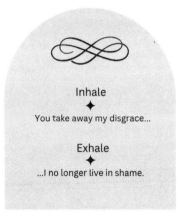

Inhale
✦
You take away my disgrace...

Exhale
✦
...I no longer live in shame.

BASED ON ISAIAH 61:7

Breathe in: Instead of shame…

Breath out: …you give me honor.

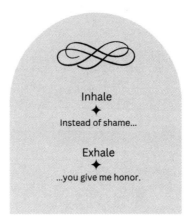

Inhale
✦
Instead of shame…

Exhale
✦
…you give me honor.

BODY SCAN

The body-scan technique is a way to observe and calm sensations throughout the body. For most people, this exercise can help promote relaxation and awareness. Slowing down and directing attention to each part of the body, while intentionally noticing sensations, can promote relaxation and enhances awareness of both physical and emotional stress held within the body.

Whole-Life Body-Scan Script

Below is a script taken from *The Whole Life: 52 Weeks of Biblical Self-Care*.[1] This script is written in a way that allows a helper to read it verbatim with the person they are caring for. As you read, you will lead the individual through an effective body-scan exercise.

1. Find a quiet room and make yourself comfortable. You may choose to sit down, or you may lie on your back. Let your hands rest in your lap or at your sides.

2. If you feel comfortable, close your eyes. Or, if you prefer, look softly in one direction instead. Begin by taking several long, slow, deep breaths, breathing in through your nose

and out through your mouth. Feel your stomach and rib cage expand as you inhale. Allow your body to relax as you exhale (reader pause here).

3. If you can hear noises or sounds around you, mentally set them aside. Shift your attention from what is happening outside your body to what is happening inside your body (reader pause here).

4. Anytime you are distracted by sounds or thoughts, simply note this and bring your focus back to your body and your breathing.

5. Starting at your feet, notice what you feel. What physical sensations do you observe? If you don't feel anything, that is okay. Just notice that (reader pause here). Wiggle your toes. Roll your ankles. Notice how they feel. Are you wearing shoes or socks? Notice how they feel on your feet. Are they tight? Soft? Warm? Sweaty? If you are barefoot, take note of how your feet feel. Take a deep breath in and imagine sending that breath all the way to your toes (reader pause here).

6. Now move your attention from your feet up to your ankles (reader pause here) and then to your calves. Take another deep breath and relax the muscles in your ankles and calves. Make whatever adjustments your body needs to be comfortable (reader pause here).

7. When you are ready, "breathe" into the rest of your legs and notice how your muscles feel. Pay attention to your hamstrings and thighs. Soften any tension that you feel (reader pause here). Has your mind started to wander? If

so, bring your attention back to your body and take a deep breath. Stay focused on your legs a little longer, paying attention to what you feel.

8. On your next inhale, move your attention to your pelvis and lower back. Exhale and then relax this area, paying attention to any discomfort as you breathe. If you need to take another breath to release the tension, do so slowly (reader pause here).

9. Moving on from your lower back, notice your abdomen and chest. Is any tension or anxiety present as you focus on this area (reader pause here)? Take a deep breath and imagine sending the oxygen to your gut, filling it completely. Exhale slowly and observe any release of negative sensations. Notice how your clothes feel on this part of your body. Where can you feel them on your belly and chest? How do they feel against your skin? Notice this and breathe (reader pause here).

10. Gently wiggle your arms. As you do, soften the muscles in your upper and lower arms. As you breathe, let your arms rest. Now pay attention to your fingers. Can you mentally soften each one of your fingers from your pinkies to your thumbs (reader pause here)?

11. Now notice your upper back and shoulders. Do you feel any pain, tightness, stiffness, or aches? Without judging what you feel, pay attention to the areas of discomfort and make any needed adjustments to help release the tension. Take a deep breath in, and as you slowly exhale, soften your shoulders. Let go of any tension. Notice any changes or shifts (reader pause here).

12. Move from your shoulders to your neck and scalp. With the same focus, notice any tense muscles. Breathe deeply, relaxing any tension you feel. The muscles in your scalp should relax from the top of your head to the base of your neck (reader pause here).

13. Next, move to your face. Soften your face and imagine your facial muscles are soft, warm clay. Breathe in slowly, and as you exhale, let those muscles rest on the bones in your face, dissolving any tension you feel (reader pause here).

14. Take a few slow, deep breaths, and notice your entire body. Feel your whole body relax into the chair or floor.

15. As you finish, shift your focus back to where you are in the present moment. Open your eyes. Recognize how much care and time you gave to your body.

SATS

An abbreviated body-scan exercise can be a valuable option in situations when there isn't enough time to do the full version. I created this simple five-step body-scan exercise that can be practiced while driving, working at a desk, or whenever there's a need to check in with the body. This can be especially useful when a person encounters an unexpected trigger or upsetting memory in the course of their day. SATS stands for Shoulders, Arms, Torso, and Settle. The acronym simplifies recall, and its brevity and straightforwardness facilitates easy implementation.

Start with a deep breath in, and slowly exhale.

1. **Shoulders**—Focus on your shoulders and the muscles that

connect to the neck. Consciously relax your shoulders and release tension from your neck. Take a deep breath.

2. **Arms**—Observe any sensations in your arms, hands, and fingers. Shake them out together or one at a time while taking a deep breath in. Then, if possible, allow them to hang down and rest for a few seconds as you breathe out. Take in another deep breath.

3. **Torso**—Feel your chest rise and fall with the natural pace of your breath and let go of any tension you notice in this area of your body as you breath normally. Take a deep breath.

4. **Settle**—Give yourself a few seconds and let whatever adjustments you made to settle in. Pause and notice any further softening you can do to your shoulders, arms, or torso. Let them all softly settle, then take one final deep breath.

NOTES

Chapter 1—What Is Trauma?

1. Tamara Hill, "Inter-Generational Trauma: 5 Ways It Impacts Families," *PsychCentral,* July 20, 2016, https://psychcentral.com/blog/caregivers/2016/07/inter-generational-trauma-5 -ways-it-impacts-families#1.

2. J.P. Gump, "Reality matters: The shadow of trauma on African American subjectivity,"*Psychoanalytic Psychology* (2010), 27(1), 42–54. https://doi.org/10.1037/a0018639.

3. Judith L. Herman, *Trauma and Recovery* (New York: Basic Books, 2022), 21.

4. Herman, *Trauma and Recovery*, 16.

5. "The History of Psychological Trauma," *New Perspectives*, https://newperspectivesinc.com/ the-history-of-psychological-trauma/. See also Herman, *Trauma and Recovery*.

6. Percival Bailey, "Hysteria: The History of a Disease," *JAMA Network*, March 1966, https:// jamanetwork.com/journals/jamapsychiatry/article-abstract/488986#:~:text=The%20name%20 hysteria%20is%20derived,Celsus%2C%20Arataeus%2C%20and%20Soranus.

7. Cecilia Tasca, et al., "Women and Hysteria in The History of Mental Health," *Clinical Practice Epidemiol Mental Health* (2012), 8:110-119; also found in the article at "Letter to the editor: Uterectomy," https://www.oatext.com/letter-to-the-editor-uterectomy.php#:~:text=Consequently%2C%20 doctors%20at%20the%20time,not%20only%20found%20in%20women.

8. Bailey, "Hysteria: The History of a Disease."

9. M. Cloitre, C.A. Courtois, A. Charuvastra, R. Carpezza, B.C. Stolbach, and B.L. Green, "Treatment of Complex PTSD: Results of the ISTSS Clinician Survey on Best Practices," *Journal of Traumatic Stress* 24 (2011): 615-27; International Society for the Study of Trauma and Dissociation, "Special Issue: Guidelines for Treating Dissociative Identity Disorder in Adults," *Journal of Trauma and Dissociation* 12 (2011): 113-212, as cited in Judith L. Herman, *Trauma and Recovery* (New York: Basic Books, 2015), 24, reference 55.

10. Herman, *Trauma and Recovery*, 23.

11. M.A. Crocq and L. Crocq, "From shell shock and war neurosis to posttraumatic stress disorder: a history of psychotraumatology,"*Dialogues in Clinical Neuroscience* (2000), 2(1), 47-55, https://doi.org/10.31887/DCNS.2000.2.1/macrocq.

12. Bailey, "Hysteria: The History of a Disease."

13. Matthew J. Friedman, "PTSD History and Overview," *U.S. Department of Veterans Affairs*, https://www.ptsd.va.gov/professional/treat/essentials/history_ptsd.asp.

14. "Trauma," *American Psychological Association*, https://www.apa.org/topics/trauma.

15. "Psych for Theology & Ministry: Preston Hill," *Blueprint 1543*, https://open.spotify.com/episode/35A94F4U0ceEcZp5pZ13PZ?si=MeKBCpQrRv6uzvk4Hk7M_Q at the 12:24 mark.

16. "Trauma-Informed Care in Behavioral Health Services," *SAMHSA*, March 2014, https://store.samhsa.gov/sites/default/files/sma14-4816.pdf.

17. Herman, *Trauma and Recovery*, 51.

Chapter 2–Why We Must Understand Trauma

1. John Murray, *Collected Writings of John Murray*, vol. 2 (Scotland: Banner of Truth, 1982), 14.

2. "Understanding Child Trauma," *Substance Abuse and Mental Health Services Administration*, https://www.samhsa.gov/child-trauma/understanding-child-trauma.

3. "The epidemiology of traumatic event exposure worldwide: results from the World Mental Health Survey Consortium," PDF document at https://www.ncbi.nlm.nih.gov/pmc/articles/PMC4869975/pdf/nihms783910.pdf.

4. J. Cockayne, S. Harrower, P. Hill, *Dawn of Sunday: The Trinity and Trauma-Safe Churches* (Eugene, OR: Wipf and Stock, 2022), 12.

5. Diane Langberg, *Suffering and the Heart of God* (Greensboro, NC: New Growth Press, 2015), 8.

Chapter 3–Trauma and the Brain

1. Bill Bryson, *The Body: A Guide for Occupants* (New York: Doubleday, 2019), 54.

2. A multidisciplinary approach adapted from the work of Bruce Perry, Daniel Siegel, Allan Schore, Loise Cosolino, Joseph LeDoux, Paul MacLean, and Alexander Luria, "The Conscious Discipline Brain State Model," *Conscious Discipline*, https://consciousdiscipline.com/methodology/brain-state-model/.

3. Perry, Siegel, et al., "The Conscious Discipline Brain State Model," *Conscious Discipline*.

4. Catherine M. Pittman and Elizabeth M. Karle, *Rewire Your Anxious Brain* (Oakland, CA: New Harbinger, 2015), 39.

5. Baby Professor, *The Human Brain: Biology for Kids* (Newark, DE: Speedy Publishing, 2017), 28.

6. Perry, Siegel, et al., "The Conscious Discipline Brain State Model," *Conscious Discipline*.

7. Pittman and Karle, *Rewire Your Anxious Brain*, 19.

8. Perry, Siegel, et al., "The Conscious Discipline Brain State Model," *Conscious Discipline*.

9. "What Is Homeostasis?" *Scientific American*, January 3, 2000, www.scientificamerican.com/article/what-is-homeostasis/#:~:text=Homeostasis%2C%20from%20the%20Greek%20words,by%20the%20physician%20Walter%20Cannon.

10. L.K. McCorry, "Physiology of the autonomic nervous system," *American Journal of Pharmaceutical Education*, 71(4), 78, https://doi.org/10.5688/aj710478.

11. Jan-Marino Ramirez, "The integrative role of the sigh in psychology, physiology, pathology, and neurobiology," *Progress in Brain Research* (2014); 209:91-129, doi: 10.1016/B978-0-444-63274-6.00006-0. PMID: 24746045; PMCID: PMC4427060.

12. "Parasympathetic Nervous System," *Cleveland Clinic*, https://my.clevelandclinic.org/health/body/23266-parasympathetic-nervous-system-psns#:~:text=Your%20parasympathetic%20nervous%20system%20is,you%20feel%20safe%20and%20relaxed.

13. Richard J. McNally, *Remembering Trauma* (Cambridge, MA: Belknap Press, 2005), 35.

Chapter 4–Trauma and the Body

1. Bessel van der Kolk, *The Body Keeps the Score: Brain, Mind, and Body in the Healing of Trauma* (New York: Penguin, 2015), 275.

2. Joshua Cockayne, Scott Harrower, and Preston Hill, *Dawn of Sunday: The Trinity and Trauma-Safe Churches* (Eugene, OR: Cascade Books, 2022), 35.

3. Jennifer Tucker, *Breath as Prayer: Calm Your Anxiety, Focus Your Mind, and Renew Your Soul* (Nashville, TN: Thomas Nelson, 2022), 26.

4. For more information on the physiological sigh and the research behind its effectiveness, see Paul Schrodt, "This 5-Minute Breathing 'Physiological Sigh' Exercise Kills Anxiety Quicker Than Mindful Meditation," *The Edge*, January 24, 2024, https://honehealth.com/edge/health/physiological-sigh-andrew-huberman/#:~:text=The%20research%20from%20David%20Spiegel,your%20anxiety%2C%20improve%20mood%2C%20and; Melis Yilmaz Balban, Eric Neri, et al., "Brief structured respiration practices enhance mood and reduce physiological arousal," *Cell Reports Medicine*, January 17, 2023, https://www.cell.com/cell-reports-medicine/pdf/S2666-3791(22)00474-8.pdf; and Ramirez, "The integrative role of the sigh in psychology, physiology, pathology, and neurobiology."

5. Schrodt, "This 5-Minute Breathing 'Physiological Sigh' Exercise Kills Anxiety Quicker Than Mindful Meditation."

6. Aundi Kolber, *Try Softer: A Fresh Approach to Move Us Out of Anxiety, Stress, and Survival Mode—and into a Life of Connection and Joy* (Carol Stream, IL: Tyndale, 2020), 143.

7. Sarah Boukezzi, Catarina Silva, Bruno Nazarian, et al., "Alternating Auditory Stimulations Facilitate Fear Extinction and Retrieval," Frontiers in Psychology (2017), June 14, 8:990, doi: 10.3389/fpsyg.2017.00990. PMID: 28659851; PMCID: PMC5470101.

8. Sam Allberry, *What God Has to Say about Our Bodies: How the Gospel Is Good News for Our Physical Selves* (Wheaton, IL: Crossway, 2021), 131.

9. Susan J. Brison, *Aftermath: Violence and the Remaking of a Self* (UK: Princeton University Press, 2002), 15.

10. Bessel van der Kolk, *The Body Keeps the Score: Brain, Mind, and Body in the Healing of Trauma* (New York: Penguin, 2015), 21.

11. Matthew A. LaPine, *The Logic of the Body: Retrieving Theological Psychology* (Bellingham, WA: Lexham Press, 2020), 351.

12. Ed Welch, "Scripture Is about PTSD," *CCEF*, February 22, 2016, https://www.ccef.org/scripture-about-ptsd/.

Chapter 5–Recognizing TRAUMA

1. Oprah Winfrey, Bruce D. Perry, et al., *What Happened to You? Conversations on Trauma, Resilience, and Healing* (New York: Flatiron Books, 2021), 87.

2. "Thalamus," *Cleveland Clinic*, March 30, 2022, https://my.clevelandclinic.org/health/body/22652-thalamus.

3. C. Bourne, C.E. Mackay, and E.A. Holmes, "The neural basis of flashback formation: the impact of viewing trauma," *Psychological Medicine* (2013), July, 43(7): 1521-32, doi: 10.1017/S0033291712002358. Epub 2012 Oct 18. PMID: 23171530; PMCID: PMC3806039.

4. "Somatization," *Oxford English Dictionary*, https://Www.Oed.Com/Dictionary/Somatization_n?Tl=true.

5. Jonathan E. Sherin, Leonard M. Miller, et al., "Post-traumatic stress disorder: the neurobiological impact of psychological trauma," *Dialogues in Clinical Neuroscience* (2011), September 13(3): 263-278, https://www.ncbi.nlm.nih.gov/pmc/articles/PMC3182008/. The first symptoms of PTSD are often delayed and they are separated from the trauma by a latency period; however, once installed, the disorder tends to follow a chronic course and the symptoms do not abate with time.

6. Bessel van der Kolk, *The Body Keeps the Score: Brain, Mind, and Body in the Healing of Trauma* (New York: Penguin, 2015).

7. "Alexithymia," *Oxford English Dictionary*, https://www.oed.com/dictionary/alexithymia_n?tl=true.

8. Ewa A. Ogłodek, "Alexithymia and Emotional Deficits Related to Posttraumatic Stress Disorder: An Investigation of Content and Process Disturbances," *Case Reports in Psychiatry* (2022), January, https://doi.org/10.1155/2022/7760988.

Chapter 6—Stages of Recovery

1. Judith L. Herman, *Trauma and Recovery* (New York: Basic Books, 2015), 223.

2. Herman, *Trauma and Recovery*, 53.

3. David Platt, Melissa Kruger, Emma Kruger, Ann Voskamp, "Raising Children with Hope," *Radical*, June 27, 2024, https://radical.net/video/raising-children-with-hope/.

4. Lawrence G. Calhoun and Richard G. Tedeschi, *Posttraumatic Growth in Clinical Practice* (New York: Routledge, 2013), 28.

5. Calhoun and Tedeschi, *Posttraumatic Growth in Clinical Practice*, 28.

Chapter 7—Starting Blocks of Care

1. Diane Langberg, *Redeeming Power: Understanding Authority and Abuse in the Church* (Grand Rapids, MI: Baker, 2020), 118.

2. Adam S. McHugh, *The Listening Life: Embracing Attentiveness in a World of Distraction* (Downers Grove, IL: InterVarsity, 2015), 163.

3. McHugh, *The Listening Life: Embracing Attentiveness in a World of Distraction*, 11.

Chapter 8—PEACE for the Traumatized

1. Viktor E. Frankl, *Man's Search for Meaning* (Boston, MA: Beacon Press, 2006), 20.

2. Charlie Mackesy, *The Boy, the Mole, the Fox and the Horse* (New York: Ebury Press, 2019).

3. Garry R. Walz, Jeanne C. Bleuer, and R.K. Yep (eds.). "Counseling Student's Perceptions of Counseling Effectiveness," *Vistas: Compelling perspectives on counseling 2006*, American Counseling Association, https://psycnet.apa.org/record/2006-03629-042.

Chapter 9–Trauma and the Bible

1. From Job 5:7.

2. Diane Langberg, *Suffering and the Heart of God* (Greensboro, NC: New Growth Press, 2015), 67.

3. John Piper, "Spiritual Depression in the Psalms," *desiring God*, June 2008, www.desiringgod.org/messages/spiritual-depression-in-the-psalms.

4. J. Cockayne, S. Harrower, P. Hill, *Dawn of Sunday: The Trinity and Trauma-Safe Churches* (Eugene, OR: Wipf and Stock, 2022), 80.

5. Ed Welch, "When Death Intrudes," Christian Counseling and Educational Foundation 2023 National Conference, Virginia Beach.

6. Welch, "When Death Intrudes."

7. Welch, "When Death Intrudes."

Chapter 10–Trauma and the Church

1. Melissa Carmona and Denise-Marie Griswold, eds., "PTSD Statistics and Facts," *The Recovery Village*, August 31, 2023, www.therecoveryvillage.com/mental-health/ptsd/ptsd-statistics.

2. Darren Slade, Adrianna Smell, Elizabeth Wilson, and Rebekah Drumsta, "Percentage of U.S. Adults Suffering from Religious Trauma: A Sociological Study," *Socio-Historical Examination of Religion and Ministry*, March 2023, 1-28, doi: 10.33929/sherm.2023.vol5.no1.01, https://www.researchgate.net/publication/369327217_Percentage_of_US_Adults_Suffering_from_Religious_Trauma_A_Sociological_Study.

3. "What Is Religious Trauma?," *Religious Trauma Institute*, https://www.religioustraumainstitute.com/.

4. Thomas Brooks, *Precious Remedies Against Satan's Devices* (Waymark Books, 2022), eBook version.

5. Tim Keller, "Puritan resources for biblical counseling," *CCEF*, April 14, 2016, https://www.ccef.org/puritan-resources-biblical-counseling.

6. J. Cockayne, S. Harrower, P. Hill, *Dawn of Sunday: The Trinity and Trauma-Safe Churches* (Eugene, OR: Wipf and Stock, 2022).

7. Cockayne, Harrower, and Hill, *Dawn of Sunday: The Trinity and Trauma-Safe Churches*, 48.

8. Diane Langberg, *Suffering and the Heart of God* (Greensboro, NC: New Growth Press, 2015), 68.

Chapter 11–Trauma and Theology

1. R.C. Sproul, *Everyone's a Theologian: An Introduction to Systematic Theology* (Sanford, FL: Ligonier Ministries, 2014).

2. Jen Wilkin and J.T. English, *You Are a Theologian: An Invitation to Know and Love God Well* (Brentwood, TN: B&H Publishing Group, 2023).

3. Lawrence G. Calhoun and Richard G. Tedeschi, *Posttraumatic Growth in Clinical Practice* (New York: Routledge, 2013), 6.

4. Calhoun and Tedeschi, *Posttraumatic Growth in Clinical Practice*, 7.

5. Timothy Keller, "Transforming Trauma: How We Integrate Traumatic Memories," *YouTube*, 2019, https://www.youtube.com/watch?v=-N_178ASBg0 (accessed July 9, 2024).

6. Dietrich Bonhoeffer, *A Testament to Freedom: The Essential Writings of Dietrich Bonhoeffer*, eds. Geffrey B. Kelly and F. Burton Nelson (San Francisco, CA: HarperSanFrancisco, 1990), 539-40.

7. Klyne R. Snodgrass, *Who God Says You Are: A Christian Understanding of Identity* (Downers Grove, IL: InterVarsity Press, 2018), 92.

8. Though I wrote down this quote in my notes, I have not since been able to find the original source, which I believe appeared on YouTube.

9. Klyne R. Snodgrass, *Who God Says You Are: A Christian Understanding of Identity* (Downers Grove, IL: InterVarsity Press, 2018), 107.

10. Calhoun and Tedeschi, *Posttraumatic Growth in Clinical Practice*, 16.

11. R.C. Sproul, "The Elements of a Christian Worldview," podcast audio, *Ligonier Ministries* (accessed July 12, 2024).

12. Richard J. McNally, *Remembering Trauma* (Cambridge, MA: Belknap Press, 2005), 106.

13. McNally, *Remembering Trauma*, 105.

14. Miroslav Volf, *The End of Memory* (Grand Rapids, MI: Wm. B. Eerdmans, 2006), eBook edition, 68.

15. Judith Herman, *Trauma and Recovery* (New York: Hachette, 2015), 12.

16. Viktor E. Frankl, *Man's Search for Meaning* (Boston, MA: Beacon Press, 2006), 113.

A Hopeful Conclusion: The Last Word

1. The original source of this quote is unknown. Through the years, a variety of authors have used variations of these words.

Appendix E

1. "About CPT," *Cognitive Processing Therapy for Posttraumatic Stress Disorder,* https://cptforptsd .com/about-cpt/ (accessed July 12, 2024).

Appendix H

1. Eliza Huie and Esther Smith, *The Whole Life: 52 Weeks of Biblical Self-Care* (Greensboro, NC: New Growth Press, 2021).

To learn more about Harvest House books and
to read sample chapters, visit our website:

www.HarvestHousePublishers.com

HARVEST HOUSE PUBLISHERS
EUGENE, OREGON